Banning Black Gods

AFRICANA RELIGIONS

Edited by
Sylvester A. Johnson, *Virginia Tech*

ADVISORY BOARD:
Afe Adogame, *Princeton Theological Seminary*
Sylviane Diouf, *Historian of the African Diaspora*
Paul C. Johnson, *University of Michigan*
Elizabeth Pérez, *University of California, Santa Barbara*
Elisha P. Renne, *University of Michigan*
Judith Weisenfeld, *Princeton University*

Adopting a global vision for the study of Black religions, the Africana Religions book series explores the rich diversity of religious history and life among African and African-descended people. It publishes research on African-derived religions of Orisha devotion, Christianity, Islam, and other religious traditions that are part of the Africana world. The series emphasizes the translocal nature of Africana religions across national, regional, and hemispheric boundaries.

Banning Black Gods

Law and Religions of the African Diaspora

DANIELLE N. BOAZ

The Pennsylvania State University Press
University Park, Pennsylvania

An excerpt of chapter 8 was previously published as part of the article "Religion or Ruse? African Jamaican Spiritual Practices and Police Deception in Canada," *Alter*nation Special Edition 22 (2018): 11–34. The author wants to thank the journal *Alter*nation for its approval for this publication.

Library of Congress Cataloging-in-Publication Data

Names: Boaz, Danielle N., author.
Title: Banning Black gods : law and religions of the African diaspora / Danielle N. Boaz.
Description: University Park, Pennsylvania : The Pennsylvania State University Press, [2021] | Series: Africana religions | Includes bibliographical references and index.
Summary: "Examines the global legal challenges faced by adherents of the most widely practiced religions of the African diaspora in the twenty-first century, including Santeria/ Lucumi, Haitian Vodou, Candomblé, Palo Mayombe, Umbanda, Islam, Rastafari, Obeah, and Voodoo"—Provided by publisher.
Identifiers: LCCN 2020058275 | ISBN 9780271089300 (hardback)
Subjects: LCSH: Religious discrimination—Law and legislation—America. | Race discrimination—Law and legislation—America. | Blacks—Legal status, laws, etc.—America. | African diaspora—Religious aspects. | Blacks—America—Religion.
Classification: LCC KDZ576.3 .B63 2021 | DDC 342.08/52996—dc23
LC record available at https://lccn.loc.gov/2020058275

Copyright © 2021 Danielle N. Boaz
All rights reserved
Printed in the United States of America
Published by The Pennsylvania State University Press,
University Park, PA 16802-1003

The Pennsylvania State University Press is a member of the Association of University Presses.

It is the policy of The Pennsylvania State University Press to use acid-free paper. Publications on uncoated stock satisfy the minimum requirements of American National Standard for Information Sciences—Permanence of Paper for Printed Library Material, ANSI Z39.48–1992.

Contents

Acknowledgments *vii*

Introduction *1*

SECTION I SANTERIA/LUCUMI, HAITIAN VODOU, CANDOMBLÉ, PALO MAYOMBE, AND UMBANDA *11*

1 | New Forms of Religious Terrorism: Physical Violence Against African Diaspora Religions *19*

2 | The Gorilla in the Room: The Right to Practice Animal Sacrifice Amidst Growing Animal Rights Activism *35*

3 | "The Dark Side of Santeria": Palo Mayombe and the Grave-Robbing Cases *53*

4 | The Best Interests of the Child? Custody of Minors and African Diaspora Religions *72*

SECTION II ISLAM, RASTAFARI, AND RELIGIOUS SYMBOLS IN THE AFRICAN DIASPORA *87*

5 | Headscarves, Dreadlocks, and Other "Disruptions": African Diaspora Religions and the Right to Education *95*

6 | Neither Litigant, nor Lawyer, nor Law Enforcement: Religious Barriers to the Justice System *115*

SECTION III THE BOUNDARIES OF RELIGION: OBEAH AND VOODOO *135*

7 | Continued Proscription: The Rights of Western Versus African "Witches" *141*

8 | "Fragmentary," "Dangerous," and "Unethical" Belief Systems: African Diaspora Faiths and the "Accoutrements" of Religion *160*

9 | Myths of African Diaspora Religions: Rumors and Religious Freedom *180*

Conclusion: The Future of Religious Racism *191*

Notes *195*
Bibliography *219*
Index *231*

Acknowledgments

First and foremost, I would like to thank Gustavo Melo Cerqueira for introducing me to the concept of religious racism and volunteering countless hours to assist me with my research in Brazil. The information about religious racism in Brazil that I learned from him and while working with him was instrumental in shaping this book and helped me to realize the importance of this project.

I am grateful to Greg Gibbs for reading and providing feedback on one of my chapters, and to Rosiane Rodrigues for sharing her insights on religious racism in Brazil, including her personal story. I would also like to thank Andrea Pitts, Elisabeth Paquette, Tamara Johnson, Karen Watts, and Umi Vaughan for their unrelenting support and encouragement as I worked on this project.

I am grateful to the Hutchins Center for African and African American Research at Harvard University and the Stuart Hall Foundation for the residential fellowship that provided me with the time and intellectual community to finish this work. Finally, I would like to thank the University of North Carolina at Charlotte for the Faculty Research Grant that funded part of the research for this book.

Introduction

In 2003, Toronto police officers suspected that two Jamaican-Canadian brothers were involved in a series of murders that plagued the city. They hatched a plan whereby an officer of Jamaican descent would pose as a spiritual advisor or "Obeah practitioner" to the suspects' mother and exert spiritual pressure on the family to convince them to confess. Over the course of several months, the police deployed an elaborate ruse to impress the family with the officer's purported spiritual power, including staging a car accident between the officer and the mother, placing dead animals on her doorstep, and even arresting the mother on manufactured charges. The brothers finally confessed to the murder during a ritual purportedly designed to end these spiritual attacks on their family, and the prosecution's entire case rested on the statements made during the ceremony. The brothers were convicted of murder, and they appealed on the grounds that confessions made to a purported spiritual advisor should not be admissible evidence against them in court. However, in 2013, a Canadian appellate court upheld the police tactics, finding that these Afro-Jamaican rituals are not "religious."[1] This case is just one brief example of the restrictions on the freedom to practice African diaspora religions in the twenty-first century.

This book is the first broad examination of the global legal challenges faced by adherents of the most widely practiced religions or belief systems of the African diaspora in the late twentieth and twenty-first centuries, including Obeah, Yoruba religions (i.e., Santeria/Lucumi and Candomblé), Umbanda,

Palo Mayombe, Rastafari, Islam, Vodou, and Voodoo. Unlike the rich anthropological and religious studies of African diaspora faiths that often discuss their relationship to politics, law, and other facets of society, this study focuses solely on a legal perspective—considering court cases, laws, human rights reports, and related materials. Using a series of case studies of specific issues, it explores how the restrictions on the right and freedom to practice African diaspora faiths demonstrate a growing social problem known as "religious racism."

"Religious racism" is a term that originates from Brazil, where devotees of African diaspora religions have been experiencing increasingly pervasive intolerance over the past several years. This terminology underscores that discrimination against African-based religions is more than mere prejudice against a faith or group of faiths; it is the intersection of religious intolerance and racism. There are at least two distinct yet overlapping ways in which intolerance against African-derived religions represents the juncture of racial and religious discrimination.

First, the case studies discussed in this book demonstrate that the recent attempts to limit the practice of African diaspora religions have all the classic hallmarks of how racial prejudice has and continues to permeate legal and justice systems across the globe. For example, Afro-diasporic religious communities struggle with overpolicing in a manner that resembles similar problems experienced by racial minorities more generally. Police officers and other criminal investigators have depicted devotees of these religions as more susceptible to unlawful behavior than those of other faiths, leading to excessive searches of places of worship, unwarranted detentions of devotees, and disproportionate use of force during those detentions (chapters 2 and 3). Furthermore, state officials and private citizens have barred devotees from courtrooms, schools, and other public spaces as well as argued that they are unfit for certain professions (chapters 5 and 6). These attempts to exclude adepts of Africana religions from public accommodations continue a long history of race-based segregation. Perhaps most significantly, vigilantes and extremists have carried out horrendous acts of violence against devotees of African-derived religions with minimal investigation and virtually no penalties for the perpetrators (chapter 1). One could cite countless other historical and present-day examples of unprosecuted acts of violence against racial minorities. In these and other ways, intolerance against African-derived religions often mirrors and works in conjunction with broader patterns of racism in legal, social, and justice systems of the Western world. However, it is a type of racism that has been almost completely ignored amid the study of other varieties of racial discrimination.

Not only does the term "religious racism" reflect that intolerance against Africana religions follows traditional patterns of racial discrimination, but it also signifies that prejudice against these faiths is typically motivated by anti-Black racism. Devotees of Afro-Brazilian religions often stress that persecution of their faiths is not new; rather, it is rooted in the era of slavery and scientific racism. This is not limited to Brazil—virtually all African-derived religions have a long and complicated relationship with legal systems in the Western world. The use of the term "religious racism" to describe these twenty-first-century cases and controversies emphasizes that they are not a recent phenomenon but rather are a reemergence of the previous ideologies and patterns of racially motivated persecution that began during slavery and continued until the middle of the twentieth century.

THE HISTORICAL PROHIBITION OF AFRICAN DIASPORA RELIGIONS

The persecution and prosecution of African diaspora religions began soon after their arrival and development in the Americas. In the eighteenth and nineteenth centuries, colonial authorities feared that enslaved persons would use religious gatherings to plan insurrections and that priests and healers would offer guidance and protection to the insurgents. Therefore, many colonies implemented laws restricting meeting without a Catholic priest, drumming, dancing, and other practices central to African-derived religions.[2] Furthermore, because Europeans thought it was their duty to "civilize" enslaved persons, colonial laws often required slaves to be baptized and instructed in Catholicism.[3] Although bans on African-derived religious practices and forced conversion to Christianity were common during slavery, perhaps the most widespread prohibitions on African diaspora faiths occurred shortly after emancipation, when legislators throughout the Americas passed statutes proscribing African religions as "primitive," "superstitious" practices and carried out campaigns of suppression against these faiths. The first nation to implement new post-emancipation bans on African-derived practices was Haiti.

In 1791, enslaved persons in Haiti (then St. Domingue) revolted against the colonists and fought a brutal and lengthy war, through which they ultimately won their independence and established a free Black nation. Following independence, other nations in the Americas and in Europe refused to recognize and trade with the fledgling country. In 1835, in the midst of and partially in response to these concerns about being recognized as a "civilized" and legitimate nation, the Haitian government passed an ambiguous penal code that prohibited fortune-telling as well as making "vaudoux," "ouangas," "macandals," or other charms. The penalty for such could be up to six months' imprisonment and a fine.[4] This was just the first step in post-emancipation suppression of African-derived religions.

The Vatican initially refused to recognize Haiti as an independent nation, and the Catholic Church had no official presence in Haiti in the first half of the nineteenth century. However, in 1860, Haiti signed an agreement with the Vatican and the Catholic Church reestablished a foothold in the country. From this point forward, the Church collaborated with various Haitian presidents to try to eradicate Vodou through "anti-superstition" campaigns. Some of the known campaigns took place in 1864, 1896, and 1912, "during which temples were destroyed and hundreds of people who admitted to being practitioners of Vodou were massacred."[5]

During this period of intermittent suppression campaigns—the late nineteenth and early twentieth centuries—rumors constantly circulated across the globe that devotees of Haitian Vodou were engaged in barbaric ritual practices including cannibalism, snake worship, and child sacrifice. For instance, in 1900, British explorer Hesketh Prichard published a book about his travels in Haiti titled *Where Black Rules White*. He devoted an entire chapter to "Voodoo" and the supposed prevalence of human sacrifice among devotees.[6] Prichard averred that the reason that Haiti had descended into such barbarism while "living in the midst of other civilized communities" was the government was too unstable to suppress it, and thus the Voodoo practitioners "carry on their rites and their orgies with practical impunity."[7] After several other chapters recounting the supposed horrors occurring in the independent nation of Haiti, Prichard concluded with a chapter explaining why "the negro" "certainly cannot rule himself."[8]

As numerous scholars have noted, these allegations of barbaric "Voodoo" practices helped lay the groundwork for the US occupation of Haiti (1915–34). Then, when the US marines arrived in Haiti in 1915, they quickly tried to suppress Vodou.[9] Only one year after the invasion began, Haiti's minister of justice and religions published a circular banning "fetishism" and "superstitions."[10] Furthermore, the marines used previously defunct legislation prohibiting "sorcery," fortune-telling, and charms to break up rituals and confiscate the drums.[11] One marine, Faustin Wirkus, who later published an account of his exploits in Haiti, describes the marines' interruption of a ceremony in 1922 wherein fifty-four people were arrested and imprisoned, and their ritual objects were confiscated. Wirkus refers to these raids as "constant."[12] This claim is supported by a report from the district of Jérémie recording the arrest of 123 people in a one-year period, from January of 1924 to January of 1925, in that region alone for violating the laws against "sorcery."[13]

Immediately following the US occupation, in 1935, President Sténio Vincent implemented broad legislation against "superstitious practices" that included explicit bans on ceremonies, dance, rites, medico-religious healing, and other spiritual practices.[14] A few years later, in 1941, President Elie Lescot once again joined forces with the Catholic Church and tried to eradicate Vodou.[15] Together, they imprisoned adherents and destroyed temples. They seized sacred drums, talismans, and other ritual objects, created a huge bonfire, and set them ablaze.

Haiti was not the only nation to implement laws restricting African-derived religions following the abolition of slavery. In 1890, just two short years after emancipation, Brazil enacted a modified Penal Code that prohibited the unlicensed practice of medicine, "popular forms of curing, or curandeirismo," as well as the "practice of spiritism, magic and its sorceries, the use of talismans and cartomancy to arouse sentiments of hate and love, the promise to cure illnesses, curable and not curable; in sum, to fascinate and subjugate public belief."[16] Paul Christopher Johnson explains that "Afro-Brazilian religions were considered a dangerous detriment to national progress," and therefore, this law prohibited them "under an alternative category to religion—namely, as a civil threat to public health."[17] The premise was that Afro-Brazilian religions were "primitive" but "contagious" and could entice even upper-class white Brazilians to participate in what was seen as degenerate spiritual and cultural practices.[18] Thus, the prohibition of African cultural and religious practices, accompanied by official policies encouraging immigration from Europe, were attempts to turn Brazil into a "modern" nation by "whitening" its population and culture.[19]

Similar to Brazil, around the turn of the twentieth century, the government of Cuba restricted the practice of African diaspora religions under the notion that they promoted criminal behavior and threatened public morality.[20] The suppression reached its height in the early twentieth century, when white Cubans claimed that Black "witches" or "brujos" were abducting white children, killing them, and using their body parts for their rituals.[21] The government censured Afro-Cuban communities and seized their religious tools. Additionally, private citizens sometimes formed lynch mobs and killed some of the purported perpetrators.[22]

Reinaldo Roman, who has written extensively about these allegations, explains that they began shortly after Cuba's independence from Spain and the end of the first US occupation of the island.[23] During this period, there were numerous internal and external debates about Cuba's ability to self-govern and the role of Afro-Cubans in the independent state. Denunciations of Afro-Cuban "superstitions" served as a justification to deny them political participation and to distance the elites from beliefs and practices that might jeopardize independence and their ability to depict Cuba as a "civilized" nation. Not only did Cuban elites worry about US or other external intervention; they also had "a general fear of African ascendancy in Cuba,"[24] and this suppression of Afro-Cuban religions coincided with "the formation of the Cuban Independence Party of Color and its agitation for social and political change."[25]

Using somewhat analogous rhetoric, US authorities also sought to suppress African American Muslims as a criminal threat in the first half of the twentieth century. This suppression campaign began in Detroit, Michigan, in 1932, after a man named Robert Harris killed his tenant on a makeshift altar in the back room of his home.[26] Harris, an African American Muslim, claimed that this sacrifice was an offering to Allah that would save the world.[27] Although authorities and the media knew that Harris had been suffering from delusions and had previously threatened the lives of his wife, his children, and his family's social worker, they depicted his actions as representative of Black Muslims in Detroit.[28] Nationwide, newspapers published stories about the leader of the "Voodoo cult" of Detroit who had hundreds of African American followers who supported his human sacrifice to Allah. Meanwhile, authorities detained actual Black Muslim leaders, questioning them about their teachings.

Ultimately, although Harris was declared insane and members of his community, then known as the Allah Temple of Islam, denied that Harris had any standing in the organization, the acts of this mentally unstable individual created severe limitations on the rights of all Black Muslims in Detroit. The authorities banished their leader, Wallace Fard, from Detroit.[29] Remaining members regrouped under the leadership of Elijah Muhammad and were forced to change their name to the Nation of Islam and move their headquarters to Chicago, all in an effort to escape this reputation.[30] However, the police and scholars continued to portray human sacrifice as part of the larger Black Muslim community and use these rumors as a basis for surveillance and harassment.

Despite the widespread persecution and prosecution of African diaspora religions in the nineteenth and early twentieth centuries, the freedom to practice these faiths expanded greatly in subsequent decades. By the mid-to-late twentieth century, most governments had repealed the discriminatory laws used to target these faiths and generally moved toward greater acceptance, or even legal recognition, of African diaspora religions. In some cases, particularly in Haiti, Cuba, and Brazil, Africana faiths became part of the public face of the nation, including statues of African-derived deities in public spaces, staged "folkloric" performances of the once-proscribed sacred music and dances, recognition of African diaspora festivals and holidays, and state support for religious tourism for ritual consultations and initiations.[31] However, this brief window of religious freedom was not to last long.

The twenty-first century has brought a renewed age of repression of African diaspora religions. As this book explores, in some ways, the limitations on African-derived faiths are connected to new phenomena such as the rise of evangelical Christianity in the Caribbean and South America. However, more than a novel occurrence, discrimination against these faiths seems to be a resurfacing of post-emancipation rationales for and methods of suppression. As the case studies herein show, each aspect of the legal restrictions on Africana religious freedom carries some rhetoric about contamination, morality, criminality, and the purported threat that Black spirituality poses to public health that resembles those popular in the nineteenth and twentieth centuries.

ORGANIZATION OF THE BOOK

This book is divided into three parts, each of which discusses one set of broader patterns of "religious racism." Each part provides a very cursory introduction to the religions discussed in that section to allow readers who have no familiarity with African diaspora religions to utilize this book without needing to acquire other introductory materials on these faiths. Each chapter focuses on a particular challenge to religious freedom for adherents of African diaspora faiths, framing these issues in transnational and transregional perspectives, wherever possible, to understand the larger human rights disputes that country-specific studies can overlook. While the manuscript is not intended to be comprehensive of every case or every issue, it is meant to provide a broad, international perspective about the right to practice each of the examined belief systems and to discuss the general freedom to practice religions of the African diaspora over the past twenty to thirty years.

Chapter 1 begins with the most egregious affronts to religious freedom in the African diaspora—physical assaults on devotees, their homes, and their places of worship. The first part of this chapter focuses on Brazil, where recent years have seen a drastic increase in physical violence against Candomblé and Umbanda adherents. Terrorists have burned, bombed, and shot at their homes and temples, as well as physically attacked the devotees themselves. This chapter provides specific examples of these assaults as well as statistics to analyze and attempt to understand this growing issue. The second part addresses Haiti, where violence against Vodou priests and devotees became a serious issue following the devastating 2010 earthquake and subsequent cholera outbreak. It discusses the violent murders of Vodou priests by vigilantes and the Haitian government's lackluster response.

Chapter 2 explores the most significant litigation over the practice of orisha/orixá religions—the ritual slaughter of animals. It begins with the dispute that led to the US Supreme Court's ruling in the *City of Hialeah* case in 1993. It surveys some of the dozens of cases that US courts have heard since then, where local officials have attempted to restrict the ritual slaughter of animals in other ways. It also compares these cases to growing controversies over animal sacrifices in Brazil and Venezuela.

Chapter 3 examines a body of cases that has rarely, if ever, been discussed in the context of religious freedom. It focuses on Palo Mayombe, an Afro-Cuban religion that is one of the most controversial belief systems of the African diaspora. Palo Mayombe adherents develop reciprocal relationships with the spirits of departed persons; they create shrines where they communicate with and make offerings (food, drink, etc.) to these spirits, and the spirits provide supernatural protection and guidance to the adherents. To create a more powerful connection, devotees ("Paleros") often use the remains of the departed person (skulls and other bones) in the shrines. This chapter explores a series of cases where Paleros and devotees of other African diaspora faiths were charged with unlawful possession of human remains and grave robbing.

The fourth chapter, the last in the first part of the book, discusses cases that have called into question the rights of devotees of African diaspora religions to gain or retain custody of minor children. These cases intersect with the others discussed in the first three chapters, stemming from the rampant discrimination against devotees that is leading to physical assaults in Brazil, concerns about animal sacrifice, as well as disputes over whether Palo Mayombe rituals are protected by religious freedom. The proceedings covered in this chapter range from criminal charges for taking children to religious ceremonies to civil disputes over custody between practitioner and nonpractitioner parents.

The second section of the book, chapters 5 and 6, introduces an interrelated set of problems about adherents' access to public facilities and spaces such as courthouses, schools, and even places of employment. Mostly centering on controversies over hair and headscarves, chapter 5 explores cases where devotees have been barred from schools because of their religious beliefs or practices. Chapter 6 examines a range of situations where litigants, lawyers, police officers, and corrections officers have been expelled from legal facilities because of disputes over their religious practices.

The third and final section centers on the modern boundaries of the concept of "religion." It begins with chapter 7, which discusses the continued proscription of Obeah and highlights the contrast to the decriminalization of "witchcraft" in other parts of the former British Empire, particularly to protect the religious freedom of Spiritualists and white "witches." Chapter 8 moves from proscription to prosecution, analyzing a range of recent cases where courts in the Americas have opined that African diaspora faiths are not religions. Finally, chapter 9 concludes with the discussion of a centuries-old issue—myths and misconceptions that taint public views of African diaspora religions.

Together, these nine chapters attempt to provide a clear picture of the major challenges to religious freedom for adherents of African diaspora faiths in the twenty-first century. They cover the most significant controversies involving the most well known and widely practiced African diaspora religions, providing the background of the controversies and the outcome of the disputes. This book introduces new issues that have never been considered as a question of religious freedom before, such as the right of Palo Mayombe devotees to possess remains of the dead. It places controversies in conversation that have not been previously regarded as analogous, such as the right to wear headscarves and the right to wear dreadlocks in schools.

The hope is that this book will be specific enough in its legal content that instruction on African diaspora religious freedom can finally reach law and legal studies courses while including enough history and background that laypeople and practitioners can appreciate the text. I have incorporated as much detail about the practitioners and their proceedings as possible to give voice to the devotees, not just the courts' interpretations of the proceedings. For too long, the only acknowledgment of these charges has been the loud voice of the media and government officials, skewing and sensationalizing these cases. The first step toward religious freedom in the African diaspora is ending the silence surrounding these abuses of rights and ensuring that the problem of religious racism can be acknowledged and discussed in scholarly and policy contexts.

SECTION I

◇◇◇

Santeria/Lucumi, Haitian Vodou, Candomblé, Palo Mayombe, and Umbanda

The first part of this book centers on five African diaspora belief systems that share a history of persecution and prosecution. During the post-emancipation period, colonies and nations throughout the Americas banned all of these religions as a threat to "progress," "morality," and "public health." Today, they continue to experience intersecting challenges in the enjoyment of religious freedom, including violence against devotees, constraints on the ritual slaughter of animals, arrests for the possession of human remains, and restrictions on devotees' parental rights.

PART I: HAITIAN VODOU

Margarite Fernandez Olmos and Lizabeth Paravisini-Gebert argue that Vodou is "the most maligned and misunderstood of all African-inspired religions in the Americas."¹ It has been known by a diverse set of monikers in the centuries since its development in the Americas. The word "Vodou" likely originated from the Fon-Dahomey language and had multiple meanings, such as spiritual energy or force, a group of deities, the process of worshipping those deities, as well as the ritual dances performed for them.² The French adopted the term "Vaudoux" to refer to a variety of African spiritual practices in their colonies, especially St. Domingue (modern-day Haiti). In the nineteenth and twentieth centuries, "Voodoo" became the most common pronunciation and spelling for both Haitian and New Orleans religious practices. Most recently, scholars and some devotees have stressed that "Vodou" is the most phonetically appropriate spelling and have preferred this term to distinguish the faith from the negative reputation that Voodoo has garnered over the years.³ However, many devotees do not deploy even the term "Vodou" to refer to their faith; they simply say that they "serve the spirits."⁴

Vodou adherents believe in a supreme being whom they call Bondye or Grand Mét.⁵ However, Bondye is a remote deity who has little interactions with humans on a regular basis.⁶ Instead, entities known as the *lwa* (also spelled *loa*) serve "as active agents whom Bondye has placed in charge of the workings of specific aspects of the world."⁷ Each of the lwa is multidimensional, having many incarnations or manifestations of their essence with "both constructive and destructive dimensions."⁸

Vodou worship takes place in a temple known as an *ounfo*.⁹ It is often located within a *lakou*, or a large complex of homes that includes a community of devotees and a cemetery where the ancestors are buried.¹⁰ Each ounfo is led by a senior male priest (*oungan*) or female priest (*manbo/mam'bo*), whose responsibility it is "to organize the various liturgies, prepare adherents for initiation, offer individual consultations for clients in need of divination or spiritual advice, and use his or her knowledge of herbs to prescribe and prepare remedies to improve health or potions, 'packages,' or bottles to bring luck or ensure protection."¹¹

The lwa have a reciprocal relationship with Vodou adherents in which they provide "help, protection, and counsel" in exchange for devotees worshipping and honoring them in many ways.¹² Methods of worshipping or honoring the lwa can include prayers and invocations, singing, dancing, drumming, food offerings, and animal sacrifice as well as the holding of public feasts or services on the lwa's sacred holiday.¹³ Vodou is a decentralized faith in which beliefs and rituals can vary greatly between different communities.¹⁴

PART II: AFRO-BRAZILIAN RELIGIONS

A. Candomblé

Candomblé is "a complex religion of the diaspora characterized by ritual dance, spiritual healing, divinatory science, spirit possession, sacrificial offerings, spiritual powers, and the celebration of living religious memories in Afro-Brazilian communities."[15] The term "Candomblé" can be traced back to at least 1826, when it was used in reference to "a house where a group of rebellious slaves had taken refuge."[16] Scholars believe that the term "Candomblé" is likely of Bantu-Kongo origin; however, the religion itself is derived from many peoples of West and West Central Africa.[17]

Candomblé is centered on the veneration of a pantheon of spirits or deities, known as orixás, who serve as intermediaries between adherents and god (Olorun).[18] Orixás are powerful spirits who embody and exercise control over the elements of the natural world—mountains, oceans, rivers, forests, and so forth. However, they also resemble human beings in many respects; they have emotions, personalities, desires, strengths, and flaws.[19] Candomblé is a decentralized faith, divided into several different "nations," each of which has its own beliefs, rituals, knowledge, and deities.[20] These nations are further divided into spiritual houses or *terreiros* that are under the direction of high priests known as an Iyalorixá (*mae de santo*) or a Babalorixá (*pai de santo*).[21] The physical building of the terreiros may be an entire compound with meeting spaces, shrines, reception areas, and other indoor spaces surrounded by gardens and other natural habitat.[22] It is a sacred space, where an initiate's spiritual lineage is anchored.[23]

B. Umbanda

Umbanda originated in Rio de Janeiro in the 1920s and has its roots in African religions as well as Kardec Spiritism. The fundamental tenet of Umbanda is the idea that "every living person has a spirit, and this spirit survives the death of the body," and that "the spirits of the dead or the not yet born reside in the realm of pure nonmateriality."[24] Like Candomblé adherents, Umbanda devotees also believe in the existence of the orixás. However, many regard the orixás as "too elevated to deal directly with earthly beings and so they send instead their emissaries" "to do their work among the human beings who come to Umbanda."[25] These emissaries or spirits include, but are not limited to, the spirits of the *pretos velhos* (the "old Blacks," referring to the formerly enslaved), the *caboclos* (indigenous persons), or *crianças* (children).[26] These spirits "seek to help humans in order to gain merit themselves and advance to higher levels of the spirit world."[27]

Paul Christopher Johnson explains that "a typical [Umbanda] ceremony uses drum rhythms and songs to call the spirits to descend (baixar) and mount their mediums, who then consult privately with participants in the stylized manner specific to their kind. Most often the spirits offer advice on topics like love, finances, and future plans."[28] Renato Ortiz adds: "All Umbanda sessions consist of invocations to the spirits, during which the spirits descend in order to understand and resolve the problems which afflict devotees. The problems include illness, unhappiness in love, or financial failure. The close of each session comes only after the spirits listen attentively to the problems of devotees and bestow charity on them."[29]

Because it incorporates beliefs and practices from a variety of European, Native American, and African religious traditions, some scholars have questioned whether Umbanda is properly classified as an Afro-Brazilian religion, arguing that it is rather a true Brazilian religion.[30] Around the end of the twentieth century, it had between thirty and fifty million followers.[31]

PART III: CUBAN RELIGIONS

A. Santeria/Lucumi

Santeria/Lucumi is the most widely practiced African diaspora religion in Cuba and has spread through the Cuban diaspora to places such as the United States and Venezuela. "Santeria" is a derogatory term that Spanish colonists used to refer to this belief system, implying that Africans worshipped Catholic saints. "Lucumi" may have originated as a Yoruba greeting, *oluku mi*, that enslaved persons used in Cuba.[32] "Lucumi" or "Regla de Ocha" (rites/rule of the orishas) are preferred terms that practitioners use to describe their faith. I use both "Santeria" and "Lucumi" throughout this text because "Santeria" is widely utilized in court cases and media reports about this faith; however, I also wish to honor the terminology preferred by devotees.

Santeria/Lucumi developed in Cuba, predominantly from the influence of enslaved persons who were trafficked to the island during the Atlantic slave trade. Although Cuba received a diverse array of enslaved persons with different ethnic origins, the Yoruba and the Kongo peoples had the most apparent impact on religious practices on the island.[33] Like Candomblé, Santeria/Lucumi is based on the veneration of orishas (orixás), who function as intermediaries between god and humans. They are more present than god, Olodumare, who is considered to be remote and does not directly interact with humans. Nathaniel Murrell explains: "Orishas receive prayers, sacrifices, and other worship, and they respond to devotees through oracles, spirit possession, and mediumship. The ritual means of communication are designed to make more potent ashe [spelled *aché* in Cuba, the spiritual energy that permeates all things] in the world to aid human accomplishments and the work of spiritual entities."[34]

Most important rituals in Santeria/Lucumi are prescribed by some form of divination. The methods of divination and the deities consulted range according to who is doing the divining and the seriousness of the questions posed, but in each instance, the devotee receives instructions from the ancestors or the spirit world about how to proceed with religious practices.[35] During divination, priests will often prescribe rituals, known as ebbos or ebós, through which devotees encourage the favor and support of the orishas. These ebbos can "range from a simple offering of fruit, candles, food, or flowers appropriate to the attributes of a particular orisha to a blood sacrifice involving a specific sacrificial animal for a serious problem, if so indicated by divination. The offering is then transformed into aché to carry out the needs of the petitioner."[36] If an animal is sacrificed, it is typically consumed by devotees. However, there are certain exceptions, such as when an animal is offered to counteract "harm caused by witchcraft."[37] Divination sessions and rituals usually take place in private buildings, frequently the home of a priest. Typically, there are no specific temples or other permanent prescribed places set aside solely for religious worship that would compare to a Christian church, a Muslim mosque, or even a Candomblé terreiro.[38]

B. Palo Mayombe

The Afro-Cuban religions known as Reglas Congos ("Kongo Religions/Rites") are derived primarily from the Bantu and Bkango peoples of West Central Africa.[39] Cuba received approximately 890,000 Africans in the Atlantic slave trade, of whom around 280,000 were from West Central Africa, the area between modern-day South Cameroon and Northern Angola.[40] However, these Africans were not the exclusive contributors to these faiths nor the only people who practiced them.[41] For example, when Africans from the Kongo arrived in Cuba, they already shared a worldview with the indigenous peoples that included ancestor reverence, spirit-conjuring, and a relationship with the land. When these societies interacted with one another, they exchanged some spiritual practices, forming multiple religious communities.[42] Today, Reglas Congas consist of several branches, such as Palo Monte/Palo Mayombe, Kimbisa, and Briyumba, among others.[43] For purposes of this book, I focus on Palo Monte/Palo Mayombe, which has experienced the most legal challenges of Cuban-Kongo religions.

The terms "palo" and "monte" mean "stick,"[44] and "mayombe" is "a deep-forested area in the Central African region."[45] These words form the name of the faith because sticks and other greenery, as well as forest animals, are important symbols in Palo Mayombe, which is a "naturalistic" religion.[46] As Jualynne Dodson explains, these forest materials "represent the concentration of the creative life force that the religion holds in sacred esteem."[47]

Palo is a decentralized religion, so there is a lot of fluctuation in how the religion is practiced.[48] However, devotees generally believe in the existence of a creator god, Nsambi (also spelled Nsambe), but this entity is remote and is not typically invoked by individual Paleros during rituals.[49] They also believe in nature spirits and spirits of powerful ancestors that resemble the orisha and are known as "mpungas" and "minkisi."[50] Despite the belief in a creator god as well as nature and ancestral spirits, most Palo practices involve the building of a reciprocal relationship with spirits of the dead.[51] These spirits, known as *muertos*, can assist the living by providing guidance, knowledge, power, and healing, but the living must maintain a connection with them in order to receive that assistance.[52] The dead can be invoked to do positive or negative things.[53]

A three-legged pot known as a *nganga* houses the spirit of the dead. Inside a nganga, "there can be dirt from farreaching corners of the earth; sticks from an assortment of specialty trees and bushes; and expressly empowered rocks from oceans, rivers, mountains, and valleys, as well as skeletal fragments from a wide selection of dead sacred humans and animals."[54] The human skulls that are often included in a nganga are known as *kiyumba*, and they mean that the spirit of the deceased is in the nganga waiting to be summoned.[55]

Devotees of Palo are known as "paleros," and priests are referred to as "tata" for men or "yaya" for women.[56] Paleros develop a relationship with a tata or yaya and belong to a temple known as a "munanso."[57] However, the religion is also "individualistic" and centers on developing a direct relationship with the spirits.[58]

C. The Arrival of Cuban Religions in the United States

Because nearly all of the central disputes about Afro-Cuban religions discussed in this book occur in the United States, it is important to briefly mention how and when these religions arrived. In the first two decades following the Cuban Revolution in 1959, hundreds of thousands of Cubans came to the United States. Most of them were white Cubans, because these were the individuals who had benefited from the previous regime's policies promoting capitalism and racial segregation.[59] It was not until 1980 that the first wave of more racially diverse Cubans landed in the United States as part of the so-called Mariel Exodus. More of these individuals were devotees of Afro-Cuban faiths than in previous generations of immigrants.[60] By 2009, litigants in one case reported that there were between 250,000 and 1 million adherents of Santeria/Lucumi in the United States.[61]

CHAPTER 1

New Forms of Religious Terrorism
Physical Violence Against African Diaspora Religions

On February 3, 2020, unidentified attackers threw a homemade bomb into an Umbanda terreiro (temple) in Ribeirão Preto, São Paulo, while twelve individuals were inside performing a ceremony.[1] When the devotees tried to flee the space, thirty assailants stoned, punched, and kicked them. The attackers caused severe injuries to a twenty-five-year-old male, knocking out five of his front teeth and rendering him unconscious. He was transported to the hospital in an ambulance. The devotees report that this was the fourth time that their place of worship had been bombed.

This story provides an example of the worst violations of religious freedom in the African diaspora—rampant physical violence against adherents, their temples, and their homes. This issue is closely connected to the increasing presence of certain sects of evangelical Christianity in parts of the Caribbean and South America. The rapid growth of these intolerant forms of Christianity has incited severe physical violence in some of the most iconic Black nations in the world, where African diaspora religions have historically been a symbol of national identity. The two nations where religious intolerance has recently become most prevalent are Brazil and Haiti.

PART I: BRAZIL

Brazil houses the largest population of persons of African descent outside the African continent and one of the largest populations of Black people in the world (second only to Nigeria). The 2010 census revealed that nearly 97 million Brazilians (50.7 percent of the population) self-identified as "brown" or "Black."[2] In addition to the sheer volume of persons of African descent in Brazil, Afro-Brazilian culture, such as samba, capoeira, Candomblé, and African-derived cuisine, plays a significant role in public imagery of the nation and draws a substantial number of foreign cultural tourists to Brazil. However, studies have shown a rapid increase in religious intolerance in Brazil in the past five to ten years and have placed Afro-Brazilian religions on the receiving end of most of this violence.

One of these studies is the Pew Research Center's Social Hostilities Index—an annual survey of the religious climate in 198 countries and territories across the globe. The Social Hostilities Index is based on a variety of questions such as whether the government limits preaching or proselytizing, whether the government intervenes in cases of religious discrimination, and whether there is violence based on religious hatred.[3] The index rates each country on a scale of 0.0 to 10.0. Countries on the lower end of the scale have the greatest levels of freedom, and countries on the higher end of the scale experience the greatest levels of hostilities toward religion.

More than ten years ago, in 2007, the Pew Foundation rated Brazil at 0.8 of 10 on its Social Hostilities Index. This placed Brazil in the "low" category, with few hostilities related to religion. In 2008 and 2009, Brazil jumped to 1.6 and 1.7, respectively, finding itself in the "moderately hostile" category. Between 2010 and 2015, it mostly fluctuated between 2.5 and 3.5, which is on the higher end of the "moderately hostile" spectrum. However, in the most recent report, which evaluates the year ending in December 2017, Brazil jumped to 4.3, which places it in the "high" category of social hostilities.[4] Brazil received the third-highest ranking in the Western Hemisphere (behind Mexico and the United States) and the highest in South America. To put this in further perspective, only approximately one-quarter of countries in the world (28 percent) are ranked as having "high" or "very high" levels of social hostilities involving religion.[5]

The Pew Research Center report indicated several factors that demonstrated that "social hostilities" toward religion were prevalent in Brazil. These issues were concentrated on private actions—harassment, intimidation, physical assaults, residential displacement, property damage, crimes or violence motivated by religious hatred/bias—as well as groups using violence to try to enforce religious norms or prevent other groups from operating. With regard to harassment and intimidation, the center noted that the Americas "ha[ve] the lowest levels of all the regions [of the world], but also ha[ve] experienced the largest increase in this type of hostility since 2007."⁶ The drafters of the report utilized Brazil as an example of this increase, citing "pockets of anti-Semitic and anti-Muslim sentiment" and "incidents targeting Afro-Brazilian religions" as key problems.⁷ With regard to the latter, the center explained: "In the state of Sao Paulo, arsonists burned down an Afro-Brazilian temple in September, one of eight attacks against Afro-Brazilian targets in the state in that month."⁸

The Brazilian government maintains at least two databases that confirm the increasing problem of religious intolerance against Afro-Brazilian faiths and provide some insights into what types of discrimination and violence have led to the country's recent poor evaluations on the Social Hostilities Index. The Secretary for Human Rights manages a free 24-7 hotline known as Dial 100 Human Rights ("Disque 100 Direitos Humanos"), where individuals can call and anonymously report human rights violations. The Ministry of Human Rights compiles data on the calls they receive and releases reports on some of the broad trends in their call data.⁹ The second data set also comes from the Ministry of Human Rights, which houses the National Committee on the Respect for Religious Diversity ("Comitê Nacional de Respeito à Diversidade Religiosa"). In 2015, the committee utilized data received from ten governmental bodies to produce the 147-page *Report on Intolerance and Religious Violence* (*Relatório sobre Intolerância e Violência Religiosa*).

Both data sets confirm a drastic increase in religious intolerance and discrimination over the past few years. Through the ten entities that reported to the National Committee on the Respect for Religious Diversity, the Brazilian government received an astonishing 1,031 reports of cases of religious intolerance or violence for the five-year period between 2011 and 2015.¹⁰ Unfortunately, only four of the ten government bodies sent detailed information about these incidents to the committee; therefore, the statistics in the *Report on Intolerance and Religious Violence* are based on less than 40 percent (394) of the reported cases.¹¹ However, the data from Disque 100 combined with the data featured in the *Report on Intolerance and Religious Violence* provide a meaningful glimpse into the nature of religious discrimination in Brazil in recent years.

Disque 100's first report covered 2011; during this year, the hotline received minimal data on religious discrimination—only 15 calls. In 2012, this number jumped to 109, then doubled to 231 the following year. In the past four years, denunciations of religious intolerance have more than doubled again, to an average of 590 cases per year, with a peak of 759 cases in 2016. In total, Disque 100 has received 2,862 denunciations of religious intolerance since 2011, 82 percent of which have occurred since 2015.

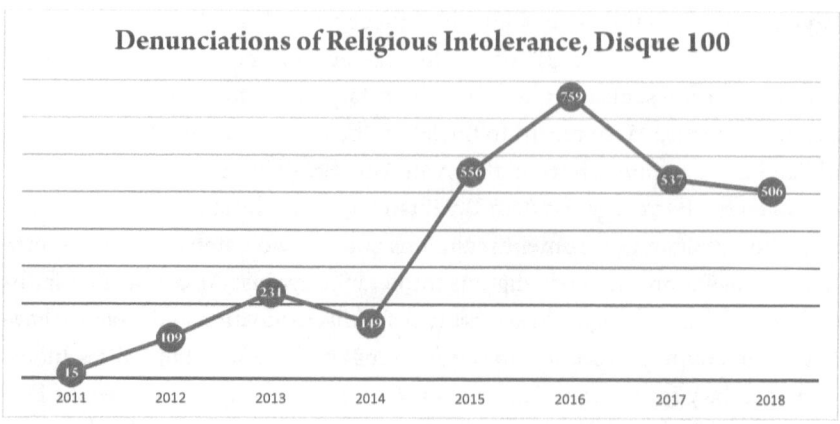

The *Report on Intolerance and Religious Violence* and Disque 100 records both confirm that adherents of African diaspora religions are, by far, the largest percentage of known victims of religious violence in Brazil. For the five-year period between the start of 2011 and the end of 2015, the National Committee on the Respect for Religious Diversity received information on the religion of the victim in approximately 65 percent (260) of the 394 cases on which they obtained specific data. Adherents of Africana religions ("Matriz Africana") were the victims in approximately 41 percent of cases in which the religion of the victim was identified.[12] Moreover, the following year, the committee issued a public notice observing the recent "significant increase" in cases of religious discrimination and violence in the country. Specifically, it expressed concern about "recent cases of aggression" and "the depredation of spaces of worship of religions of African origin."[13]

Although working with different data sources, Disque 100's report confirms that violence against adherents of Afro-Brazilian religions has increased since the committee's report. Disque 100 has received 660 denunciations of intolerance against Afro-Brazilian religions since 2011. Nearly three-quarters (73 percent) of these cases occurred in the last three reporting years—2016 to 2018. Furthermore, since 2015, devotees of Afro-Brazilian religions have represented more than 50 percent of the Disque 100 cases in which the religious affiliation of the victims was known. In 2016 and 2018, they represented nearly two-thirds—64 percent—of the known victims. These statistics are particularly striking when one considers that devotees of Afro-Brazilian religions represent a mere 1 percent of the population.[14]

State reporting centers likewise indicate that violence against Afro-Brazilian religions is rampant and disproportionate to their representation in the population. Between December 2016 and August 2017, the Center for the Promotion of Religious Freedom and Human Rights in Rio de Janeiro received fifty-two complaints of religious intolerance in the state; thirty-four (65 percent) of the complaints were from devotees of Afro-Brazilian faiths.[15] Between August and October, a state reporting center known as Fight Against Prejudice Hotline, founded in response to rising religious intolerance, received forty-three additional reports of religious discrimination in Rio de Janeiro. Ninety percent of the complaints came from adherents of Candomblé and Umbanda.[16]

In addition to these statistics, human rights experts across the globe have drawn attention to the burgeoning violence against Afro-Brazilian religions in their recent reports. For instance, in 2014, the chair of the Working Group of Experts on People of African Descent expressed concern to the UN General Assembly about "the racism, persecution and violations of cultural rights and the right to religious freedom suffered by the religious communities of African origin, such as *Candomblé* and *Umbanda*."[17] The following year, in September 2015, Rita Izsák, the United Nations special rapporteur on minority issues, made an official visit to Brazil. Ms. Izsák noted that the single exception to the general climate of religious tolerance in the country was "the situation of Afro-Brazilian religions, which are facing an increasing number of incidents of violence, intimidation and discrimination."[18]

In contrast to the high rates of victims of religious intolerance who were adherents of Afro-Brazilian faiths, the National Committee on the Respect for Religious Diversity's report shows the vast majority of the aggressors in cases of religious intolerance were Christians, especially evangelicals.[19] Although Protestants are only approximately 22 percent of the population of Brazil,[20] they were 63 percent of the aggressors in the cases in which the religion of the aggressor was known.[21] Moreover, in November 2019, the International Commission to Combat Religious Racism (ICCRR) published a report on three hundred cases of religious intolerance against Afro-Brazilian religions that occurred between 2000 and 2019. Christians were the perpetrators in 100 percent of the cases in which the religion of the aggressor was known; of these cases, at least 80 percent of the perpetrators were evangelicals.[22]

A. *Specific Incidents of Religious Racism*

Not only is intolerance against Afro-Brazilian religions prevalent, but governmental and nongovernmental sources indicate that many of these discriminatory acts are violent forms of religious intolerance. For instance, the Palmares Foundation, a federal institution tasked with preserving Black influence on Brazilian society, reported that it had documented 218 violent attacks against devotees of Afro-Brazilian religions and their places of worship from 2010 to 2015.[23] Similarly, the ICCRR found that more than half of the acts of intolerance it had documented between 2000 and 2019 were violent attacks against people and/or property. It is important to examine some of the most prevalent forms of violence against these faiths to gain a better understanding of the problem.

Perhaps the greatest threat to Afro-Brazilian religious freedom in the twenty-first century is the growing popularity of extremist sects of evangelical Christianity among drug-trafficking gangs in Rio de Janeiro and the increasing frequency with which these converts are regarding the eradication of Afro-Brazilian religions as their spiritual mandate. These attacks date back to at least 2005, when traffickers from the Comando Vermelho gang forced Umbanda and Candomblé temples to close in at least six of the favelas that they controlled in the North Zone of Rio.[24] Around the same period, Evangelized drug traffickers in the West Zone of Rio and on Ilha do Governador not only began to close Afro-Brazilian temples but also banned certain ceremonies and the wearing of bracelets or necklaces associated with Afro-Brazilian religions.[25] Over the next five years, Evangelized traffickers also increasingly began prohibiting the residents of the favelas and communities they controlled from wearing white—a ritual color of Afro-Brazilian faiths—and threatening to evict individuals who broke this rule.[26]

More recently, trafficker assaults have turned increasingly violent. For instance, in 2017, traffickers filmed themselves attacking two Afro-Brazilian temples in the city of Nova Iguaçu. In the first recording, the extremists forced a priest to destroy his terreiro and claimed to be acting in the name of Jesus as they threatened to kill him if he rebuilt the temple.[27] In the second attack, seven individuals held an Iyalorixá at gunpoint, ordering her to break everything in her temple in the name of Jesus.[28] They also "used their guns to rip ileke Orisha [religious amulets] off of [devotees'] necks" and "even urinated on the Orisa [sic], saying they wouldn't permit the practice of 'witchcraft' in that community."[29] In total, between July and early September 2017, at least seven Afro-Brazilian terreiros were destroyed in Nova Iguaçu. Furthermore, across the state, at least thirty terreiros were destroyed in a twenty-day period in September 2017.[30] Although it is unclear how many of these other attacks were carried out by the traffickers themselves or by like-minded individuals, it seems clear that Evangelized drug gangs contributed substantially to this culture of violence in 2017.

Since 2017, this issue has escalated further. In August 2019, government officials announced that Evangelized traffickers had threatened at least two hundred religious temples in the State of Rio de Janeiro.[31] In early 2020, reports clarified that at least 132 of these "threats" included physical violence against the devotees and/or their places of worship.[32] For example, on July 11, 2019, the traffickers invaded an Afro-Brazilian terreiro in the neighborhood of Parque Paulista.[33] They ordered all the devotees to leave except for the religious leader, an eighty-four-year-old woman. The traffickers held her at gunpoint and ordered her to destroy her sacred objects and shrines. After she completed this destruction, the traffickers set fire to the remnants of the temple.

In addition to the Evangelized trafficker attacks on Afro-Brazilian places of worship, private citizens have likewise committed physical acts of violence against these sacred spaces. In fact, this form of intolerance is the most prevalent in the ICCRR's report on discrimination against Afro-Brazilian religions since the start of the twenty-first century. These assaults against places of worship have taken several forms.

As the introduction to the chapter indicates, intolerant persons have attacked Afro-Brazilian temples using incendiary devices such as bombs, Molotov cocktails, and firecrackers. For example, in December 2016, unknown assailants placed a bomb on the electric meter of Mãe Elaine de Oxalá's temple while she and others were performing a religious ceremony.[34] This was not the first attack; Mãe Elaine had long endured harassment, including people throwing stones at her temple and setting the columns on fire. Similarly, between October 2016 and February 2017, an intolerant neighbor carried out three attacks on the Centro de Umbanda Oxum Apará in Salvador, Bahia, by throwing firecrackers into the building while they were holding celebrations.[35] In the third incident, 150 people were present in the center, three of whom were injured severely and transported to an emergency medical facility.

In addition to the use of incendiary devices, intolerant persons have repeatedly burned Afro-Brazilian places of worship. For instance, in September 2015, arsonists targeted a series of Candomblé temples in the State of Goiás near the Federal District. On September 5, they set ablaze two temples within a five-hour period. One of the temples was located in Santo Antônio do Descoberto and was owned by Candomblé priests Edvaldo do Nascimento and Rejiane Varjão.[36] The priests learned of the arson when their neighbors called to notify them. By the time they arrived, the fire had caused R$30,000 in damages. The second temple burned that day was located in nearby Águas Lindas. The owner of the temple, Babalorixá Djair Santos, arrived before it was completely destroyed because a neighbor warned him about strange noises on his property. Both Santos and Nascimento told reporters that they did not know who started the fires, but they speculated that the arsonists' motive might have been religious intolerance. For Nascimento, a key piece of evidence supporting this theory was that he had found a clean, unscorched bible in the rubble—an apparent calling card of the arsonists.

Afro-Brazilian places of worship also suffer from constant acts of vandalism. Some of these are minor cases, where attackers place graffiti on the outside of the temple. For instance, in August 2017, vandals targeted a new Candomblé terreiro that devotees were constructing in Lauro de Freitas, Bahia.[37] They wrote "o sangue de Jesus tem poder" ("the blood of Jesus has power") on the structure and broke an offering bowl that the adherents had placed at the base of a nearby tree. A little over a year later, in October 2018, unknown vandals wrote "Jesus é o caminho" ("Jesus is the Way") on the exterior of Casa de Oxumarê, one of the most well-known Candomblé temples in Salvador, Bahia.[38]

In other cases, assailants harass devotees by throwing objects—most frequently large stones—at their places of worship while adherents are inside hosting a ceremony. For instance, from 2016–2017, intolerant persons repeatedly launched rocks as well as rotten eggs and vegetables at Ilê Axé Obá Inã terreiro in Penha, Rio de Janeiro.[39] These rocks broke through the roof of the temple and narrowly missed hitting the devotees inside. Similarly, attackers stoned Ilê Nife Omo Nije Ogba terreiro in Maceió, Alagoas, for six hours in March 2018 while devotees were hosting a ceremony.[40] Despite placing fifteen calls to various government offices, no one came to assist the religious community and stop this attack.

The most common form of violence against Afro-Brazilian places of worship, however, is when assailants break into a temple to destroy and/or steal both sacred and secular objects. For instance, in August 2018, vandals broke down the doors and walls of an Afro-Brazilian terreiro in the city of Nova Iguaçu (Rio de Janeiro).[41] They stole the freezer, the industrial stove, the television, and ceremonial garments. They also smashed three hundred images or shrines of the orixás on the floor. The owner estimated the financial loss at R$20,000. He was so upset when he saw the damage that his blood pressure spiked and he had to go to the hospital.

In most of these cases, the perpetrators are never identified and therefore never prosecuted. However, where there is evidence of the identity of the attacker and/or their motive, it is nearly always a Christian assailant who has explicitly announced a religious motive for the attack. For instance, in May 2008, four members of an evangelical church, Nova Geração de Jesus Cristo, invaded an Umbanda temple, Centro Espírita Cruz de Oxalá, in Catete, Rio de Janeiro.[42] The attackers verbally abused the devotees who were gathered for a ceremony, calling them "devil worshippers" and announcing that the members of the evangelical church had come in the name of Jesus. The assailants forced their way into the temple and broke about thirty religious images, shelves, and a fan. More recently, in 2018, a man named Leonardo carried out a similar attack on an Umbanda temple, Flor do Matão Deus é Quem Guia, in São Luís, Maranhão.[43] Leonardo arrived with a bible in his hands and began breaking everything while shouting "Get out, Satan."

Religious intolerance in Brazil does not always take the form of violence against places of worship; there is also a concerning trend of violence directly against devotees. Many of these cases take place in public spaces as devotees are simply carrying out their regular activities. For instance, in March 2006, Mãe Jaciara, the leader of a Candomblé terreiro called Ilê Abassá de Ogum, was walking down the street in Salvador, Bahia when two evangelical males told her "Jesus loves you."[44] Mae Jaciara responded, "Ogum too [referring to an orixá]." The two men became angry and began to assault Mãe Jaciara with their bibles in hand. Police arrested the men for religious intolerance.

One of the most disturbing trends in assaults against devotees of Afro-Brazilian religions is a rise in student-on-student violence. In August 2015, a friend posted a photo of fourteen-year-old Agnes on social media that revealed that Agnes was a devotee of Candomblé. The following day, Agnes went to her school in Curitiba, Paraná, and a classmate called her a *macumbeira* (sorceress) and kicked her. Agnes fell and hit her head on a wall while other students encouraged the attacker, yelling "Kick that macumba." Agnes's mother reported that the school did not punish Agnes's attacker.[45] Less than a year later, in April 2016, classmates carried out a similar assault on sixteen-year-old Isadora, a student in Aparecida de Goiania, Goiás.[46] Like the attack on Agnes, the incident began after classmates saw a photo of Isadora on social media wearing a Candomblé necklace. Two female students knocked Isadora to the ground, then began kicking and punching her while yelling that their god was greater than Isadora's *macumba* (sorcery).

Stoning of persons is another common method through which intolerant persons have committed violence against devotees of Afro-Brazilian religions. The most famous of these cases occurred in 2015. Two adult males followed the Campos family as they were walking home from a Candomblé service.[47] The men carried bibles and called the family "devils," telling them that they were going to hell and that "Jesus will return." They threw stones at the family, striking eleven-year-old Kailane on the head. Her attackers then hopped on a bus and rode away from the scene. Kailane's family took her to the hospital for treatment; they reported that she fainted and suffered memory loss from the blow.[48] Although Kailane's family recounted the attack to the authorities and the Brazilian media extensively covered this incident, it does not appear that the culprits responsible for the attack were ever identified.

The murder of devotees, especially priests, of Afro-Brazilian religions is another growing problem. Some of these incidents represent disputes between devotees and intolerant neighbors that escalate to the point of deadly violence. For instance, in September 2012, Candomblé devotee Marcos Antônio Dias Santos Marcelino was on a ladder at the wall that separated his temple from the neighbor's property.[49] The neighbor, Manoel Correia dos Santos, arrived home drunk and became angry when he saw Marcelino on the ladder. Dos Santos threatened to kill Marcelino, then he grabbed a shotgun and fired. One of the shots hit Marcelino in the head and killed him. The Iyalorixá of the terreiro, Rosa Maria Lopes (who was also Marcelino's wife), later explained that the dispute was based solely on religious intolerance and that Dos Santos had previously shot at another member of their terreiro.

In addition to such specific disputes with witnesses and known assailants, certain cities or states have experienced rampant, unsolved murders of priests in a short period of time with no identifiable motive aside from religious bias. For instance, in late 2015, five Afro-Brazilian priests were murdered in the greater Belem region of Pará in the span of approximately three months.[50] Such cases pose a major concern with regard to religious freedom, because the perpetrators are almost never identified and it is difficult to predict future victims or protect other devotees from assault.

B. Ineffective Solutions

By and large, the Brazilian authorities have not managed to identify and arrest the individuals responsible for these violent attacks or curb them before they have happened. With regard to the Evangelized traffickers in Rio de Janeiro, these assaults have been taking place since 2005, but available records indicate that August 2019 was the first time that police managed to arrest any of the perpetrators. At that time, officers apprehended eight people who were part of a group called Bonde de Jesus (Jesus Tram), which several traffickers formed to coordinate attacks on Afro-Brazilian religions. However, these eight individuals were clearly not the sole, and perhaps not even the primary, perpetrators of these assaults.[51] Other traffickers have continued their assaults on Afro-Brazilian religious communities after these arrests.

Regarding other violent offenses, it is very rare that reports indicate that the perpetrators were apprehended. In fact, in 2016, the special rapporteur on minority issues wrote that she had received reports of "widespread impunity" in cases of assaults on Afro-Brazilian religions. The special rapporteur warned that the "lack of responsiveness to complaints filed, or failure to investigate allegations, further contributes to a sense of marginalization and discrimination on the part of the communities. Moreover, the lack of accountability and trust in law enforcement services has meant that followers of Afro-religions report feeling unsafe in their neighbourhoods and cities."[52] The special rapporteur urged Brazil to improve "police and judicial training" and take "swift action" "against any incident of religious intolerance against Afro-religions, and [that] the perpetrators of violence must be held directly accountable."[53] Around this same time, an Afro-Brazilian activist organization, the Collective of Black Entities, announced its intent to file complaints with the United Nations and the Organization of American States to seek "accountability from the government for failing to investigate acts of religious intolerance and prosecute perpetrators."[54]

Instead of arresting the perpetrators, prosecuting them, and incarcerating them, the Brazilian government has focused on other measures to combat religious intolerance.[55] Over the past few years, the government has developed a series of films, tv shows, and educational materials promoting religious diversity; held workshops to promote interfaith dialogue; and established (in 2007) a national day for the fight against religious intolerance.[56] In 2014, the Secretariat for Human Rights created the National Committee on the Respect for Religious Diversity, which produced the 2015 report discussed earlier. In 2015, the Human Rights Ombudsman Office created a specific unit of the Disque 100 hotline for adherents of Afro-Brazilian religions. The following year, the National Committee on the Respect for Religious Diversity discussed creating a victim protection network for persons who experience religious violence.[57] However, none of these mechanisms for interfaith dialogue or reporting violence appear to be eradicating or even curbing the problem. Other than recording these incidents and "promoting dialogue," the government has made little meaningful effort to increase the protection of Afro-Brazilian religions or condemn and curtail the religious terrorism carried out by evangelicals.

PART II: HAITI

Haiti is an iconic nation in the African diaspora. In the early nineteenth century, it was a beacon of hope to enslaved Blacks in the Western Hemisphere as people of African descent overthrew their masters, defeated the French and thwarted other European attempts to seize the island, and ultimately formed the first free Black nation in the Americas. Popular legend says that Vodou played an important role in Haitian liberation; perhaps most significantly, a Vodou ceremony held in an area known as Bwa Kayiman (Caiman Woods) purportedly united and empowered insurgents to participate in what would become the only successful slave rebellion in the Western Hemisphere. However, in recent years, Haitians and outsiders have questioned whether Vodou is detrimental to Haitian society and reinterpreted the legendary ceremony at Bwa Kayiman as something sinister rather than liberatory.

The violence against Vodou adherents in Haiti can be directly connected to the tragic series of natural disasters in 2010 and the growing influence of Protestantism in the small Caribbean nation. In January 2010, a 7.0-magnitude earthquake hit Haiti, displacing more than a million people and killing more than 200,000.[58] Approximately nine months later, in the middle of October, the largest cholera outbreak in the world began sweeping the country.[59] In two months, cholera had killed approximately 2,600 people,[60] hospitalized more than 60,000, and infected more than 120,000.[61] Before the decline of the outbreak in 2015, it had "infected hundreds of thousands and killed upwards of nine thousand."[62] Vodou adherents would be blamed for both of these disasters and suffered substantial violence such as lynching, temple destruction, physical assault, and denial of basic aid such as food and water.

A. *The Post-Earthquake Protestant Threat*

Historically, the predominant religions in Haiti were Vodou and Catholicism. However, there has been an increasing Protestant presence on the island for several decades. Following the 2010 earthquake, there was an immediate influx of Protestant missionaries, supposedly to provide financial aid and other assistance. Patrick Bellegarde-Smith explains that approximately 64 percent of the international community's post-earthquake aid to Haiti went to nongovernmental organizations (NGOs),[63] many of which are religious organizations. Similarly, writing in 2012, Nicole Payne Carelock asserted that there were a minimum of ten thousand religious NGOs in Haiti. Carelock averred that following the earthquake, "tiny cinderblock churches were being built at breakneck speed; pastors and ministers report that they were four or five times over capacity."[64]

In the immediate aftermath of the earthquake, many Protestants expressed negative perspectives on Vodou, outright blaming devotees for the devastation. Most of these opinions centered on the infamous ceremony of Bwa Kayiman as the original sin that prompted this disaster. Most notoriously, just days after the earthquake, controversial evangelical minister Pat Robertson claimed that Haitians had made a pact with the devil (rather than Vodou spirits/lwa) to obtain their independence from France. Although Robertson's comments were the most publicized, this rhetoric surfaced over and over in the years following the earthquake. For example, Carelock, who traveled to the Dominican Republic just three short days after the earthquake struck neighboring Haiti, asserts: "When I arrived, the only thing I heard about was this great religious revival. I heard about how the quake was God's way of punishing the evil in Haiti."[65] Carelock explains that "the majority of Haitian Protestants I have interviewed in Santo Domingo and Haiti did not view *Bwa Kayiman* as a libratory moment but as a moment when the fledgling nation of Haiti was 'consecrated to the Devil.' Many have developed an oppositional view of *Bwa Kayiman* that is a key to their religious identity. This act, in turn, ensured a legacy of misery in Haiti that is evidenced by the underdevelopment that grips it today."[66] Carelock gave the example of Joshua, a missionary from Tennessee, who told her: "I'm talking about pure historical fact here; the nation of Haiti was dedicated to Satan 200 years ago."[67] He continued, "It was a blood ritual ... a pact for 200 years, and guess what? Time's up."[68]

Protestants did not limit their attacks on Vodou to mere verbal denigration. In the immediate aftermath of the earthquake, some missionaries denied aid to Vodou adherents. The most well-recognized example comes from controversial evangelical pastor Frank Amedia of Touch Heaven Ministries.[69] Just one month after the earthquake, Amedia said the following about the organization's post-earthquake aid: "We would give food to the needy in the short term, but if they refused to give up Voodoo, I'm not sure we would continue to support them in the long term because we wouldn't want to perpetuate that practice. We equate it with witchcraft, which is contrary to the Gospel."[70] Several sources have also quoted a well-respected Vodouisant, the late Max Beauvoir, as stating that Protestant churches had indeed refused supplies to Vodou adherents.[71] Scholar Felix Germain, in an article published just one year after the earthquake, succinctly explained that denying aid to Vodou worshippers was part and parcel of how missionaries in Haiti and the rest of the "global south" "capitalize on material deprivation and insecurity to advance their theological agenda."[72] Germain asserts, "Overtly or covertly, they trade food, services like education and health care, and even emotional and psychological support for 'their God.'"[73]

In the months following the earthquake, Vodou adherents also experienced physical assaults on their persons and their shrines, likely as a result of the widespread attribution of the devastation to their "devil worship." Paisley Dodds, in an article published for the Associated Press in February 2010, described such violent attacks: "[They] pelted them [Vodou adherents] with rocks and halted a ceremony meant to honor victims of last month's deadly earthquake. Voodooists gathered in Cité Soleil where thousands of quake survivors live in tents and depend on food aid. Praying and singing, the group was trying to conjure spirits to guide lost souls when a crowd of evangelicals started shouting. Some threw rocks while others urinated on Voodoo symbols. When police left, the crowd destroyed the altars and Voodoo offerings of food and rum."[74] Carelock, who conducted doctoral research in Haiti from late April to August 2010, confirmed these media observations: "In Haiti, the anti-Vodou fervor reached fever pitch when Christian fundamentalists took to the streets in an attempt to stone Vodouisants. Many were injured and feared for their safety. In many instances, United Nations police were called to the scenes."[75] In her dissertation, Carelock includes photos of people stoning the participants in a Vodou ceremony and the adherents running away or protecting themselves with chairs. She also shows armed UN soldiers coming in to protect devotees.[76]

B. The Cholera Escalation

Toward the end of 2010, violent assaults on Vodou adherents resumed and escalated as devotees were blamed for the cholera outbreak that had seized the country in mid-October and would continue to wreak havoc until 2015. Some Haitians believed that the cholera outbreak was a result of Vodou adherents poisoning the water supply with a substance known as *poud kolera*, or cholera powder.[77] By late November, mobs began to lynch Vodou devotees.[78]

According to Frantz Lerebours, a representative of the national police, by the first few days of December, the mobs had killed twelve persons, many of whom they hacked to death with a machete before incinerating their bodies.[79] Others were burned alive with fires fueled by gasoline and tires.[80] By late December, vigilantes had killed at least forty-five Vodou priests in the Department of Grand'Anse alone.[81] However, Carelock, who interviewed both Vodouisants and Christians after the earthquake, suggested that "informants with whom I have spoken lamented (or boasted) that it had actually been at least three times that amount."[82]

In April 2011, Michel Forst, the UN Human Rights Committee's independent expert on human rights in Haiti, acknowledged "the difficulty of prosecuting the perpetrators, because the murders are carried out by anonymous crowds and, more often than not, people conspire to conceal the identity of the perpetrators."[83] However, Forst urged the government to "launch inquiries, thereby reminding everyone that, under the rule of law, no one is entitled to take justice into their own hands."[84] In July 2011, the Haitian government reported to the Human Rights Council that "measures (sensitization campaigns and strengthening of police units assigned to concerned areas) were taken to protect voodoo practitioners from lynching after some of them were accused of witchcraft at the time of the fresh cholera outbreaks in May 2011."[85] In January 2013, the Haitian government reported to the Human Rights Committee that "some practicants [sic] of Vodou have nevertheless been accused of sorcery and lynched, most recently during the time of the cholera epidemic, which was seen in some rural areas as having been caused by evil spells. The victims were principally in Jérémie, a town in the south-west. The State subsequently had to intervene to punish the perpetrators and protect the practicants of Vodou."[86] Ironically, in that same report, the government later seemingly downplayed the issue, asserting: "Religions and faiths may be freely practised. There is no discrimination against the practicants of Vodou."[87]

In April 2014, the Human Rights Committee asked Haiti to clarify how many people had been arrested for lynching Vodou devotees, how they had been punished, and what reparations had been awarded to the victims. They also asked the Haitian government to describe what they were doing to combat religious discrimination and prevent vigilante violence from reoccurring.[88] As of the publication of this book, more than five years after the committee's queries, I have found no official response from the Haitian government nor any evidence of these purported efforts to curb violence against Vodou adherents or to bring the criminals to justice.

PART III: CONCLUSION

As the statistics and stories in this chapter demonstrate, there have been widespread problems of physical violence against adherents of African diaspora faiths in Haiti and Brazil in the twenty-first century. These incidents share three significant similarities that are important to recognize in addressing these problems and preventing future attacks. This physical violence is emerging primarily in predominantly Black countries that are known for the prevalence of Afro-diasporic faiths. One must analyze the importance of religious racism as a possible backlash to the very notoriety of these faiths. Second, in each country, there is a direct connection between the growth of evangelical Christianity and physical violence. Yet, when one discusses religious extremism in international forums, the emphasis remains almost exclusively on Islam. These evangelical groups have not been denounced as terrorists, and policies have not been developed to curb the spread of violent, extremist sects. Third, the governments of Brazil and Haiti have actively documented (though likely underestimated) and openly admitted that these acts of religious terrorism have taken place. Yet, when asked about concrete action plans to protect Vodou and Candomblé adherents, the response has been a lackluster promotion of interfaith dialogue or even deafening silence.

To prevent violence against these faiths from continuing or even increasing, these governments need to ensure that investigations into these attacks are undertaken both swiftly and seriously, and that the perpetrators are sentenced to an appropriate punishment. The acknowledgment of these events without subsequent plans to eradicate the violence suggests to adherents and to the people carrying out the attacks that the government has given its tacit consent for the violence to resume or continue. The lack of broader denunciations of evangelical extremists likewise undermines the governments' purported commitment to protecting religious freedom for all. Unwillingness to investigate and suppress religious groups that, as the governments' own reports confirm, are carrying out systematic attacks on African-derived religious communities strongly suggests significant bias toward evangelical Christians and against these vulnerable faiths.

CHAPTER 2

The Gorilla in the Room
The Right to Practice Animal Sacrifice Amid Growing Animal Rights Activism

In May 2016, a four-year-old African American boy crawled into an enclosure that housed a seventeen-year-old silverback gorilla named Harambe at the Cincinnati Zoo in Ohio.[1] The gorilla grabbed onto the child and began dragging him around the enclosure. To save the boy, a zoo employee shot and killed Harambe. Within two days, more than twelve million people viewed and forty thousand people commented on the video of the incident that someone uploaded to YouTube.[2] Shortly thereafter, Sheila Hurt began an online petition called "Justice for Harambe," which demanded that the child's parents "be held accountable for lack of supervision and negligence that caused Harambe to lose his life."[3] It gained more than five hundred thousand signatures and led to the development of #JusticeforHarambe, which many have argued was a mockery of similar hashtags that called for justice for Black Americans who had been wrongfully killed by police officers.[4] These events suggest that many people in the United States prioritize the life of an animal over the *life* of a four-year-old African American boy. This story lays the groundwork for understanding the overwhelming trend to weight the life of an animal as a higher priority than the freedom to practice religions that require ritual animal slaughter. Keeping the Harambe controversy in mind as an indicator of current public opinions regarding animal rights, it is not difficult to imagine why the restrictions on animal sacrifice have been a common mechanism for limiting African diaspora religious freedom in the twenty-first century.

PART I: THE UNITED STATES

The United States has perhaps the earliest and most extensive history of litigating the rights of African diaspora religious devotees to engage in animal sacrifice. These cases can be divided into three parts. First and most well known, there have been two lengthy cases about local ordinances prohibiting animal sacrifice within city limits. Second, there have been several incidents of police harassment and interruption of ceremonies. These cases rarely result in formal charges but undoubtedly have a chilling effect on religious freedom, as police officers traumatize adherents when they issue threats, display weapons, and/or disrupt sacrificial rituals. Third, recent years have seen increasing charges of animal cruelty against devotees regarding their care of animals before or during a sacrifice. These cases are becoming the most common threat to the right to engage in animal sacrifice in the United States and represent a pretext for police and animal control officers to investigate other conditions at the adherent's home or other properties.

A. Zoning Cases

The earliest and most high-profile cases related to the right to engage in animal sacrifice in the United States were grounded in regulations about zoning, or the location and form of slaughtering animals. These cases began with distinct intentions—the first with the purposeful suppression of Santeria/Lucumi through the creation of new ordinances and the second with the application of long-standing regulations about animal care to sacrificial practices. Despite their different origins, these cases share some strong similarities in the singling out of sacrificial practices as posing a distinct risk to other methods or reasons for slaughtering animals, such as hunting, fishing, farming, or pest control. Local governments presented Santeria/Lucumi religious slaughters, particularly in residential areas, as a means through which disease and other contaminants (both mental and physical) might spread. This language can be regarded as a resurfacing of nineteenth- and early twentieth-century narratives about African diaspora religions as a threat to public health and morality.

i. *Church of the Lukumi Babalu Aye, Inc., v. City of Hialeah* (1987–1993)

In 1987, a group of Santeria/Lucumi adherents, the Church of the Lukumi Babalu Aye, sought to establish a permanent physical location for their church as well as a school, cultural center, and museum in Hialeah, Florida.[5] In direct response, the Hialeah City Council issued Resolution 87-90, which documented the public's supposed "great concern regarding the possibility of public ritualistic animal sacrifices," a practice central to Santeria.[6] Shortly thereafter, the City Council passed three ordinances that prohibited possessing, slaughtering, or sacrificing an animal unless the primary intention was to use it for food and made it unlawful to kill an animal for food outside of a properly zoned slaughterhouse.[7]

The Church of the Lukumi Babalu Aye filed a lawsuit challenging the City of Hialeah ordinances on several grounds, including that the city ordinances violated their religious freedom and conflicted with state laws prohibiting animal cruelty, which contained express exemptions for ritual slaughter. When this case reached the District Court, the judges found in favor of the City. Ignoring the obvious correlation between the passage of these ordinances and the church's plans to establish a place of worship, the court opined that the laws were not discriminatory but rather were an attempt to regulate the growing "problem" of animal sacrifice in residential spaces, which posed a threat to "public health and the control of disease" as well as a "risk to children, and animal welfare."[8] As for the alleged conflicts with state statutes that protected "ritual slaughter," the court explained that these laws only applied to Jewish and Muslim ritual slaughter because these were conducted for the primary purpose of food consumption and occurred within a space analogous to those used for the secular killings of animals for sale and food consumption.[9] The church appealed the case to the Eleventh Circuit, which affirmed the District Court's decision without drafting a separate opinion.[10]

Four years later, the Supreme Court reversed the lower courts' decisions and found in favor of the Church of the Lukumi Babalu Aye. It determined that the City of Hialeah ordinances were invalid because they impermissibly targeted Santeria sacrifices while creating exemptions for virtually every other method of killing an animal, such a kosher slaughter, "hunting, slaughter of animals for food, eradication of insects and pests, and euthanasia."[11] The court characterized the city's actions as "religious gerrymandering," or the intentional suppression of Santeria/Lucumi through the proscription of animal sacrifice, one of its central practices.[12] The Supreme Court also believed that the city's purported concerns about public health and cruelty to animals could be addressed through narrower regulations on the care and disposal of animals instead of the blanket proscription of ritual sacrifice.

Although on the surface the Supreme Court ruling appears to represent a great victory to adherents of African diaspora religions, this decision can only be interpreted to bar intentional discrimination against any faith. The court did not unequivocally protect Santeria/Lucumi from legal attacks nor suggest that animal sacrifice could not be regulated by animal welfare or public health legislation. Because of the limited scope of the Supreme Court's decision in favor of the Church of the Lukumi Babalu Aye, lawmakers and police officers continue to try to restrict animal sacrifice. However, as a result of the *City of Hialeah* case, they tend to rely on existing laws and policies to avoid the appearance of intentional discrimination. Santeria/Lucumi adherents have spent the past twenty-five years in litigation trying to determine the boundaries of the *Church of the Lukumi Babalu Aye v. City of Hialeah* case.

ii. *Merced v. Kasson* in Euless, Texas (2006–2009)

The next high-profile animal sacrifice case in the United States began thirty years later in Euless, Texas. José Merced is a priest of Santeria/Lucumi and the president of a religious organization known as the Templo Yoruba Omo Orisha Texas.[13] Merced was born in Puerto Rico but moved to Euless, Texas, in 1990. For sixteen years, Merced conducted ceremonies, including animal sacrifice, in the garage attached to his house. He typically obtained these animals from nearby markets and had them delivered to his home within a few hours of when he intended to sacrifice them. Whenever possible, the animals were cooked and consumed after the blood had been offered to the orishas. During these sixteen years, there was no record of anyone ever improperly disposing of the carcass of a sacrificed animal (they were placed in a dumpster owned by Merced's colleague) or becoming ill from eating the meat.[14]

Merced performed these rituals with apparently little intervention from the city of Euless until September 4, 2004.[15] At that time, Merced was hosting a ceremony and a neighbor called the police, who then requested the presence of animal control officers. They permitted Merced to proceed with the ceremony. However, on May 4, 2006, another neighbor complained to the city authorities, alleging that Merced was preparing to sacrifice goats at his home. Animal control and police officers returned to Merced's home, and Merced informed them that he was planning a ceremony for the following day. The officers warned him that local laws prohibited animal sacrifice and told him to consult with the appropriate city authorities before proceeding.[16]

The ordinances that the officers referenced had been passed in 1974, sixteen years prior to Merced's arrival in the city, and, unlike the City of Hialeah ordinances, did not have any connection to the practice of Santeria/Lucumi.[17] They forbade keeping four-legged animals such as goats and sheep within one hundred feet of any building used for human habitation.[18] They also proscribed slaughtering or killing any animal "except domesticated fowl considered as general tablefare" within the city limits.[19] A person who violated these laws was guilty of a misdemeanor; each offense was punishable by a fine of up to $2,000.[20] Every day that a person violated the statute was considered a separate offense.

Merced's residential lot was within the city limits and was insufficient to permit him to house the four-legged animals necessary for his religious practices. Merced and another priest, Ventura Santana, went to the appropriate city offices and asked whether they could obtain a permit that would exempt them from these laws.[21] The city responded that there was no room for variation from the ordinances. Merced had to postpone initiating a new priest because he could not perform the necessary sacrifices of four-legged animals.

Several months later, in December 2006, Merced sued the city of Euless, alleging that they had violated his constitutional right to religious freedom as well as the Religious Land Use and Institutionalized Persons Act (RLUIPA), which requires local governments to demonstrate that they have a compelling interest in limiting religious land use and that the law or policy limiting religious land use advances that interest in the least restrictive manner possible. The case proceeded to trial before the United States District Court for the Northern District of Texas.

During the trial, the city argued that the government interests underlying zoning laws were more important than Santeria devotees' free exercise rights.[22] They hired expert witnesses who testified that these statutes were designed to protect public health and safety. The experts specifically highlighted concerns that the disposal of carcasses could attract bugs and mice, and that contact between humans and animal blood could spread diseases such as salmonella and typhoid.[23] The District Court found in the city's favor, concluding that the city's concerns about sanitation were compelling and that the laws addressed these issues in the manner that was least restrictive to Merced's religion.[24]

Merced appealed the decision, and in 2009, the United States Court of Appeals for the Fifth Circuit reversed the District Court, finding that the city's enforcement of the ordinances violated RLUIPA.[25] The Circuit Court noted that there were several inconsistencies in the city's evidence that made their purported concerns about public health appear to be a "red herring." First, although the city mentioned concerns about the proper disposal of dead animals, there was no evidence that Merced, in his sixteen years of performing sacrifices, had ever discarded animal remains in an unsanitary manner. Second, the court noted that the city allowed restaurants to dispose of organic waste in dumpsters and permitted the butchering and discarding of hunted animals in Euless, so long as they were not killed in the city. The judges believed that these practices would raise analogous concerns about the spread of disease and attraction of vermin that the city claimed justified the restriction of animal sacrifice. The court also dismissed concerns about animal welfare, opining that the method of sacrifice in Santeria/Lucumi was no more harmful to the animals than that used in commercial slaughter for food. Finally, the judges explained that there were several less restrictive means of protecting public health than the complete prohibition of animal sacrifice, such as creating a permit system for Santeria adherents to obtain approval to conduct ritual slaughter and dispose of carcasses in accordance with public health guidelines.[26]

For all the foregoing reasons, which closely resemble the discrimination concerns discussed by the Supreme Court in the *City of Hialeah* case, the Circuit Court prohibited the city of Euless from enforcing these ordinances to ban Merced's religious sacrifices.[27] Merced's attorneys demanded $350,000 in fees from the city of Euless following their victory. In January 2010, the parties settled on $175,000.[28]

Since the *Merced* case, local authorities have rarely, if ever, attempted to use zoning laws to prohibit animal sacrifice in the United States. However, these two lengthy litigations demonstrate the importance of such laws in the imposition of restrictions on African diaspora religious freedom. The idea that the slaughter of animals, whether religious or otherwise, must take place in properly zoned areas gave authorities a basis to resurrect twentieth-century arguments that African-based religions posed a threat to public health. Although focusing now on physical rather than mental or social contamination, authorities attributed the spread of disease, the attraction of pests, and the abuse of animals to Santeria sacrifices. However, the Church of the Lukumi had not yet opened its doors, and Merced had never, in sixteen years, generated such problems with his religious practices.

B. State Intrusions on Religious Practice

In the mid-to-late 2000s, there were several instances where state officials (i.e., police or state inspectors) barged into devotees' homes and businesses after receiving complaints about animals on the premises. They shut down religious ceremonies and business operations to conduct fruitless investigations. Although no charges ultimately resulted from these cases, government authorities explored options for sanctions, ranging from parking violations to animal cruelty. This practice of overpolicing Afro-diasporic religious communities, like the racial profiling of any minority group, makes devotees even more vulnerable to arrest and incarceration than the rest of the population. Additionally, the process of being targeted and detained undoubtedly left devotees feeling vulnerable and threatened, questioning whether their religious freedom, and sometimes their very lives, were in jeopardy.

i. Jesus Suarez, Coral Gables (2007–2008)
The first of these police harassment cases in the 2000s began around the same time as the Euless, Texas, case. On June 8, 2007, a Santeria/Lucumi priest named Jesus Suarez was conducting an initiation ceremony in Coral Gables, Florida, and around twenty devotees had gathered at his house.[29] A neighbor called 911, stating that he had heard sounds of animals and thought there was a religious ceremony going on at Suarez's residence.[30] Shortly after they had sacrificed the first goat, approximately twenty-five officers in nineteen police cars arrived. Officers drew their guns on the adherents and detained them for three hours before releasing them without arrest.[31] The Church of the Lukumi Babalu Aye intervened in this case, filing a lawsuit demanding that the police turn over all records related to this incident.

The following year, and in direct response to the Church of the Lukumi Babalu Aye's 2007 lawsuit, the Miami-Dade Police Department issued a legal memorandum stating that "officers must be mindful of the religious rights of all individuals, including practices involving the humane slaughter of animals, prior to effecting arrests pursuant to Florida Statutes §828.12, Cruelty to animals."[32] This language would later be added to the police department's handbook under a section titled "Freedom of Religion and Animal Sacrifices."[33] This section describes the *City of Hialeah* case, explaining that the Supreme Court determined that the city's ban on animal sacrifice violated the First Amendment of the constitution. The handbook emphasizes that "the handling, preparation, and ritual slaughter of livestock is not a crime."[34] However, it also reminds officers of other options for sanctioning devotees, indicating that if they arrive at a place where Santeria rituals are taking place, they should assess whether there has been excessive noise or parking violations.

ii. William Camacho, New Bedford, Massachusetts (2011)
The next government involvement with animal sacrifice also involved a temporary infringement of rights that ended without criminal charges. In August 2011,

an anonymous tip came in to the police station in New Bedford, Massachusetts, claiming that there were loud animal cries emanating from a barber shop called Bad Boyz Cutz.[35] City inspectors arrived and found several chickens in cages and cardboard boxes in the basement of the building. William Camacho, who owns the barbershop, admitted that the animals belonged to him. He reported that he is a Palero and the birds were being used for animal sacrifice to the spirits of departed persons. However, he averred that the sacrifices were not conducted at the shop; they took place in a rural area.[36]

Initial reports suggested that Camacho would be charged with animal cruelty.[37] City inspectors also closed the barbershop, citing supposed unsanitary conditions. The mayor of New Bedford, Scott Langley, maintained that the shop was shut down because it did not have running water and because there were animal feces and flies in the basement.[38] However, only a week later, Camacho reopened the barbershop (after removing the birds), and there were no charges pending against him.[39]

C. Animal Cruelty

Most recent cases regarding animal sacrifice following the *City of Hialeah* litigation have centered on questions of whether animal cruelty has occurred during religious rituals. Like the police intrusion incidents in the 2000s, these cases usually commence following a complaint from a neighbor or during the investigation of other alleged crimes. Charges of animal cruelty pose the greatest challenge for the freedom to engage in ritual slaughter because the state usually pursues these charges when they have at least the slightest basis. Furthermore, convictions in these cases can create misconceptions of African diaspora religious communities because they usually involve the care of nonsacrificial animals (i.e., pets), the treatment of sacrificial animals before religious rituals, and/or methods of slaughter that are not widely recognized or sanctioned by the broader religious communities.

i. *State v. Zamora* in Miami, Florida (1993–1996)

Shortly after the Supreme Court decision in favor of the Church of the Lukumi Babalu Aye, on June 26, 1993, a Santeria priest in Miami, Florida, named Rigoberto Zamora invited journalists to his apartment to witness him perform the ritual sacrifice of fifteen animals over the course of two hours, including "five chickens, three goats, two hens, two pigeons, two guinea-hens and a lamb."[40] He explained that his decision to extend this invitation was a celebration of the Supreme Court ruling and an effort to open his faith to the public to break down some of the misconceptions about it. However, unlike most priests, who exclusively sacrifice animals by quickly severing the carotid artery or pulling out a bird's spine, Zamora reportedly used a blunt knife to cut the goat's throat and threw one of the guinea hens against the floor.

The police arrested Zamora on four counts of unnecessary killing of animals in a cruel or inhumane manner in violation of Florida Statute Section 828.12(1)—a misdemeanor punishable by imprisonment for up to one year and/or a fine of up to $5,000. Zamora filed a motion to dismiss, arguing that the case violated his freedom of religion. Judge Marilyn Milian ruled against him, finding that "there is not one scintilla of evidence or argument before this court that the Santeria faith requires that animals suffer during ritualistic slaughter."[41] On September 16, 1996, more than three years after the sacrifices and seven months after the court denied his motion to dismiss, Zamora pled guilty to one charge of animal abuse and Judge Betty Capote sentenced him to two years' probation and four hundred hours of community service.[42]

In addition to criminal prosecution, Zamora also received substantial backlash from other Santeria/Lucumi devotees. When Zamora announced his intention to perform these sacrifices in front of television cameras, other devotees, including members of the Church of the Lukumi Babalu Aye, discouraged him from proceeding.[43] After the televised rituals, approximately two hundred priests signed a petition seeking to rescind Zamora's priesthood status. As Santeria/Lucumi is a decentralized belief system with no high council capable of ousting an ordained priest, Zamora responded that no one had the authority to sanction him. However, he did apologize and state that he would never again perform a public ceremony.

ii. Jorge Badillo, Monmouth County, New Jersey (2011–2014)

Jorge Badillo is a Santeria priest who resides in Freehold, New Jersey. On March 17, 2011, a local sheriff went to Badillo's home to execute a domestic violence warrant and to search for a firearm that Badillo's brother had allegedly hidden in the home.[44] While searching for the gun, the sheriff, Captain Martin, entered the shed behind the house and saw Badillo's shrines and some dead chickens. Although Martin did nothing at the time, the following day he called Chief Amato of the Society for the Prevention of Cruelty to Animals (SPCA), who, along with several SPCA officers, went to investigate what Martin called "possible animal cruelty."[45] Without a warrant or probable cause, Amato went to the back of Badillo's house and, before notifying Badillo or requesting permission, opened the gate and began taking pictures of the chickens and the shrines.⁴⁶ Amato then knocked on the front door and spoke with Badillo and his sister, Leyda, who explained that the animals had been sacrificed in the practice of their religion, Santeria. Although there was no ordinance prohibiting keeping animals on the property and there was no evidence that Badillo had abused the birds prior to or at the time of their deaths, Amato averred that they "had no right to practice Santeria in Monmouth County or in New Jersey or anywhere in the United States."⁴⁷ He furthermore claimed that he "was familiar with Santeria, that he targeted Santeros and had just arrested two Santeros in Spring Lake [a nearby town] recently."⁴⁸

Amato asked the Badillos whether there were any other animals on the property aside from the dead chickens and a dead pet turtle that he had seen outside. They showed him three guinea hens and a pet rabbit; Amato ordered the family to send these animals to a farm. He told the Badillos that he would arrest them if they did not remove the live animals and dispose of the dead ones properly. However, giving the Badillos little time to comply with his demands, Amato returned the following day and placed nine summonses for Jorge in his mailbox—four animal neglect charges for the three guinea hens and the pet rabbit, three animal abuse charges for the birds that had been sacrificed, and two additional charges for failing to properly keep the pet turtle and for causing its death.⁴⁹ Each of these misdemeanor charges carried a potential term of imprisonment of up to six months and a potential fine of up to $1,000. Therefore, if convicted on all charges and sentenced to the maximum terms, Badillo would have served four and a half years in prison and paid $9,000 in fines.

Amato also called a local newspaper, the *Asbury Park Press*, and told them about the animal abuse charges and the practices that led to them.⁵⁰ The *Asbury Park Press* printed the story, and in response, the Badillo family received numerous threats, and their car and home were vandalized. Jorge Badillo was also trying to adopt two children through the Department of Children and Family Services, and he claimed that the charges "adversely affected" the process.⁵¹

Badillo went to court on the animal cruelty charges and all but one count was dismissed. The remaining charge related to neglect of their pet rabbit, which Amato claimed had no water. Badillo pled guilty and paid a $200 fine. On March 8, 2013, Badillo subsequently filed a lawsuit against Amato and Sheriff Martin, alleging that the two had targeted him as a Santeria devotee and conspired to deprive him of his religious freedom. He also sued the assistant prosecutor who refused to intervene to prevent Amato's discriminatory practices. All parties moved to dismiss the cases against them.

Judge Freda Wolfson of the United States District Court for the District of New Jersey denied the motion to dismiss the case against Amato but granted the motion against the other parties for technical reasons. Thereafter, Badillo's lawsuit proceeded against Amato alone, seeking damages for unlawful search and interference with religious freedom. On October 24, 2014, the parties entered into a settlement agreement whereby Amato refused to admit liability but promised to pay $40,000, of which $13,000 went to Badillo for the violations of his rights and $27,000 to his attorneys' fees.[52]

iii. Robert Talamantez et al., San Antonio (2018)
The most recent of these animal abuse cases began on March 16, 2018, when Bexar County Animal Control Services and Sheriff's Department traveled to a residential neighborhood to investigate a complaint of animal cruelty. The deputies interrupted a priesthood initiation at the home of Robert Talamantez, a babalawo, and his wife, Irma. They had already sacrificed "a goat, three roosters, a pigeon and some chickens before deputies arrived, bringing it to a premature halt."[53] Eleven people were charged with violating Texas Penal Code §42.09, which governs the care of livestock animals. This law prohibits a person from "intentionally or knowingly" torturing or abandoning an animal; failing to provide water or care; or seriously overworking, poisoning, or causing animals to fight with one another.[54] There are explicit exceptions for scientific research, fishing, hunting, trapping, animal husbandry, and wildlife management, but not religious rituals. Any violation of the statute is a Class A misdemeanor, which is punishable by a fine of up to $4,000 and/or a jail sentence of up to one year.[55]

Each person appears to have been held in jail overnight before being released on bonds ranging from $2,000 to $3,500 on March 17, 2018. On March 26, 2018, several of the devotees filed a civil lawsuit against Nicolas LaHood, criminal district attorney of Bexar County, and other county officials.[56] On May 2, 2018, the prosecutor dismissed the criminal charges against the devotees. The civil lawsuit against Bexar County is still pending as of August 2020.

D. Conclusions About US Animal Sacrifice Cases

These cases reflect that opponents of African diaspora religions and/or animal sacrifice have changed tactics since the early zoning cases, where they argued that these practices posed a threat to public health. Perhaps realizing that direct challenges to the sacrifices would not succeed, police and neighbors have resorted to harassment and surveillance to try to catch devotees in a criminal offense. Analogous to the purported "concerned citizen" who calls the police on Black communities for having a barbeque in the park or walking through an affluent area, if someone witnesses livestock animals in residential spaces or hears their cries, particularly when accompanied by drums and singing, they report devotees to the authorities. These allegations give police the opportunity to surveil other conditions in homes and places of employment, and to charge devotees with violations of policies relating to sanitation and parking, or cruelty charges related to pets. Like other forms of racial profiling, this creates an environment where devotees are unfairly surveilled in comparison to other people and are forced to be extremely cautious about their secular lives to avoid criminal offenses arising from their religious activities. Moreover, like other victims of overpolicing, devotees have been harassed, threatened, denigrated, and held at gunpoint in the process of these detentions, as well as subjected to the trauma of being jailed for charges that ultimately had no merit.

PART II: ANIMAL SACRIFICE AND ORISHA RELIGIONS IN SOUTH AMERICA

While police officers and courts in the United States have struggled to understand the meaning of the *City of Hialeah* case, courts and lawmakers across the globe have increasingly attempted to limit the practice of animal sacrifice. In both Brazil and Venezuela, regional laws regulating or prohibiting the practice of animal sacrifice have recently reached the nations' federal supreme courts. These laws stem from nearly identical controversies, both of which began with the passage of local or state ordinances that regulated animal welfare. After orisha devotees sought clarification that religious freedom would not be restricted through these ambiguous new policies, some legislators pushed back, seeking explicit bans on animal sacrifice. These disputes closely resemble that which occurred in the *City of Hialeah* case in the 1980s and 1990s, once again resurrecting these ideas that African diaspora religions are "uncivilized" and pose a threat to public health. Moreover, they began to explicitly raise the question of whether animal life is more important than African-derived religious beliefs.

i. Rio Grande Do Sul, Brazil (2003–2019)

The controversy over animal sacrifice in Brazil began in 2002, when Manoel Mario, a state assemblyman in Rio Grande do Sul, introduced a bill regarding the protection of animals,[57] which prohibited, among other things, causing suffering or injury to any animal.[58] This bill only allowed an animal to be killed "suddenly and painlessly," and for purposes of food consumption.[59] In May 21, 2003, the governor approved the bill, which became Law No. 11,915.

Candomblé adherents quickly became concerned that this law would be applied to prohibit animal sacrifice. They wrote an open letter in opposition of the law, stating that it created the opportunity for prejudiced neighbors, especially evangelicals, to file complaints against Afro-Brazilian devotees. To answer these concerns, Assemblyman Edson Portillo proposed an amendment to the law that explicitly stated: "This prohibition shall not include the free exercise of the cults and liturgies of religions of African origin."[60] The State Assembly passed Portillo's amendment, Law No. 12,131, a year after the law first went into effect.

After passing the Assembly, Law No. 12,131 went to the governor, Germano Rigotto, who had the option to approve or veto it. Representatives of nonprofit animal rights organizations issued official statements asking the governor to veto the bill, claiming that neighbors reported seeing animals still alive after Afro-Brazilian sacrifices and that devotees intentionally caused the animals a slow and painful death.[61] Animal rights activists also marched in front of the governor's palace holding signs in opposition of the bill; however, the governor signed the bill into law.

In late 2004 and early 2005, the State Court of Justice evaluated the constitutionality of Law No. 12,131. Despite continuing vocal protests from animal rights groups,[62] on April 18, 2005, the court issued a decision upholding the constitutionality of Law No. 12,131. Rapporteur Araken de Assis wrote first, emphasizing the paramount importance of the constitutional protection of religious freedom, citing the US Supreme Court's decision in the *City of Hialeah* case as a precedent that should serve as a general guideline for how Brazil should handle such matters.[63] De Assis also opined that animal sacrifice is no greater cruelty than the processes through which animals are killed for food consumption.[64] Antonio Carlos Stangler Pereira and José Antônio Hirt Preiss both emphasized that animal sacrifice or the ritual slaughter of animals was a relatively common practice across religious communities, occurring among Jews and Muslims or even indigenous populations of Brazil.

However, the decision was not without opposition. Some justices, such as Maria Berenice Dias and Alfredo Foerster, believed that creating an exemption for Afro-Brazilian religions gave an unconstitutional preference or privilege to one religion, violating principles of equality. Other justices expressed concern that the exemption would give devotees the impunity to treat animals cruelly and mask it as religious practice. Two judges, Osvaldo Stefanello and Foerster, argued that the constitution's guarantees of the right to life applied to animals, and that in a conflict between religious liberty and the right to life, the latter was paramount. This argument would become central in later debates about this exemption.

In the days following the court's decision, a local newspaper published an article about the case, creating a special site for responses and asking readers to weigh in on the ruling. More than 80 percent of the fifty-six people who replied wrote in opposition of the law, calling it a disgrace and a step backward for the country. Several also suggested that devotees of Afro-Brazilian religions practiced human sacrifice, and that they would soon ask the government to approve that now that they had protected the ritual slaughter of animals.[65]

The controversy over animal sacrifice in Rio Grande do Sul appears to have died down for approximately ten years following the State Court of Justice's decision. However, in 2015, Representative Regina Fortunati proposed bill 21/2015, which would amend the original animal rights law and repeal Law No. 12,131 (the section specifically protecting animal sacrifice).[66] Fortunati argued that animal rights is an evolving concept and that her bill reflected the fact that more people in society are choosing not to eat meat and are fighting against the death of animals in laboratories and religious rituals.[67] She asserted that human beings have a duty to protect all living things and that this duty supersedes religious freedom. Whether knowingly or unknowingly, Fortunati also replicated the language of the country's 1890 penal code provisions that had limited Afro-Brazilian faiths, by contending that these ritual practices pose a threat to public health.

In May 2015, the legislative assembly's Commission of Constitution and Justice (CCJ) determined that Fortunati's bill was unconstitutional because it infringed on the guarantee of freedom of religion. Fortunati responded to the CCJ's decision, arguing that the rights in the constitution were not absolute and invoking a rule that allows the entire assembly to vote on whether or not to adopt their decision. During those debates, Fortunati's supporters centered on one now familiar theme—that an animal's "constitutional" right to life superseded devotees' right to religious freedom. Opponents of the bill, however, demonstrated that Fortunati had focused on animal sacrifice while ignoring greater threats to animal welfare throughout the country, such as slaughterhouses, product testing on animals, and the rodeo. Even cars colliding with animals on Brazilian roadways, one legislator pointed out, killed far more animals than were sacrificed in Afro-Brazilian rituals. Manuela D'Ávila, a member of the CCJ, opined that the bill was rooted in prejudice against Afro-Brazilian faiths. Ultimately, the assembly sided with the CCJ, voting 27–14 to adopt their opinion.

The controversy did not end there. In 2016, the Federal Supreme Court agreed to evaluate the constitutionality of the Rio Grande do Sul amendment, specifically to determine whether it violated principles of secularism by granting Afro-Brazilian religions protections that were not given to other faiths.[68] On March 28, 2019, the court dismissed the appeal, finding that the Rio Grande do Sul amendment was constitutionally valid. Ultimately, they believed that the amendment did not privilege Afro-Brazilian religions; rather, it recognized a long-standing prejudice against these faiths and sought to ensure that devotees of Afro-Brazilian religions enjoyed the same rights as members of other faiths by preventing prejudiced officials from manipulating the animal protection law to prosecute them. The only remaining concerns were raised by Minister Marco Aurélio, who agreed that animal sacrifice should be constitutional but desired explicit guarantees that the animal would not be mistreated prior to the sacrifice and that the meat of every sacrifice would be consumed.

ii. Libertador, Venezuela (2015–Present)
The practice of Santeria/Lucumi has been growing in Venezuela, particularly due to an agreement that the late president Hugo Chavez made with Cuba—that the latter would send thousands of doctors to Venezuela in exchange for subsidized oil.[69] As this African diaspora faith's popularity has increased, so too has the controversy about it. Similar to other countries in the Americas, one of the primary debates about Santeria/Lucumi in Venezuela has centered on the perceived tensions between animal rights and animal sacrifice.

Legal controversies about animal sacrifice date back to at least 2009, when the National Assembly (Asamblea Nacional) began debating a law providing certain protections for plants and animals.[70] Gonzalo Báez, president of the Yoruba Society of Venezuela (Sociedad Yoruba de Venezuela), and other leaders in Venezuelan orisha communities met with the National Assembly to discuss what authority the law would give to municipalities to regulate ritual animal slaughter.[71] They expressed concern that this bill would authorize police officers to attend their ceremonies and look over their shoulders while they conducted sacrifices. Báez stressed to the legislature that their religious practices provided important benefits to their communities. He contended that most of the meat from the animals that his organization sacrificed were used to feed the poor at the Misión Negra Hipólita. He also emphasized that the sacrifices were conducted for healing purposes, to save the lives of people who are sick.

A year later, in 2010, Venezuela passed the Law of Protection of Domestic Fauna, Free and in Captivity, which may have been the final version of the unnamed legislation that concerned Yoruba religious practitioners the year before. This law provides protection to domestic animals, delineating only a few reasons to kill them (for food consumption, scientific reasons, or euthanasia) and dictating that animals must be slaughtered without causing them pain and away from the presence of children.[72] Perhaps because Yoruba leaders had emphasized that they typically consumed the meat following their sacrifices or used it to feed the poor, religious or ritual sacrifice is not one of the listed exceptions.[73] The law also gave municipalities some authority to regulate animal welfare.

Despite whatever ambiguities may have existed about national legislation, local officials in Libertador, a municipality in the capital city of Caracas, clarified their position on animal sacrifice in February 2015. They passed an amendment to Libertador's Ordinance on the Tenure, Control, Registration, Marketing and Protection of Domestic Fauna (Domestic Fauna Ordinance)[74] that prohibited the sacrifice of animals for ritual purposes.[75] Shortly after the passage of the ordinance, several Venezuelans spoke out in favor of the restriction of animal sacrifice. Carlos Ruperto Fermín of Aporrea wrote a detailed list of the incidents of purported animal abuse in Venezuela.[76] Among these, he referenced the purported "serious problem" of Santeria/Lucumi. He asserted that orisha devotees were illiterate, ignorant, and evil, and claimed that the bodies of sacrificed animals that were left in the street had traumatized children. He contended that Santeria adherents ask for respect but do not respect the lives of other living things. María Arteaga, founder of the Fundación Amigos Protectores de Animales, likewise reasoned that the rights of a person end where the rights of another living thing (including nonhuman animals) begins.[77] Daniel Cabello, president of the Fundación de Ayuda y Protección Animal, described ritual slaughter as torture and argued that religious freedom should be limited when it interferes with morality and public order.[78] Roger Pacheco, director of an NGO called AnimaNaturalis, highlighted purported public health concerns associated with killing animals in residential or public spaces.[79]

Later that year, on October 8, 2015, Yoruba priests filed an action with the Supreme Court of Justice (Tribunal Supremo de Justicia) to repeal this amendment to Libertador's Domestic Fauna Ordinance. They argued that the law was too vague to provide any clarity about what was prohibited and that it was an unconstitutional attack on their religious freedom. The priests also contended that the municipal ordinance exceeded the boundaries of the authority that the national Law of Protection of Domestic Fauna gave to municipalities.[80] They requested that the court issue a "precautionary measure" that would prevent the enforcement of the ordinance until the court could determine its validity. In May 2016, the Supreme Court agreed to hear the action but refused to grant the precautionary measure.[81]

On July 21, 2016, Vanessa Padron of Maracay, Venezuela, created a petition in response to this action before the Supreme Court, asking that it refuse to impose the injunction on the animal sacrifice ordinance and continue to protect animals from these "perverse" and "inhumane" acts of "mistreatment."[82] As of February 5, 2020, 40,780 people had signed this petition from numerous different countries, including Colombia, Mexico, Argentina, Spain, Ecuador, El Salvador, Uruguay, the United States, and, of course, Venezuela itself. However, due to the constitutional crisis of 2017, the Supreme Court has spent the past few years embroiled in controversy and is presently operating in exile. It is unclear when or even whether the court will return to hearing ordinary matters such as this case.

PART III: CONCLUSION

The Harambe incident reminds us that these global debates about animal rights are never devoid of racial undertones and impact. Whether carried out through zoning restrictions, animal welfare claims, or environmental protection laws, all these efforts to restrict the ritual slaughter of animals in African diaspora religious communities replicate and reinforce other forms of racism in the Americas. They lead to unwarranted calls to the police, excessive surveillance, abuse of authority, baseless detention, and costly litigation. Moreover, they resurrect nineteenth-century ideologies about Black culture and religion as a contaminating influence that threatens public health and morality, including claims that they promote human sacrifice.

It is also important to reflect on the prejudices revealed in animal rights activists' willingness to fight endlessly for animals while disregarding the systematic violations of the rights of people of African descent. Just as the widespread outrage from the killing of Harambe and the development of #JusticeforHarambe denigrated the value of Black lives and mocked movements to end police brutality, the disputes over animal sacrifice place the rights of people of African descent below animal welfare. As Hédio Silva Junior, one of the attorneys in the Brazilian Supreme Court case about animal sacrifice, explained: "The life of black people doesn't have any value. But the chicken used in black religion has to be radically protected."[83]

CHAPTER 3

"The Dark Side of Santeria"

Palo Mayombe and the Grave-Robbing Cases

On February 9, 2006, Myrlene Severe, a thirty-year-old Vodou priestess, arrived at Fort Lauderdale/Hollywood International Airport on a flight from Cap Haitien, Haiti. Severe was carrying a human skull inside her checked luggage.[1] When Customs and Border Protection officers questioned Severe about the skull, she reported that the bones had been purchased in Haiti and were "part of her voodoo beliefs," and had been designed "to ward off evil spirits."[2] Severe had not declared the skull on her customs form.

The following day, an Immigration and Customs Enforcement agent filed a complaint against Severe in the United States District Court, alleging that Severe had violated federal law by knowingly and intentionally smuggling human remains into the United States, making a false representation on her customs form, and "transporting hazardous material in air commerce."[3] Each of these offenses carried a potential penalty of up to five years' imprisonment.[4] Therefore, if sentenced to the maximum penalty for each offense and to consecutive terms of imprisonment, Severe potentially faced up to fifteen years' imprisonment for bringing a human skull into the United States.[5]

Severe was in federal custody for four days before she was released on a $100,000 bond. The following month, the federal court reduced the charges against her to the misdemeanor offense of "knowingly and unlawfully storing and maintaining human remains."[6] On April 12, 2006, Severe entered a plea of guilty, and on July 26, 2006, the judge sentenced her to a $1,000 fine (the maximum for this offense) and two years of probation.[7]

Severe's case represents one of the most contentious aspects of the right to practice some African diaspora religions—devotees' use of human remains for religious rituals. These controversies are grounded in the tensions between the Eurocentric notion that deceased persons should be interred in the ground and African-derived beliefs that the remains of the dead should be kept among the living to communicate and develop a relationship with spirits of the departed. They are also rooted in a multitude of contradictions, wherein white Americans have long used the bodies of people of African descent in medical experimentation, autopsies, circus attractions, and souvenirs of lynching; meanwhile, devotees of African diaspora religions have been arrested for possessing and exhuming human remains for spiritual purposes.

PART I: US BELIEFS AND POLICIES REGARDING HUMAN REMAINS

The United States has very strict legislation regarding the treatment of the bodies of deceased persons that typically requires interment in a cemetery, or other designated burial ground, and criminalizes otherwise possessing or disinterring human remains. As a former British colony, US laws regarding the dead are derived from English perspectives and principles. In early modern England, the country was divided into church districts known as parishes, and each typically had only one appropriate place to dispose of a dead body—in a "consecrated graveyard."[8] Prior to the early sixteenth century, there were some exceptions to this idea that bodies must be buried. A person might keep the bones of a saint, for example, because they "were thought to work miracles and cures, ensure good harvests, and protect the owner from harm."[9] However, the Protestant Reformation, which began in 1517, put an end to these practices because it "attempted to eliminate from Christianity those practices considered more magical than religious."[10] Since at least the early seventeenth century, English law criminalized disinterring or disturbing buried bodies based on the idea that a corpse no longer belonged to any individual but must be protected by the public.[11]

Because of the separation of church and state in the United States, its lands were not divided into parishes as they were in England, so the country is not composed of consecrated burial sites maintained by the state.[12] However, the general principle of protecting the remains of the dead was carried over during the colonial period. R. F. Martin explains that the "normal ultimate destiny" of a person in the United States, at least "so far as his bodily parts are concerned, is a single and permanent commitment to the soil."[13] Martin contends that the idea of allowing a corpse to lay undisturbed in its "final repose" is so ingrained in US society that one might "hear it spoken of as a 'right' of the dead and a charge on the quick [living]."[14]

By the late nineteenth century, some US courts had ruled that the public has a right to ensure that a corpse has a decent burial, and "any interference with that right, by mutilating or otherwise disturbing the body, is an actionable wrong."[15] In the twenty-first century, almost every state in the United States has laws that proscribe the disposition of human remains in any place other than a cemetery or disinterring a buried body and removing any parts of the corpse or any item buried with the deceased under threat of lengthy terms of imprisonment and substantial fines.[16] Such widespread legislation and harsh punishments emphasize most states' purported commitment to preventing persons from possessing the remains of departed persons and "protecting" corpses from being disinterred once they have been buried. However, in the history of England and the United States, the purported "right" to a permanent burial has been far from universal.

PART II: RACIAL AND ECONOMIC LIMITATIONS ON THE RIGHT TO PEACEFUL REPOSE

Despite these harsh laws about possessing and exhuming bodies in England and the United States, protections of the right to peaceful repose have historically been limited with regard to racial minorities, persons convicted of a crime, and poor and homeless persons. For hundreds of years, both England and the United States used the bodies of convicted criminals to supply medical schools with materials for anatomy classes.[17] In the United States, participants in slave uprisings were among those "criminals" commonly dissected. After Nat Turner's rebellion in 1831, a Virginia medical school allegedly dissected Turner's body.[18] Similarly, the *New York Tribune* reported that after John Brown's raid in 1859, the bodies of the rebels were dug up and taken to a nearby medical school for dissection.[19] By contrast, several Southern states passed laws in the 1860s specifically exempting indigent Confederate soldiers and their spouses from having their bodies sold to medical colleges.[20]

The disinterment of Black bodies was not just a punishment for crimes or rebellion; it served the purpose of providing materials for medical training, which grew exponentially from 5 schools in 1810 to 130 in 1890.[21] This growth translated to greater demand for bodies, which were often acquired by illegal methods, such as theft before and after burial, purchase, and even murder.[22] In the late nineteenth century, scholars estimate that approximately five thousand cadavers were procured for medical dissection each year. The majority of these were obtained illegally and most were African American.[23] For instance, in 1829, a white medical doctor described how he paid the manager of a public graveyard for fifty to eighty-five bodies a month to supply Philadelphia medical schools.[24] Similarly, a New England professor of anatomy admitted that he received approximately twenty-four African American bodies per semester in the 1880s and 1890s.[25]

A later discovery in Georgia provides some context for understanding the vast quantity of African Americans who were resurrected from their supposedly "final repose." In 1989, when construction workers were renovating the building that had once housed the Medical College of Georgia in Augusta, they discovered nearly ten thousand human bones in the basement of the college along with medical tools that made it clear that this was an autopsy room. Analysis determined that the bones were from the period between 1835 and 1912, and that around 80 percent of the bones were from the bodies of African Americans.[26] Many of them had been stolen from a single African American graveyard, Cedar Grove Cemetery.[27]

There were many reasons that African Americans were more commonly exhumed than Americans of European descent. In part, this reflected contemporary power dynamics—Blacks had no control over their bodies during slavery, so plantation owners could give them to the hospital if they got sick to the point that they couldn't work. This was also a way for plantation owners to terrify enslaved persons—threatening them with dissection to discourage them from rebelling or doing something else that was punishable by execution.[28] Black cemeteries were often easier to pillage because they didn't have guards, gates, or other protections.[29] Furthermore, Blacks were expected to allow their bodies to be subjected to autopsy and dissection as a sort of "payment" if they received free medical care in hospitals.[30]

The unearthing of these bodies would have had a very traumatic effect on the deceased person's family. In the eighteenth and nineteenth centuries, because medical professionals found decomposed bodies less useful, grave robbers focused on newly deceased persons who had been buried for fewer than ten days.[31] Therefore, the families would have still been mourning this new loss. Furthermore, once in the possession of medical professionals or others who made use of human remains, the bodies of African Americans were frequently treated with unthinkable irreverence and brutality. For instance, after spending several years with her (often naked) body on public display, Saartjie

Baartman died in 1815. Baron Georges Cuvier, who is credited with founding comparative anatomy, cut Baartman to pieces, placing her "brain, vulva and anus in glass jars."[32] Twenty years later, another woman of African descent, Joice Heth, endured similar abuses. Famous circus figure P. T. Barnum put the elderly Heth on display in the northeastern United States, claiming that she was 161 years old and had been the "mammy" for George Washington.[33] The following year, Heth died and Barnum arranged for a professor of surgery to publicly dissect Heth's corpse in the City Saloon in New York in an alleged attempt to prove that she was truly as old as Barnum claimed.[34] Barnum made a substantial sum on this spectacle, charging fifteen hundred people a viewing fee of fifty cents per person.[35]

The medical students' handling of corpses was often much worse than these irreverent public dissections. In the early twentieth century, they took staged photos gathered around Black cadavers, writing captions referring to the deceased as "coons" and "niggers."[36] It is also important to recall that throughout the late nineteenth and mid-twentieth centuries, mobs of white Americans would murder African Americans and steal pieces of the body as souvenirs or keepsakes to remember these lynchings.[37] Ironically, given the repulsion with which many regard the use of human remains in religious rituals, Harvey Young labels these body parts as "fetishes" and contends that lynching witnesses used them as good luck charms or magical items.[38]

Even today, the likelihood that Black bodies will be dissected rather than laid to rest is disproportionately high. Many states require prisons, morgues, hospitals, and other public offices to notify a local medical school if they are in possession of an unclaimed body or the body of a person whose family cannot afford their burial.[39] After a certain period of time, usually somewhere between thirty and ninety days, the medical school can use the body for dissection. These bodies are frequently racial minorities.

PART III: AFRICAN AND AFRICAN DIASPORA BELIEFS ABOUT DEATH AND BURIAL

While US and English legal systems criminalize interactions with the burial sites and bones of departed persons, in many African and African diaspora communities, they are used as a conduit to communicate with the deceased.[40] Historically, earth from a burial site served as a "near universal element in the pharmacopeia of African American supernaturalism" used "to symbolize the presence of spirits in transitional places."[41] African American conjurers temporarily buried charms in a cemetery to capitalize on the power of the spirit(s) who lingered or resided there.[42] In the eighteenth and nineteenth centuries, persons of African descent in the Caribbean and North America ingested grave dirt as a component of an embodied oath to participate in an uprising, presumably to invoke the assistance of the departed in battle.[43]

Some persons of African descent also "may keep part of the dead body as a symbol of the abiding presence of the departed."[44] Historically, in many African communities, the dead were buried in close proximity their descendants' home or even inside it, to facilitate the performance of sacrifices, offerings, and divinations by the living; it was extremely rare for the dead to be buried long distances from their living relatives.[45] Similarly, in rural societies in modern Haiti, there are family compounds with burial grounds where people can directly make offerings to their ancestors.[46]

The remains of deceased persons are particularly important in Palo Mayombe and other Kongo-derived religions. Adherents work with the spirit of a deceased person or persons who assist the practitioner in their physical, mental, spiritual, and emotional needs.[47] The devotee creates a vessel for this spirit(s) to reside within, called a nganga, which is filled with plants, dirt, stones, water, and herbs as well as animal and human bones, to create a "microcosm embodying these objects and the qualities they represent."[48]

A. The Palo Mayombe Cases

Devotees of several African diaspora religions have been arrested for possession and acquisition of human remains; however, Palo Mayombe adherents have been the defendants in the most numerous and widely publicized cases. In part, these cases stem from the ideals discussed earlier, that there is only one proper resting place for a deceased person—a designated graveyard. However, these cases are also a product of the time period in which they emerged and represent a growing trend for "scholars" and specially trained police officers to target African diaspora religions as "cults" that are prone to criminal activity.

i. Background of the Palo Cases

One cannot understand the limitations on the freedom to practice Palo Mayombe without discussing the 1989 murders in Matamoros, Mexico, and the increasingly popular concept of African diaspora religions as "narco-cults," or religions prone to adoption by violent criminals. At the end of the 1980s, Santeria/Lucumi was making national headlines in the United States because of the animal sacrifice court case that was slowly making its way through appellate courts. By contrast, Palo Mayombe, another Afro-Cuban belief system that had also blossomed in the United States with the massive influx of Cuban immigrants following the Cuban Revolution, was relatively unknown. However, all this would change in 1989, when a series of a gruesome sacrificial murders in Matamoros, Mexico, made international headlines.

On March 14, 1989, a University of Texas student, Mark Kilroy, disappeared while he was on spring break in Matamoros. In early April, Kilroy's body was discovered along with the remains of numerous other people buried on a ranch twenty miles outside the city.[49] Authorities later learned that a group of drug dealers known as the Cartel del Golfo had tortured and killed Kilroy and the others.[50] They found a cauldron containing blood, organs, and a human brain on the property. Cartel members who were arrested claimed that the deceased were Santeria sacrifices that "would bring them good luck and protection in their drug trade."[51] However, on April 11, 1989, a US anthropologist identified the cauldron as a Palo Mayombe nganga.

Within a year, a few books on the murders emerged emphasizing the purported role of Palo Mayombe in these already sensationalized events. For instance, Jim Schutze, in his book *Cauldron of Blood: The Matamoros Cult Killings*, claimed that "Palo Mayombe is a bad one, in part because it is almost always practiced by people who are in some way involved in violent criminal life."[52] He asserted that the leaders of Palo Mayombe, or "Tata Nkisi," are "an especially evil kind of witch or bruja," who are "very savage and very un-European" and whose primary function is murder.[53]

Since the Matamoros murders, scholars who examined the crimes have argued that Constanzo and his associates actually learned their religious "rituals" from repeatedly watching a horror film, *The Believers*.[54] However, countless scholars and forensic anthropologists have continued to spread a false impression that African diaspora faiths, especially Palo Mayombe, have an intricate connection with illegal activities. For example, in 2009, Ronald Holmes and Stephen Holmes published the fourth edition of *Profiling Violent Crimes: An Investigative Tool*.[55] In a chapter titled "Profiling Satanic and Cult-Related Murder," they contend that "there is a dark and evil side, a criminal side, to Santeria that is called Palo Mayombe."[56] To prove their characterization of Palo, they cite the Matamoros murders. Similarly, Tony Kail has written a series of books claiming that Santeria/Lucumi, "Voodoo," Palo Mayombe, and related religions are "narco-cults" or "magico-religious cults" that are designed to provide spiritual protection for drug traffickers and other criminals. Kail cites the

Matamoros incident as "one of the most notorious examples of a narco-cult" and attributes these practices to Palo Mayombe "combined with elements of Mexican brujeria."[57] Unfortunately, biased scholars and police officers such as these have "trained" some of the main witnesses against Palo adherents in court cases, and the notoriety of these murders has had a very negative impact on Palo.[58]

ii. The New Jersey Cases

The majority of arrests of Palo Mayombe adherents for possessing human remains or exhuming graves took place in and around Newark, New Jersey, between 1999 and 2007. They represent the earliest meaningful assessments of whether Palo Mayombe is a protected religion and whether possession of human remains is ever permissible. Several of the New Jersey cases relied on the aforementioned "cult" experts to investigate and testify about the "dark" and "criminal" nature of Palo. Additionally, in most of the New Jersey cases, the state would position themselves as the defenders of long-dead families who supposedly suffered from the exhumation of their kin. Despite the lack of a living victim and multiple inconsistencies in many of the cases that should have raised questions about the defendant's guilt, the prosecutors and judges proceeded as if Palo devotees were some of the most dangerous criminals in their communities.

a. Franklin Sanabria Jr.

On January 13, 1999, twenty-eight-year-old Franklin Sanabria Jr. broke into a mausoleum at Holy Sepulchre Cemetery in Essex County, New Jersey.[59] He opened the coffin and took the remains of Leonard Perna, a local bar owner who had died of cancer in the 1980s.[60] Police arrested Sanabria after they identified him by a fingerprint that he left behind. After he was taken into custody, Sanabria reported that he had stolen the remains with the assistance of a senior Palo Mayombe adherent who was teaching him about the religion. However, the prosecutor discovered that Sanabria lied about his alleged Palo Mayombe accomplice, who was actually in prison on unrelated charges at the time of the burglary.

The grand jury indicted Sanabria for third-degree burglary, and he pled guilty to the offense. The judge sentenced him to four years of probation, two hundred hours of community service at a local park, and a fine of $4,200, which would be used to repair the mausoleum. Perna's remains were recovered years later, in 2002, in the home of Palo adherents Eddie Figueroa Sr. and

Eddie Figueroa Jr., whose cases are discussed later.[61] At the time the remains were recovered, Perna's son reported that he believed his father's bones had been chosen because Paleros mistakenly thought he was a mob boss (several individuals with the last name Perna were reputed members of the Lucchese crime family in New Jersey) and presumably believed his spirit was powerful.

b. Alberto Lima

About six months after Sanabria's conviction, on August 13, 1999, workers at Arlington Memorial Park Cemetery in Hudson County, New Jersey, observed that one of the mausoleums had been broken into and symbols such as circles and arrows had been drawn around it. Inside, they discovered two dead roosters, lit candles, and two dolls.[62] The body of an infant, James Scrimshaw, had been taken from the tomb. The police also found evidence of other rituals including candle wax and cigars in other parts of the cemetery.

Detectives surveilled activity at the cemetery for several weeks, hoping to observe the people who took Scrimshaw's body. They arrested Alberto Lima, a Cuban immigrant, who they saw entering the cemetery one evening.[63] Police searched Lima's car and found a nganga in his trunk. They also later searched the home of Lima's associate and found several other ngangas. On September 21, 1999, prosecutors charged Lima with "theft of human remains, desecration of a grave, burglary, criminal mischief."[64] Nearly two months later, on November 15, 1999, media reports of the case indicated that Lima was still in the county jail because he could not afford to post his $100,000 bail while he awaited trial.

The evidence against Lima seems to have been scant. Scrimshaw's body was not recovered in Lima's car or at his associate's home; in fact, none of the ngangas contained any human bones. Furthermore, police explained that an expert had (accurately) told them that Palo adherents were not likely to take the body of an infant because the spirit was too young to work with. Police officers offered a competing motive, opining that perhaps the body had been sold to drug dealers, who they believed would pay a substantial sum of money for the body of a pure, virgin child to provide spiritual protection from arrest for their trafficking and other crimes.[65] Despite the lack of a body or a clear motive, Lima was sentenced to a year in prison for these charges.[66]

Detectives pursued this case of their own accord, with no pressure from the boy's family, who was never located. Both Scrimshaw and the eight-year-old boy who shared his tomb had died around the turn of the twentieth century, 1916 and 1908, respectively, and, likely due to the age of the corpses, detectives concluded that the family was probably also deceased.[67]

c. The 2002 Series: Cruz, Delgado, Figueroa, and Miraballes

In 2002, police arrested at least six Palo Mayombe adherents and priests in connection with bones found during the raids of a local religious supplies store (*botanica*) and the basement of a family home that was used as a ritual space. Two men, Mario Delgado and Ramon Gonzalez, were charged with removing the bones from two local cemeteries. Three men, Oscar Cruz, Eddie Figueroa Jr., and Eddie Figueroa Sr., were charged with possessing stolen remains. Miriam Miraballes, the alleged ringleader of local Palo devotees, was arrested for ordering the thefts. These cases all began with the arrest of Ramon Gonzalez, one of the alleged bone thieves.

1. Ramon Gonzalez and Oscar Cruz. In the 1990s, Ramon Gonzalez met Miriam Miraballes at a botanica owned by Miraballes's son. Gonzalez later described Miraballes as a "high priestess"[68] who was the "most influential Palo leader in Newark" and had initiated every devotee he knew.[69] He developed a relationship with her over several years when he attended a series of religious ceremonies she conducted. Gonzalez then moved to Florida for a few years and was arrested there for firearm, cocaine, and marijuana possession, for which a judge sentenced him to two years' probation.[70]

In November 2001, Gonzalez returned to New Jersey, violating the terms of his probation in Florida.[71] He reconnected with Miraballes, who advised him that initiation into Palo would improve his circumstances. About a month after he returned to New Jersey, Miraballes allegedly asked Gonzalez to help two other men remove human remains from a local cemetery. On December 18, 2001, Gonzalez claims he drove these men to Mount Pleasant Cemetery and waited in the vehicle while they entered and returned with two bags, which they placed in Gonzalez's trunk. Gonzalez drove to meet with Miraballes and transferred the bags to her car, then Miraballes paid Gonzalez $100. Gonzalez never saw the contents of the bags; however, he assumed that human remains were inside of them because the following morning, the assistant manager of the cemetery discovered that someone had broken into a mausoleum and removed the bones of Richard and Emily Jenkinson, who had died in the 1920s and 1930s.

The next month, Miraballes allegedly asked Gonzalez to remove the remains of Joseph Rovi, who died in 1969, from Holy Sepulchre Cemetery.[72] She purportedly promised him that she would pay him $500 and initiate him into Palo if he did so. Miraballes supposedly gave Gonzalez, who later testified that he had only a sixth-grade education and "could bearly [*sic*] read," a sheet of paper with Rovi's name and directions to the body.[73] On January 23, 2002,

Gonzalez told his girlfriend, Ruth Santiago, that he needed to collect some grave dirt from the cemetery and asked her to drive him. When they arrived, Gonzalez jumped a fence at the cemetery and broke into the mausoleum. Gonzalez put Rovi's body in the back of Santiago's truck and went home, then called Miraballes. She arrived with another person to get the body; however, she never paid Gonzalez the $500 nor performed the promised rituals.

While Gonzalez was transferring the remains to Miraballes, Santiago saw that there was a body, not dirt, in the bag. Santiago, who was a secret informant for the FBI on another matter, reported Gonzalez to the bureau. The FBI contacted Newark Police Detective Donald Stabile, who interviewed Santiago and Gonzalez, convincing the latter to become a paid informant assisting the Newark police in capturing the devotees who received and used the remains. However, nothing further transpired until several months later, when Gonzalez again found himself in legal trouble.

On August 11, 2002, Gonzalez was arrested for attempting to break into a botanica owned by fifty-year-old Palo Mayombe priest Oscar Cruz.[74] After his arrest, Gonzalez spoke to Detective Stabile again, reporting that Cruz was keeping human remains in the basement. Based on Gonzalez's confession, the police obtained a search warrant and raided the botanica. They found an altar with candles; bones; and plates containing food, money, and other things in one room. In another, they found three ngangas containing fruits, sticks, machetes, animal remains, and the bones of five different people.[75] Police were able to trace the origins of three sets of bones to thefts. They identified two sets of remains as those that Gonzalez admitted to taking—the bones of Joseph Rovi from Holy Sepulchre Cemetery and Richard Jenkinson from Mount Pleasant Cemetery. The police also identified one set of remains as belonging to a man named Jacob Schmidt, whose bones had been taken from Mount Pleasant prior to Gonzalez's removal of the Jenkinsons.[76]

Police arrested Cruz and charged him with three counts of receiving stolen property.[77] In addition to the evidence of the skulls themselves, which were produced at trial for the jury to view and touch, the prosecution relied on the testimony of Mario Delgado, another Cuban immigrant, to secure a conviction. Delgado confessed to removing Schmidt's skull from the mausoleum in December 2001 and made a deal with the prosecution, who, in exchange for Delgado's confession and identification of Cruz, would reduce the charges against him to one count of cemetery desecration and recommend that his sentence be limited to the eleven months he had served in prison awaiting trial.[78] When Delgado was arrested for cocaine possession shortly after his release, he made another deal with the prosecutors to serve just under a year in jail for the drug charges if he would also testify against Cruz.[79] Delgado testified that Cruz had offered him $500 to steal Schmidt's skull; however, Cruz had failed to pay him.

Cruz's attorney, Ann Sorrel, offered several arguments to undermine Delgado's testimony and defend her client. She countered that Paleros often purchase the bones used in their ceremonies and that Cruz had been unaware that the remains had been stolen.[80] Sorrel also tried to discredit Delgado by asking him about his extensive criminal history in the United States, which included twenty-six arrests as well as multiple convictions for possessing drugs and weapons in the twenty-four years since he had arrived in the country.[81] Sorrel's final tactic was to demonstrate that the concept of using human remains in religious ceremonies might be unusual in the United States, but it was very normal to Cuban-born Cruz. Cruz took the stand and explained that he had first become involved in Palo Mayombe over forty years prior, when he was just seven years old. He estimated that he had conducted hundreds of rituals involving human remains. Even the prosecutor, Dean Maglione, admitted that "it was obvious that Mr. Cruz did not feel he was doing anything wrong," though he knew that taking the bones from the cemetery was against US law.[82] After a lengthy trial, the jury found Cruz guilty of two counts of receiving stolen property. The judge sentenced Cruz to five years' imprisonment.[83]

2. *Eddie Figueroa Sr. and Eddie Figueroa Jr.* About two months after police raided Oscar Cruz's botanica, in October 2002, Gonzalez told Detective Stabile that Palo Mayombe rituals were being conducted in a temple located in the basement of a multifamily home where fifty-six-year-old Eddie Figueroa Sr. and his thirty-five-year-old son, Eddie Figueroa Jr., resided.[84] They discovered three skulls, one of which belonged to Leonard Perna, whose remains had been removed from the cemetery by Franklin Sanabria back in 1999.[85] The father and son were charged with desecrating graves and possession of stolen property.[86] They faced ten years' imprisonment on the possession of stolen property charge, a second-degree felony, and eighteen months on the charges of desecrating graves, a fourth-degree felony.[87] Unfortunately, I have been unable to determine the outcome of these cases in the extensive newspaper coverage of these Palo cases or in the New Jersey court record system.

However, the reports of their arrests represented two important legal and social shifts in these prosecutions. First, in the midst of the Figueroas' trials, the New Jersey assembly introduced a bill that would increase the desecration of human rights from a fourth-degree felony to a second-degree felony and allowed the state to charge devotees for ritual use of stolen bones without proving knowledge that the remains had been unlawfully obtained. The bill was a response to large-scale fraud committed by a crematory in Georgia, but prosecutor Dean Maglione told *The Herald News* the following when discussing the bill: "Some people say that we should spend police money working on the living rather than the dead"; however, "I'd like to shake Palo Mayombe up a little bit so that they're not stealing bones or stealing people's money through shoddy practices."[88]

The second shift was the vocal response of experts and other religious communities to reports of these arrests. *The Herald News* interviewed Felix Mota, a Santeria priest who owned a botanica in Passaic. Mota averred, "I know people from Palo who practice good, but a lot of people from Santería don't want to be associated with Palo because it's evil."[89] Similarly, the *New York Times* published an article on this arrest in which they interviewed Babalawo Oloye Ifa Karade, author of several books about Afro-Cuban religions. Karade described Palo Mayombe as "a mutation of Yoruba in much the way that satanism, which sprang from Christianity, is a misguided mutation."[90] When the most famous trial regarding Palo Mayombe began the following year, one would see these descriptions of Palo as an "evil," "misguided" "mutation" continuing to be put forth in explanation of why adherents must be prevented from possessing human remains.

3. *Miriam Miraballes*. After most of the other cases had been resolved, in early 2003, the state began to build a case against Miriam Miraballes, the alleged mastermind behind the series of thefts that had occurred from 1999 to 2002. This case is important because it was the first to seriously discuss Palo Mayombe as a religion. The prosecution relied on one of the "cult" experts discussed previously to explain the use of human remains in Palo and to convince the jury that Miraballes was involved in the crime. This case also became the first Palo Mayombe decision to be heard by an appellate court in the United States.

The only significant evidence that the state had tying Miraballes to these offenses was the statement of Ramon Gonzalez, who alleged that he had stolen remains at Miraballes's request. Gonzalez made a deal with the prosecution that in exchange for his testimony against Miraballes, Gonzalez would receive a reduced sentence for the New Jersey cemetery thefts as well as receive assistance with his weapons and drugs charges in Florida.[91] On April 22, 2003, the state indicted Miraballes on three counts of burglary, three counts of theft of human remains, and conspiracy to commit both of the foregoing offenses. She pled not guilty and was held on $500,000 bail.[92]

Gonzalez testified at Miraballes's trial, and the prosecutor, Dean Maglione, also introduced evidence of the remains recovered at Oscar Cruz's botanica. To tie the remains more firmly to Miraballes, the prosecution called a New York City detective, Marco Quinones, an alleged expert in "nontraditional religions such as Santeria and Palo Mayombe," to explain the function of human remains and the process of initiation.[93] However, the qualification of Quinones to testify in this matter represented a serious controversy.

Quinones represented himself as an expert witness on nontraditional faiths, including Santeria and Palo Mayombe, explaining that he conducts training seminars on these belief systems for other police officers.[94] However, Guzman, Miraballes's attorney, questioned the adequacy of Quinones's qualifications as an expert witness on several grounds. First, over the course of nearly twenty years, between 1986 and 2004, Quinones reported that he had a mere one hundred hours of training (and no formal education) related to nontraditional religions—fifty hours related to Santeria, thirty hours related to Palo Mayombe, and twenty hours related to other faiths.[95] During this same twenty-year period, Quinones reported that he had dealt with around fifty cases related to Santeria but only five directly related to Palo.

Perhaps the most controversial aspect of Quinones's qualifications was a lack of publications on nontraditional religions (a typical method of proving that an individual is an "expert" on the subject in question) aside from some PowerPoint slides and internal police memorandums.[96] Quinones admitted that he had never published anything on so-called cult crimes outside the NYPD nor ever put together any documents on Palo, even within the police department. Trying to redeem himself, Quinones referenced the case in Matamoros, Mexico, stating: "The practitioners of that case were involved in Palo. They were actually committing human sacrifices."[97] He explained, "I used the actual crime scene video of that case in the criminal investigation course to elaborate on the perspective in handling that particular case."[98] However, on cross-examination, Quinones clarified that he was not an expert in the Matamoros case and hadn't even gone to the crime scene; he just used the case for training purposes in the NYPD. Apparently unbeknownst to Miraballes's attorney, Quinones's reference to the Matamoros case also undermined his credibility because it demonstrated that long after true experts had debunked the idea that African diaspora faiths were involved, Quinones continued to present this horrific crime as an example of Palo Mayombe.

Since, by Quinones's own testimony, he had only dedicated thirty hours to independent research on Palo since 1986, had only participated in perhaps five cases related to Palo, had no formal education in Palo or other African diaspora religions, and had no traditional publications about the subject, Miraballes's attorney sought to have him disqualified as an expert. However, the court disagreed and allowed the state to use Quinones's "expert" opinion to bolster their case. The court noted that in New Jersey the requirement for expert testimony is that the witness have more information than the average juror and that Quinones had "occupational experience" that could help him explain why the remains and other ritual items are used by devotees.

Quinone's testimony about the function of human remains was just as sensational as one would expect from a person not formally trained or personally engaged in the practice of African diaspora faiths. Likely intentionally cultivating images of the witches of European mythology, Quinones referred to the nganga as a "cauldron," where human remains were placed alongside sticks, animal bones, graveyard dirt, and other things. He also added the unfounded claim that in addition to ritually slaughtering animals, "some people will feed [the nganga] human blood from a human sacrifice."[99] To support these outrageous assertions, during the trial, the prosecutor left a plastic bag containing one of the skulls on the counsel's table in the jury's direct line of view.[100]

In addition to trying to shock the jury by conjuring images of witch's cauldrons and human sacrifice, part of the prosecution's strategy appears to have been to undermine the very idea that Palo is a religion. In his initial testimony about his qualifications as an expert in "nontraditional religions," Quinones responded that he was responsible for training other police officers about "cults" since 1986.[101] Over several pages of the court transcript, the judge, the prosecutor and Quinones debated with Miraballes's attorney about whether "cult" is an appropriate term for Palo Mayombe. Ultimately, the judge asked the jury to strike Quinones's references to "cults," and the parties agreed to use the term "nontraditional religion."[102]

Barred from referring to Palo Mayombe as a cult, Quinones proceeded to describe Santeria, the Afro-Cuban religion that the US Supreme Court had already recognized, and then distinguish Palo Mayombe from it. He emphasized the supposedly syncretic nature of Santeria but claimed that Palo Mayombe was a purely African, "nature oriented religion" involving the worship of spirits, ancestors, and the dead that "oppose[s] the Christian God."[103] Quinones bluntly argued that "[Palo] is considered by many practitioners of Santeria as the dark side because Palo basically works with spirits that are evil in their nature," and that "many Santeros will not incorporate any practices of Palo within their Santeria practices."[104]

This idea that Palo Mayombe is evil was prevalent throughout Quinones's testimony. He repeatedly used phrases such as "whatever god or demon" Paleros worship or whatever "saint or devil" that they are interacting with.[105] In contrast to the "good people" who practice Santeria, including judges, secretaries, and other professionals, Quinones averred that 90 percent of the people who practice Palo are associated with an evil form of the religion.[106] In particular, he stressed that people who were in possession of human remains "in all likelihood [were] practicing something evil."[107]

At the end of the two-and-a-half-week trial, the jury convicted Miraballes on all seven counts of the indictment.[108] At the time, Miraballes was sixty years old and walked with a cane. In one instance, reporter William Kleinknecht observed that Miraballes appeared in court "looking more like a grandmother than a grave robber."[109] However, her age and "feeble" appearance garnered no sympathy from Judge Ravin, who sentenced her to fifteen years' imprisonment with seven and a half years of parole disqualification—the highest end of the possible sentence range for her offenses and the maximum length of parole disqualification.

In the list of aggravating factors contributing to Miraballes's sentence, Judge Ravin listed the high likelihood that she would continue to break the law. Ravin added, "The immense need to deter others generally who would consider burglarizing crypts and stealing human remains is self-evident."[110] To explain why he listed no mitigating factors in the case, Ravin explained that this last "aggravating factor" (deterring people from stealing bones) "vastly outweighs any single or collective mitigating factors."[111] Furthermore, even though Quinones had testified that Paleros preferred the remains of individuals who had been deceased long periods of time, Ravin gave a lengthy speech when he issued this sentence, calling Miraballes's alleged offenses a "serious harm" because "there was an obvious threat of emotional devastation to any relative of the dead which you through your accomplices wrenched from their final resting places."[112]

Because of the impropriety of certain hypotheticals that the prosecution posed to Quinones, Miraballes's attorney appealed the jury's decision. The Appellate Division of the Superior Court of New Jersey reversed Miraballes's conviction and remanded the case for a new trial. Ultimately, in March 2008, more than five years after Miraballes was indicted, she pled guilty to one count of conspiracy to commit burglary, and the state dismissed the other charges against her. Miraballes's case marked the end of the five-year span of constant arrests of Palo Mayombe adherents and priests for possessing and "stealing" human remains. However, she would not be the last devotee of an African diaspora faith to face police harassment and/or criminal charges for this religious practice.

iii. Amador Medina

One of the most recent cases of unlawful possession of human remains stems from Massachusetts. In the summer of 2015, someone broke into a mausoleum in Hope Cemetery in Worcester, Massachusetts, and removed the remains of five persons.[113] Six months later, a woman walking through the cemetery noticed that one of the mausoleums appeared to have been broken into. She contacted cemetery employees, who then notified the police.[114] One of the mausoleums was built in 1903 for Charles Chandler Houghton, "a prosperous boot manufacturer and real estate developer," and his family.[115] Houghton's wife was buried there in 1911, and their adult children were interred in the mausoleum between 1926 and 1944. Mausoleum caretakers report that two children were also buried there.[116] At the time of the break-in, the mausoleum had long been out of use. The last individual had been interred in the mausoleum in 1944, over seventy years prior to the thefts.[117]

In December 2015, approximately two months after police discovered the thefts, the City of Worcester issued a press release that indicated that despite extensive investigation they had been unable to locate any family members of the persons whose bodies were missing. However, one week later, *CBS Boston* interviewed Bob Doezema, alleged great-grandchild of Charles Houghton (interred 115 years prior to the thefts) and grandchild of an unnamed person who was buried in the mausoleum (but does not appear to have been one of the bodies removed from it). Although Doezema, who did not appear to be over seventy years old, unlikely met any of the individuals whose bodies were removed, *CBS Boston* emphasized that he was "feeling a pain that's hard to imagine."[118]

That same month, a 911 operator received a tip that thirty-two-year-old Amador Medina in Hartford, Connecticut, was keeping human remains on the porch of his apartment. Two police officers and two detectives went to Medina's home to investigate the claim. Medina admitted that he was a Palo Mayombe priest and that he had five sets of human remains that he used for religious rituals.[119] Medina showed the officers garbage bags containing bones and dirt and led them through his house past shrines with protruding human bones. These bones were later identified as belonging to the bodies stolen from Hope Cemetery. Medina initially reported that he had bought the remains from another individual for approximately $3,000; he also allegedly showed the police photos on his phone of open caskets with the remains still inside with a visible sign labeling the location as Hope Cemetery. Hartford police contacted Worcester police, who decided to arrest Medina.

The prosecutor in Worcester charged Medina with disinterring the bodies, disturbing graves, and breaking and entering with intent to commit a felony. In February 2018, Superior Court Judge Shannon Frison granted the defense counsel's motion to suppress the statements that Medina allegedly made to Hartford police on the grounds that he was not notified of his right to remain silent or his right to an attorney. A little more than a week later, the prosecutor announced his intent to appeal Judge Frison's order because, without the confession and the remains, there was little grounds to proceed with the case. On July 24, 2020, the Supreme Judicial Court of Massachusetts reversed Judge Frison's order, finding that Medina was not in police "custody" at the time that he made these statements; therefore, the police were not required to notify him of his rights.[120] As the prosecution can once again use the bones and Medina's alleged confession as evidence, they will likely move forward with the case.

PART III: CONCLUSION

Of the dozen cases discussed in this chapter, it is important to recall that only one involved the remains of a person who had living relatives, and that the family speculated that this rare incident stemmed from the incorrect assumption that they were members of a crime family. Although most of the deceased persons had no family members to claim ownership over their remains or object to the exhumation of the bodies, Palo and Vodou adherents were charged with felony offenses carrying potential penalties of imprisonment for eighteen months to ten years for each count. Therefore, the state is using its power and authority to enforce the type of burial that they regard as a "right" of the dead, without any living person invested in the outcome. Black bodies had been exhumed and used for private purposes for years, but adherents of African diaspora religions are now prosecuted for doing the same.

While many in the Western world might struggle with the possession of human remains as an issue of religious freedom, one must recall that in most African diaspora religions, adherents believe that the dead can still communicate with the living. Palo Mayombe adherents and others belonging to similar faiths do not believe that they are stealing bodies; they believe that these spirits, many of whom have long been neglected by the living, have agreed to enter a reciprocal relationship with the devotee. Their spirit has consented to the use of their bones and, rather than rotting alone and unattended in a grave or mausoleum, the bones become a conduit that receives offerings of food, liquid, and the lifeblood of animal sacrifice. If the standard policy for dealing with the bodies of persons who have no one to claim them or pay for their burial is to send the corpse to medical schools for testing and dissection, one must wonder why religious rites are not equally as valid once decades have passed and no living relatives can lay claim to the remains.

CHAPTER 4

The Best Interests of the Child?
Custody of Minors and African Diaspora Religions

Dr. Rosiane Rodrigues is a journalist, Candomblé priestess (Iyalorixá), and researcher in anthropology who lives in Rio de Janeiro, Brazil.[1] When her youngest son, Marquinhos, was a few months old, she separated from his father. As is customary in Brazil, the father asked a family court to determine his visitation rights. The standard procedure in cases involving the custody of young children is for a social worker and psychologist to examine each parent and their residence. Rosiane's social worker was rumored to be a member of the Universal Church of the Kingdom of God—a Pentecostal church known for its prejudice against Afro-Brazilian religions.

The social worker's report noted that Rosiane was a devotee of Candomblé who had religious shrines in every room of her home and took her children with her to ceremonies. The psychologist opined that Rosiane was "vengeful" and suffered from emotional problems. After reviewing these reports and learning that Rosiane was a Candomblé adherent, in May 2007, the family court judge determined that "the father would have better moral conditions to raise the boy." Although the father had only sought visitation once every two weeks, the judge terminated Rosiane's custodial rights and placed the boy with his father. He restricted Rosiane's contact with her son to supervised visits during a four-hour window on Saturdays.

Finding that a person who has Candomblé images throughout their residence might have "irreversible mental disorders," the judge ordered a police escort to go to Rosiane's home to seize the child. After being taken to the police station and held for eight hours, Rosiane relinquished custody of her son to an officer. The following day, the father showed up on her doorstep with Marquinhos, explaining that he didn't want custody; he only wanted visitation. He left the child in Rosiane's care but refused to return to the court and officially explain his preferences on the record.

Over the following weeks, Rosiane reports that her son's father harassed, blackmailed, and assaulted her. He threatened to tell the court that she had kidnapped Marquinhos if she didn't comply with his every whim. Rosiane consulted lawyers, women's rights advocates, and human rights experts. She was evaluated by a battery of psychologists and social workers. After three months, Rosiane was able to regain provisional custody of Marquinhos. It was more than three years before she regained permanent custody. The entire controversy began and ended because of her affiliation with Candomblé.

Rosiane is not alone. Over the past few years, courts in the United States and Brazil have increasingly been asked to consider whether adherents of African diaspora religions are fit to be awarded guardianship of children in adoptions and custody proceedings, as well as whether devotees have endangered their children by allowing them to witness or take part in religious ceremonies. In the United States, this dates back to some of the earliest litigation over the right to practice African diaspora religions and centers on the question of whether witnessing the "violent" act of animal sacrifice endangers the welfare of children. In Brazil, the issue of whether such faiths pose a threat to minors is typically raised in child custody proceedings by a nonpractitioner parent. In all these cases, courts are split as to whether they consider affiliation with African diaspora religions to be a negative factor in the custody proceedings. However, even in cases that reach a favorable conclusion, the courts' inconsistencies with respect to these claims and the devotees' resulting confusion about their rights has a chilling impact on religious freedom.

PART I: THE UNITED STATES

In the United States, animal rights activists and other opponents of African diaspora religious freedom have argued for more than thirty years that the ritual slaughter of animals has a negative effect on children. Although rarely, if ever, leveling similar complaints against farmers, hunters, or other persons who slaughter animals in the presence of children, they contend that witnessing the death of animals can turn a child into a violent criminal or otherwise damage a child's psyche. Beginning with the *City of Hialeah* case, challengers of the right to practice animal sacrifice have reasoned that its effects on children should justify banning the practice and/or removing children from the custody of their parents. As animal rights activists gain influence and the general population of the United States grows more disconnected from its food sources, cases such as those described in the following sections pose an increasing threat to religious freedom.

A. *The Santeria/Lucumi Cases*

US courts have heard at least three cases with overt or veiled suggestions that animal sacrifice can be detrimental to children. Ultimately, even though litigants tried to push animal sacrifice as a deciding factor in two of these cases, other issues formed the backbone of these opinions. However, the ambiguous responses in these cases underscores yet another unsettled issue of the right to practice animal sacrifice following the Supreme Court's decision in the *City of Hialeah* case. The uncertainty in these cases also lays the groundwork for later decisions finding that Palo Mayombe ceremonies do pose a threat to children.

This argument that animal sacrifice damages children began with the *City of Hialeah* case itself. At the District Court level, the City of Hialeah argued and Judge Spellman agreed that one of the compelling interests to ban animal sacrifice was "to prevent the adverse psychological effect on children exposed to such sacrifices."[2] Early in its decision, the District Court noted that "children as young as seven years have been initiated" during ceremonies in which between "24 to 56 four-legged animals and fowl are sacrificed," and that "children of all ages are permitted to witness the public sacrifices during the annual ceremonies, as long as the parents are present."[3] The city's expert, a research psychologist named Dr. Raul Huesmann, asserted that witnessing animal sacrifice, "particularly in the circumstances of the initiation rite where a number of animals are sacrificed," would desensitize children to violence and aggression as well as increase the likelihood that the child would behave violently toward animals and humans and become a danger to their community.[4]

The Church of the Lukumi Babalu Aye presented their own witnesses about the impact that observing animal sacrifices would have on children. A clinical psychologist named Dr. Angel Velez-Diaz disputed the idea that there was a strong correlation between violent behavior and witnessing violence. Velez-Diaz argued that there had to be other factors before witnessing violent behavior would cause a child to engage in that behavior. However, the

District Court dismissed Dr. Velez-Diaz's testimony as less "credible" than Dr. Huesmann's.[5]

The church's other expert, Ms. Hendrix, was a professor at Miami Dade Community College (now Miami Dade College) and had conducted a study on children's attitudes toward death. Hendrix testified that children who had observed the death of animals or humans tended to see death as a natural occurrence, and that children who were prepared for the sacrifice would likely view it as a normal religious experience. The court said that Hendrix's opinions were not "persuasive," because Hendrix did not know Huesmann's studies, she hadn't interviewed children who had observed animal sacrifices, and her studies focused on death rather than violence.[6]

After dismissing the church's experts, the District Court concluded that the ordinances barring animal sacrifice helped safeguard the welfare of children. The judges opined that the city had proven, through this testimony about the likelihood that children would become more aggressive and violent from witnessing animal sacrifice, that "the risk to children justifies the absolute ban on animal sacrifice."[7]

The Eleventh Circuit chose not to adopt this aspect of the District Court's reasoning when it affirmed this decision on appeal. However, when the case proceeded from the Eleventh Circuit to the Supreme Court, several animal rights groups submitted amicus briefs that argued that witnessing animal sacrifice would harm children.[8] For example, the Humane Society of the United States opined that "a growing body of evidence suggests that violence toward animals in childhood may be a leading indicator and precursor of adult criminal and antisocial behavior, that animal abuse within families often goes hand in hand with spousal and child abuse, that permitting a child to abuse animals without punishment or correction can lead to progressively more violent and antisocial acts as the child develops, and that children exposed to animal abuse are being taught to devalue sentient life."[9] Therefore, they concluded that "the state interest in protecting animals from cruelty and unnecessary death is part and parcel of the broader, irreducible, and paramount state interest in societal peace, order, health, and safety. It is against that very concrete interest that [Santeria adherents'] desire to kill animals for reasons of abstract religious ideology must be weighed."[10]

The Supreme Court did not address the question of the psychological impact of animal sacrifice on children in its decision finding in favor of the Church of the Lukumi Babalu Aye. Therefore, their ruling did not silence the discussions about the purported negative impacts of animal sacrifice on children. In fact, the same year that the Supreme Court issued its decision in the *Church of the Lukumi Babalu Aye* case, another case arose suggesting that animal sacrifice was a factor in child care and custody.

Judge Marks of the Family Court of New York County, New York, was deciding a case regarding whether Child Services should be able to conduct an investigation of a prospective adoptive parent and submit the findings to the court. In support of her decision that the Probation Department should conduct an independent study of the home instead of Child Services, Judge Marks explained: "In another adoption case, the agency's home study failed to report the foster mother was a priestess of the Santeria religion which practices animal sacrifice. The Probation Department's independent report stated those facts. Although constitutional, it is certainly an important fact to be disclosed."[11]

A similar discussion about Santeria sacrifices and adoption emerged in 2008, again raising the question of whether adherents should be permitted to expose children to their faith. The case began in November 1999, when Ronald A.'s children were removed from his custody because of his history of drug abuse and trafficking as well as physical and sexual violence against the children and their mother.[12] In December 1999, the children were placed with the "S." foster family.[13] In June 2006, Mr. and Mrs. S. became the children's legal guardians, and in 2008, they were going through proceedings to formally adopt those who were still underage.

However, in October 2008, the Department of Children and Family Services received a complaint that one of the children, M.A., was being sexually abused by C.S., the adult son of Mr. and Mrs. S. When the caseworker interviewed M.A., she said that this abuse had been ongoing since she was ten or eleven years old. She also asserted that "the S. family practiced the religion of Santeria and sacrificed chickens for a cleansing ritual, though she denied ever seeing a chicken being sacrificed or that the family used spells."[14] The biological father, Ronald A., filed a petition to terminate the S. family's guardianship over the children and prevent the adoption, referencing the alleged sexual abuse of M.A. and asserting that Mr. and Mrs. S. "forced the children to practice Santeria and threatened them with witchcraft."[15] He also asked the court to order that Mr. and Mrs. S. not practice Santeria in the home while the children remained in their custody.

Ultimately, Ronald A.'s petitions were unsuccessful. When the Department of Children and Family Services investigated the allegations, M.A. recanted her story about sexual abuse and about Santeria. She "informed the social worker that she had never seen the S.'s sacrifice any animals or use any spells."[16] The S. family denied that they practiced Santeria but reported that they had once purchased and butchered a live chicken to make soup.

Ronald A. appealed the Los Angeles Superior Court's denial of his petitions to the Second District Court. Judge Doi Todd affirmed the Superior Court's decision, stating in relevant part and citing the *Church of the Lukumi* case: "Even if the S.'s practiced Santeria, which they denied, [the] father does not explain under what authority the juvenile court could order them to stop practicing any particular religion."[17] Therefore, unlike Judge Marks in New York, the Second District Court in California seemed to rebuke the idea that animal sacrifice around children could impact one's right to custody.

These three cases demonstrate that US courts have varied greatly in their rulings regarding whether Santeria/Lucumi devotees endanger children by exposing them to animal sacrifice. Courts' responses have ranged from the Supreme Court's notable silence to Judge Marks's suggestion that it was a "factor" to consider, to the Second District's ruling that there was no authority to stop someone from practicing their religion. The following year, however, the courts in Newark, New Jersey, would take a very clear position that animal sacrifice endangered children and was not protected by religious freedom.

B. *The Palo Mayombe Case*

In 2009, Yenitza Colichon, a Palo Mayombe adherent in Paterson, New Jersey, was charged with felony child endangering for involving her daughter in an initiation ceremony where she was ritually marked and witnessed animal sacrifice. This case stands out as the only US court decision after the *City of Hialeah* case that has limited the religious freedom to engage in animal sacrifice without regard to how the animals were treated. It is also the only one since the *City of Hialeah* decision to find that animal sacrifice in the presence of children constituted child endangering. It is therefore critical to explore this case in detail and interrogate why the courts may have reached this conclusion.

On May 15, 2009, Yenitza Colichon was preparing to depart for Army basic training.[18] Colichon was concerned about the welfare of her seven-year-old daughter while she was away, and she asked two Palo Mayombe priests, twenty-five-year-old Zahira Cano and thirty-two-year-old Julio Cano, to perform a protective ceremony for the child.[19] This ceremony appears to have been an initiation into the religion, during which the priests sacrificed several chickens and a goat. They also stuck the child with needles and made ten small incisions on the child's body—on her forehead, the front and back of her shoulders, as well as her feet, wrists, and calves.[20] Researchers who study Palo Mayombe have described a similar initiation process, which is referred to as being "marked" in Palo.[21]

After the ritual, Colichon's daughter reported to her teacher that she was having nightmares and she explained some of the details of what occurred during the ceremony. A school official examined the child and found pin marks on her body. The school called the Division of Youth and Family Services (DYFS), who assigned a caseworker, Kenrick Lawrence, to investigate the situation.[22] Lawrence went to Colichon's home and asked her about the allegations. Colichon initially denied her daughter's account of her injuries and claimed that the child had an active imagination. She reported that the marks on her daughter's body were the result of skating or fighting with her cousins.[23] Colichon asserted that she did not believe in the kind of rituals that her daughter described. However, Lawrence also interviewed A.C., who repeated the story she had told to her teacher. Lawrence and a female coworker then examined A.C. and observed the pin marks and cuts on the child's body. Finding the markings inconsistent with Colichon's story, DYFS ordered an emergency removal of A.C. from Colichon's home and placed her with relatives.

Once A.C. was placed with relatives, DYFS continued their investigation. They contacted the police, who executed a search warrant on the Canos' home and found a number of items that seemed consistent with A.C.'s story, such as "dolls, a shrine, religious statues, bones, machetes and bundles of sticks bearing numbers and names," as well as animal blood and hair.[24] Additionally, approximately three days after A.C. was removed from her custody, DYFS held another meeting with Colichon. At that time, Colichon admitted that A.C.'s marks were from a "ceremony," described the man who performed the rituals as A.C.'s godfather, and explained that this was intended to be a ritual of protection.[25] She reported that she did not initially disclose how the injuries occurred because the rituals were supposed to be a secret. Another caseworker assumed that Colichon was an adherent of Santeria and asked her about her involvement with this faith. Colichon denied that she was a Santeria/Lucumi devotee, but she does not appear to have clarified to DYFS workers that the ritual she described was a Palo Mayombe rite.

DYFS continued with proceedings alleging that Colichon had abused and neglected A.C. by "bringing her daughter to the rituals and allowing others to inflict pain and fear on the child."[26] Under New Jersey law, an abused or neglected child is one "whose physical, mental, or emotional condition has been impaired or is in imminent danger of becoming impaired as the result of the failure of his parent or guardian, as herein defined, to exercise a minimum degree of care ... (b) in providing the child with proper supervision or guardianship, by unreasonably inflicting or allowing to be inflicted harm, or substantial risk thereof, including the infliction of excessive corporal punishment; or by any other acts of a similarly serious nature requiring the aid of the court."[27] On December 9, 2009, Judge Arthur Bergmann found that A.C. had been neglected and abused. A.C. and Colichon participated in counseling after this decision, and A.C. returned to Colichon's home once the counseling was complete.

Colichon appealed Judge Bergmann's ruling to the Appellate Division of the Superior Court of New Jersey, arguing that it violated her right to freely practice her religion. The court affirmed Bergmann's decision, explaining that it found "no merit" to her argument because "she failed to produce any legally competent evidence that subjecting her daughter to this ceremony was based on [her] religious beliefs, or even that the ceremony was religiously based."[28] In part, the court seized on a statement that Colichon's attorney had made in closing arguments that this case was not about "the appropriateness of the practice of Santeria" but rather on "whether the child was harmed" by the ritual.[29] In hindsight, this seems to have been an innocent plea to not judge Colichon based on her religious beliefs but rather to scrutinize the scant evidence that the child had suffered any physical harm from the ceremony. However, the court apparently took this argument to mean that the rituals were not religious. In fact, in a footnote to a section describing witnessing animal sacrifice as "terrifying" and "traumatic" for a small child, the court clarified: "Our decisions should not be read as opining on the practices of any religion. There is no evidence that this ritual was part of the child's family's culture or religion."[30]

The appellate court's decision is striking because, although Colichon denied that she was an adherent of Santeria, she gave numerous indications that the ceremony was religious. As discussed earlier, Colichon reported to DYFS that the rituals were designed to protect her daughter while she was serving in the Army. Furthermore, she described the priests who performed the ceremony as A.C.'s godparents. This raises the question: if this was not a religious ritual, what was it?

The court's determination that a Palo Mayombe ceremony was not religious is also significant because, although most courts in the United States have likely never heard a case involving this Afro-Cuban faith, the Appellate Division of the Superior Court of New Jersey had issued its decision regarding Miriam Miraballes just three years earlier.[31] In that case, the court heard extensive testimony about Palo Mayombe from Detective Quinones, including significant details about the use of animal sacrifice in Palo rituals. The court's decision itself described Palo Mayombe as a "nontraditional religion."[32] Therefore, it is unclear why, in Colichon's case, the court found that there were no free exercise issues at stake.

After setting aside the argument of religious freedom, the appellate court ruled against Colichon's appeal, finding that the combination of animal sacrifice and cutting the child presented a clear record of child abuse. The court opined that witnessing animal sacrifice alone would "be terrifying to a young child," but when compounded with "having strange adults stick her with needles all over her body," which subjected her to "the risk of blood-borne diseases," it was obvious to the court that Colichon had "subjected the child to physical pain, emotional trauma, and the risk of very serious physical harm."[33] The court also regarded the fact that Colichon had reported that the marks on her daughter's body were the result of skating or fighting with her cousins as evidence that Colichon knew there was something wrong with the rituals. They further noted that even when she did admit to attending the ceremony, she told Child Services workers that she did not believe in the rituals.[34] Yet Colichon had explained to Child Services officials that she had initially lied about attending the ceremony because it was supposed to be kept a secret. Furthermore, Colichon's hesitance to openly profess adherence to a nontraditional faith would be understandable under threat of losing custody of her child and going to prison if local officials determined that this constituted abuse.

In addition to the juvenile court proceedings regarding Colichon's custody of A.C., Colichon also had to defend herself against criminal charges for her family's participation in this Palo Mayombe ritual. On July 8, 2009, less than two months after the rituals took place, the prosecutor charged Colichon with child endangerment, a second-degree felony with a maximum sentence of ten years' imprisonment and a $150,000 fine, as well as abuse of a child, a fourth-degree felony with a maximum sentence of eighteen months' imprisonment and a $25,000 fine. The prosecutor charged Julio and Zahira Cano with third-degree felony child endangerment for performing the ceremony, which carries a maximum sentence of five years' imprisonment and a $25,000 fine.

On April 12, 2010, Colichon's attorney, Joseph Manzo, filed a motion to dismiss the indictment because it violated her religious freedom. Manzo argued that the sacrifice was part of a religious ritual, and that the marks on the child's body were a religious symbol that had been scratched on her as part of an initiation ritual that was akin to baptism for Catholics and no more harmful than Jewish circumcision.³⁵ However, on January 21, 2011, Judge Joseph Portelli denied the motion. Portelli distinguished this Palo Mayombe initiation from circumcision because it involved a stranger taking a child into a "darkened room" and performing an "unsanitary ordeal."³⁶ By contrast, Portelli argued that circumcision "is performed by a trained, sometimes, licensed practitioner under sterile conditions."³⁷

In May 2011, the Canos entered a pretrial intervention program through which they would serve one year of probation and then their records would be expunged. Joseph Del Russo, chief assistant prosecutor for Passaic County, proudly announced to the press that the Canos had "since parted ways with the Palo Mayombe religion."³⁸ A few days later, Colichon made a plea bargain with the prosecution. She pled guilty to abuse of a child and the other charges against her were dismissed. On June 24, 2011, the judge sentenced her to probation for eighteen months.³⁹

Although the sentences for Colichon and the Canos were arguably minor, this case has important implications for the broader spectrum of African diaspora religious freedom. In some ways, since the Eleventh Circuit dropped the issue of psychological damage to children in the *City of Hialeah* case, Colichon's case is the only valid appellate court decision in the United States to directly interrogate whether animal sacrifice poses a threat to minors. Although this question was raised regarding Santeria sacrifices in prior cases, it was not the central issue in the 1993 custody dispute before the New York Family Court, and the claims that the S. family practiced Santeria were disproved before the court really had to evaluate them. Nevertheless, both of these courts suggested that animal sacrifice, while possibly relevant information, would not be decisive in determining custody. Therefore, one could argue that this is the first clear court decision finding that animal sacrifice is a form of child abuse and that involving a child in ceremonies containing this practice can result in criminal charges and termination of parental rights.

However, two elements of this case distinguish it from prior animal sacrifice decisions. First, part of the court's decision terminating Colichon's temporary custody of her daughter was because she took her to a ceremony where she was stuck with small pins. The judge opined how "terrifying" that must have been for the child and found Colichon guilty of inflicting severe physical harm on her daughter. Would the court have been so quick to find that the child had been abused without this physical marking?

The second distinct element of this case is the controversial nature of Palo Mayombe and the long history of previous disputes regarding Afro-Cuban religions in the Newark area. For example, in October 2003, Passaic, New Jersey, a town about ten miles northeast of Newark, erupted in controversy over Afro-Cuban animal sacrifice rites. A Santeria priest, Felix Mota, who desired to change community perceptions of his faith, made a formal announcement that he intended to hold a public ceremony in the back room of his botanica.[40] He invited television and newspaper reporters to photograph and film the sacrifice of two chickens and a lamb. However, his plan backfired and police were forced to send officers to protect Moya against the approximately one hundred protesters who gathered outside his store.[41] The Humane Society of the United States and the American Society for the Prevention of Cruelty to Animals demanded that Mota be arrested for violating animal cruelty laws.[42] The police chief issued a statement explaining that he had a discussion with Mota's lawyers and believed that the ceremony was protected by the First Amendment. He promised to investigate Mota if he violated any law but clarified: "We're not going to go down there and stop him from conducting a religious service."[43] This appears to have been the first major controversy related to animal sacrifice in the Newark area.

Probably more significantly, as outlined in chapter 3, between 1999 and 2004, several purported Palo Mayombe adherents were charged with burglary, possession of stolen property, disinterring bodies, and related charges for removing human remains from local mausoleums to use in their ceremonies. These cases were many officials' first encounters with Palo Mayombe, and they would have tainted the images that police and judges had of adherents. The last of these cases, that of Miriam Miraballes, was resolved in 2007 and arguably in Miraballes's favor. The idea that the alleged ringleader of a grave-robbing "cult" escaped any significant punishment for ordering the removal of the remains and for conducting many of the ceremonies that would have initiated other adherents into this faith might have encouraged authorities to target Paleros and send a message that it would not be tolerated.

It is also significant that in March 2009, newspapers across the United States featured articles reflecting on the twenty-year anniversary of the Matamoros murders, resurrecting negative stereotypes that Palo Mayombe devotees played a central role in this astonishing case.[44] Colichon's case cannot be viewed as entirely separate from the memory of these recent events. Were judges reflecting on Mota, Miraballes, or the Matamoros cases when they heard DYFS officials' complaint that Colichon had initiated her child into Palo Mayombe?

Third, if Colichon were a Santeria adherent, as the DYFS officials had initially suspected, her case would have unquestionably raised issues about religious freedom and concerns about conflict with the Supreme Court's recognition of Santeria/Lucumi as protected by the First Amendment of the constitution. Since Colichon was engaged in a Palo Mayombe ritual, however, it is unclear whether Colichon's case resurrects the debates in the *City of Hialeah* case about the damage that animal sacrifice has on children or whether the courts simply did not recognize Palo Mayombe as a religion. Colichon's initial reluctance to claim these as religious rituals further complicates the interpretation of this case, as it is conceivable that the judges were more swayed by the tardiness of the religious defense than the nature of the faith itself.

Regardless of these distinguishing factors, the Colichon decision is troubling. Palo Mayombe adherents have faced a series of legal challenges to their practices in the United States in recent years and have never clearly been recognized as a protected religion. Public misconceptions of their religion dating back to the Matamoros murders likely have a chilling effect on this faith that may be reflected in this case, even thirty years later.

The Colichon decision could also have very negative implications on the freedom to engage in animal sacrifice more generally. As the United States and Europe move further toward the support of animal rights at the expense of religious freedom, and as the West becomes further and further disconnected from the sources of meat production, it seems likely that challenges such as this will continue to surface and devotees must be prepared. However, if future courts are asked to tackle this question, the judges should ask themselves whether cattle and pig farmers, butchers, hunters, fishers, or others who professionally or recreationally expose their children to the death of animals will likewise be charged with child endangerment. If the answer is no, then to single out adherents of African diaspora religions constitutes religious racism.

PART II: BRAZIL

Discussions of belief or participation in African diaspora religions often arises in Brazilian child custody cases as well. In the past ten to fifteen years, there have been a series of custody disputes between a devotee of an Afro-Brazilian faith and a nonpractitioner, where courts have been asked to determine whether a parent's custodial rights are impacted by the adherent's possession of religious iconography, attendance at Afro-Brazilian ceremonies, or status as a practitioner/priest. The mere assertion that such evidence would support the limitation of visitation or the termination of parental rights underscores the significant biases against these faiths in Brazil. However, it is even more troubling that several courts have revoked custody, temporarily or permanently, solely because of their religious affiliation.

The Commission to Combat Religious Intolerance shared three stories on its official website between 2009 and 2010 that recount the potentially catastrophic effect of the introduction of evidence of Afro-Brazilian religious affiliation during a custody dispute and confirm state interference to prevent children from participating in Afro-Brazilian ceremonies. The first was that of Candomblé priestess Rosiane Rodrigues, who lost custody of her youngest child in 2007 after a social worker visited her home and observed Candomblé images and ritual implements.[45] This case is discussed in the introduction.

The Commission to Combat Religious Intolerance reported a similar case in 2009.[46] A family court in Rio de Janeiro terminated the parental rights of a twenty-five-year-old woman after the father of her three-year-old son filed a lawsuit claiming that she was an unfit mother because she was a Candomblé priestess. The Commission to Combat Religious Intolerance, in collaboration with an NGO called Projeto Legal, filed an appeal demanding the immediate reversal of the opinion and the return of custodial rights to the mother. At the time of the commission's report, the child was temporarily placed with his paternal grandparents.

The following year, the commission shared another story about state interference with parental rights to practice and introduce their children to Afro-Brazilian faiths. In early May 2010, the parents of an eleven-year-old girl, identified only as "L," brought their child to Ilê Axé Oxalá Tababy terreiro in Paulista for a ritual related to the child's health.[47] On May 5, the Tutelary Council of the City of Paulista (a municipal council tasked with overseeing the rights of children with the ability to call for loss of parental guardianship or custody),[48] and the military police became involved. They conducted a "visit" to the temple, claiming that they had received an anonymous tip that a child would be offered up as a sacrifice in a black magic ritual. The temple priestess, Mãe Dada de Oxalá, permitted the council member to see the girl to prove that she had not been harmed, and the mother was called out of work to bring written authorization for L to participate in the ritual. The council member warned the mother that L could not be at the terreiro for so long and that it did not "look good." The council member and military police left without ever providing any written authorization for their investigation of the temple or any clear information about the origins of the alleged complaints. The following day, L's mother received a phone call from a council member named Mércia Baraxó, who told L's mother that she would lose custody of L if she left her at the terreiro.

On May 7, Baraxó and other tutelary council members returned to the terreiro, again accompanied by the military police. This time, the council alleged that the reason for their visit was that L was missing too many days from school. The council insisted that the child would have to leave immediately and the ritual could not be completed. Baraxó took the complaint to the juvenile court. However, the tutelary council returned later that evening, apologizing for the previous interventions, explaining that the judge had instructed them to convey that there had been a mistake and that they valued Candomblé as a religion. The following day, the stress of the repeated tutelary council and police interventions caused Mãe Dada to suffer from unspecified health problems that required medical attention. Additionally, despite the apparent resolution of the situation, the adherents reported to the commission that Baraxó returned the following week to both the temple and L's house to further harass them.

Court records indicate that in recent years, disapproving nonpractitioners have continued to appeal to family courts that involvement in Afro-Brazilian faiths should be a factor in custody rulings. For instance, in 2012, the Court of Justice of Rio Grande do Sul heard a custody dispute between the parents of seven-year-old Kerolainy. The trial court had granted custody of Kerolainy to the father, and the mother appealed the decision to the Court of Justice. Kerolainy's mother argued that the trial court had not had proper jurisdiction to hear the custody action and that the father had been preventing Kerolainy from having contact with her mother and maternal grandmother. She also alleged that the paternal grandparents took Kerolainy to Umbanda rituals, which supposedly scared the child.[49] The Court of Justice did not directly address this claim about Umbanda rituals in the published appeal. However, they affirmed the award of custody to the father and dismissed the mother's appeal, suggesting that they were not persuaded by the mother's concerns about Umbanda.

That same year, Court of Justice of Paraná also heard a case where the noncustodial parent alleged that the practice of Afro-Brazilian religions created grounds to terminate parental rights. An unnamed father filed for custody of his children, claiming that his former wife and eldest daughter had both converted to Umbanda or Candomblé and that their "fanaticism" had created an unstable environment for the younger children.[50] Unfortunately, the Court of Justice did not address this claim in the published appeal because the lower court had modified its decision while the appeal was pending, rendering the case moot.

Most recently, in 2017, André Amâncio Fogaça sued the mother of his child, Luciana Soeiro Purissmo, for moral damages because she "baptized" their infant child in Luciana's religion, Umbanda.[51] Fogaça, a Catholic, stated that this "baptism" in a religion different from his own, without consulting him or asking him to participate, shocked him and his entire family. He demanded 7,500 *reais* in compensation. The court determined that although learning that his daughter underwent an Umbanda ritual was upsetting to Fogaça and his family, it is natural for parents who subscribe to different faiths to want to expose their child to their own faith. This is particularly true when, as was the case here, the child is in that parent's custody. The court explained that such cases are not appropriate for moral damages.

Although the court found in Purissimo's favor, it still provides some evidence of the bias against Afro-Brazilian religions. One must wonder whether Fogaça would have felt so "shocked" and believed that he was entitled to financial compensation if Purissimo had introduced their daughter to Judaism or another mainstream faith, rather than Umbanda.

PART III: CONCLUSION

As the aforementioned cases have demonstrated, litigants and courts in the United States and Brazil have frequently debated what impact the practice of African diaspora religions has on a person's ability to properly parent a child. In the United States, these cases have generally centered on a single factor—the practice of animal sacrifice. Early opponents of these rituals suggested that participating in animal sacrifice would make a child more prone to violence in the future. More recently, courts have ruled that allowing a child to witness the ritual slaughter of an animal is traumatizing and constitutes criminal child abuse.

In Brazil, noncustodial parents and government officials have contended that merely being a devotee or priest of an African diaspora faith should be grounds for limiting or terminating parental rights. As recently as the late 2000s, judges have removed custody from practitioner-parents, and local officials have used the power of the police to intimidate devotees into removing their children from Afro-Brazilian temples. In the midst of the largely unchecked religious terrorism against adherents of Afro-Brazilian religions, the threat of losing visitation or custody of one's children represents yet another kind of state-sanctioned violence against these communities.

SECTION II

❖❖❖

Islam, Rastafari, and Religious Symbols in the African Diaspora

Islam and Rastafari, might, at first glance, seem to have little connection; however, they actually have much in common. First, in places such as Algeria, Jamaica, and Brazil, Muslims and Rastafarians have led resistance movements against slavery or colonialism. For this reason, European colonists regarded these religions as dangerous and sought to suppress them. Second, both are Abrahamic faiths that regulate adherents' dress, limit or prohibit the consumption of alcohol, and bar devotees from consuming certain foods, among other things. In particular, many adherents of these faiths maintain certain religious hairstyles and/or wear religious head coverings in public places. Third, devotees of both religions have faced significant limitations on their rights as they have moved to different parts of the world such as Europe and the United States and, for Rastafarians, Africa as well. Last, these limitations are closely related to controversies about race and identity as well as gender norms.

PART I: INTRODUCTION TO ISLAM

Islam requires little introduction in comparison to the other religions discussed in this book. With well over 1.6 billion followers, this faith is the second-largest religion in the world.[1] As a monotheistic, Abrahamic religion, it shares much with the largest religion in the world—Christianity. Therefore, this section focuses on explaining why Islam is included here as a religion of the African diaspora and on introducing the reader to a key difference between Islam and other well-known Abrahamic religions that results in the litigation discussed in this book.

There are two strong arguments for including Islam as a religion of the African diaspora. First, Islam spread to the African continent very early after its inception and, consequently, was dispersed to the Americas and Europe with mass movements of African people such as the Atlantic slave trade and postcolonial migrations to Europe. Second, startling percentages of the world's Muslims live in Africa, and these figures are increasing every day, particularly in "Sub-Saharan" or "Black" Africa. These statistics about the prevalence of Islam on the African continent and its significance in the history of the African diaspora set the stage for thinking about the importance of race in global controversies over Islam.

A. History of Islam in the African Diaspora

Islam formed in the beginning of the seventh century based on revelations that the Prophet Muhammad received from God. Within approximately twenty-five years after the Prophet's death in 632, Islam had spread across North Africa.[2] By the fourteenth and fifteenth centuries, key West African empires such as Mali and Songhai came under the control of Muslim leaders and were major centers of trade and knowledge transmission.[3]

Because of its early spread throughout the continent, Islam has long been present in the African diaspora. Harold Lawrence argues that the Islamic Mali Empire sent approximately 2,400 ships to the Americas between 1307 and 1312, nearly two hundred years prior to Columbus's supposed discovery.[4] He contends that the Mali people introduced Islamic symbols (e.g., the crescent) and customs (e.g., refusal to eat pork) to societies that Europeans thought were simply indigenous to the Americas.[5]

African Muslims also arrived in the Americas, alongside devotees of other African religions, in the Atlantic slave trade. Muslims were very important in the history of Atlantic slavery because they led some of the most significant rebellions in the Americas. For example, scholars have speculated that Francois Makandal, one of the most famous eighteenth-century rebels in St. Domingue (present-day Haiti), was Mandingo (from the Mali Empire) and spoke Arabic.[6] They have suggested that Boukman, one of the purported leaders of the Bwa Kayiman ceremony in 1791, was also a Muslim.[7] Additionally, studies have shown that Muslims led five and participated in at least seventeen slave uprisings in Bahia, Brazil.[8] Perhaps most significantly, in January 1835, Muslim Africans led an important rebellion in Bahia in which seventy Africans were killed and more than three hundred were arrested.[9]

The importance of Islam in the African diaspora, particularly as a form of resistance against oppression, did not die out with the end of slavery. In the twentieth century, Black communities in the United States formed successive waves of Muslim communities. Two of the most famous are the Moorish Science Temple and the Nation of Islam. Of course, of the latter, Malcolm X would become one of the most well-known civil rights leaders in US history.

Today, Islam continues to play an important role in the African diaspora. In response to a 2015 Gallup Poll, 36 percent of all US Muslims self-identified as "non-Hispanic Black."[10] Today, at least 13 percent of all Muslim adults in the US are African Americans, and an additional 5 percent are foreign-born persons from "Sub-Saharan Africa."[11] Furthermore, when Donald Trump issued his January 27, 2017, Executive Order 13769 banning US visas to nationals of certain countries, widely referred to as the "Muslim ban," three of the seven countries (Libya, Somalia, and the Sudan) were located on the African continent. For this and other reasons, a recent National Public Radio study highlights that Black Muslims face "double jeopardy" in the United States—contending with both racial and religious biases.[12]

African Muslims are also at the center of controversies over the rights of Muslims in France. Mostly due to the influx of North Africans from France's former colonies, in the mid-twentieth century, Africans represented more than 50 percent of all immigrants in France.[13] Islam became the second-largest religion in France by the end of the twentieth century, with Muslims representing around 10 percent of the country's population.[14] Today, Africans continue to constitute more than 44 percent of all immigrants in France, and Muslim Africans continue to be 34 percent of all immigrants.[15]

B. The Significance of Islam in Africa and African Muslims in the Twenty-First Century

In addition to the contributions that individual Muslims and Islamic organizations have made to the history of the African diaspora, the sheer number of African Muslims warrants the consideration of Islam as a religion of the African diaspora. According to the Pew Research Center, there were 1.618 billion Muslims in the world in 2010.[16] An astonishing 27 percent of Muslims, 437,742,000 people, lived on the African continent.[17] This is more than three times the number of Muslims who resided in the Middle East in 2010 (126.6 million). The Pew Research Center projects that by 2030, there will be approximately 638,896,000 Muslims in Africa, and they will constitute nearly one-third of the world's Muslim population (29.17 percent).

Even if one were to analyze these figures in relationship to the problematic, illusory boundary between North and "Sub-Saharan Africa," the figures remain staggering. In 2010, there were 242.5 million Muslims in "Sub-Saharan Africa"—50 million more Muslims than in North Africa. By 2030, the Pew Research Center projected that the population of Muslims in "Sub-Saharan Africa" would increase by 60 percent to 385.9 million people. These figures are not just the result of disparities in the population density of the regions. The Pew Research Center estimates that nearly one-third (29.6 percent) of the population of "Sub-Saharan Africa" is Muslim and eight of the forty-six countries in "Sub-Saharan Africa" have populations that are at least 90 percent Muslim.[18] The growing number of Muslims in "Sub-Saharan" or "Black" Africa is important to understanding global struggles over the rights of Muslim immigrants. Black Muslim females, triple minorities, are often at the center of controversies over headscarves and veils.

C. The Significance of Headscarves and Veils

Cultural, social, and religious norms of women covering their head, hair, and/or face in public have been around for millennia—long before the advent of Islam. The earliest-known records of such practices come from thirteenth century BCE Assyrian laws requiring married women to veil themselves in public but prohibiting enslaved women and prostitutes from doing so.[19] Veiling later served as an indicator of social position in many ancient societies, including the Greek, Roman, and Persian Empires.[20] Veiling was also a common practice in early Christian and Jewish societies, often serving as a symbol of modesty.[21] Despite these broad cultural and religious roots, some of which continue to play a role in global veiling practices today, in the twenty-first century, many regard wearing a head covering or veil as synonymous with Islam.

In general, "Islam focuses on modesty in dress and behavior," and the Qur'an, "believed to be the direct word of God,"[22] instructs all believers to "cover your nakedness" with "garments."[23] Within the Qur'an, there are two mentions of the "hijab," an Arabic word that "stems from the word hajaba, meaning 'to prevent from seeing.'"[24] The first instructs Muslim women to "draw veils over their bosoms" and "not display their beauty and ornaments" or "charms" except to their immediate male family members, other women, or children "who are not yet aware of women's nakedness."[25] The second says that female believers should "draw their cloaks close round them" or "make their outer garments hang low over them" so that they can "be recognized" and not be "insulted" or "annoyed."[26] The Hadith, "the recorded sayings and actions of the Prophet Muhammad,"[27] expands on this, explaining that in the presence of men who are not part of the woman's immediate family, a woman who is past the age of puberty should wear loose-fitting clothing covering her body except her face, hands, and feet.[28] There are a range of different manifestations of this mandate for women to dress modestly, including "the headscarf (hijab), via the twopiece veil, the alamira, the long rectangular scarf or shayla worn widely in the Gulf states, the waistlength cape or khimar, the Iranian chador, the fullface veil or niqab, up to the most concealing of Muslim veils, the burqa, covering the entire face and body."[29]

Scholars have stressed that wearing headscarves, veils, and other coverings signify more than just a type of clothing; they are about a general principle of modesty or piety and moving away from emphasis on a woman's physical body.[30] The act of covering oneself, whatever form it may take, "is not only meant to guard women from inappropriate leering male attention, but it is considered to be a liberating experience to be free from societal expectations and judgments over a woman's body and other physical characteristics."[31] Hera Hashmi argues that one of the reasons that women wear the hijab is "out of respect for themselves. Instead of potentially being treated as a sexual object, wearing the hijab allows people to judge a woman according to her character and personality rather than physical appearance."[32] The principle of hijab, Hashmi contends, is "not to deny a woman's sexuality but rather is to preserve and channel it into the private life."[33] It is also important to note that, at least in principle, women are responsible for their own piety or faith. Islam does not give men the authority to force women to veil themselves or engage in any other religious behavior; it is a woman's choice.[34]

PART II: INTRODUCTION TO RASTAFARI

Although it had its roots in a variety of different beliefs and movements, Rastafari religion began in the early 1930s. Many scholars believe that the religion was deeply influenced by the teachings of Marcus Garvey, who foretold that a Black ruler would come to power "as a sign of the deliverance of Africans around the world from the bonds of poverty, exploitation, and colonialism."[35] Some of the founders of the faith believed that Garvey was a prophet and that his words had been fulfilled with Haile Selassie's rise to power as the emperor of Ethiopia in 1930.[36] Thus, one of Rastafarians' central beliefs is that Haile Selassie "is the Black Messiah who appeared in the flesh for the redemption of all Blacks exiled in the world of White oppressors."[37]

Rastafari is a bible-based faith, and, historically, many of their members were disillusioned Christians.[38] However, they do not interpret the bible in the same ways as Christians and other Abrahamic faiths. Rastafarians believe that Black people wrote the bible but that some parts have been "corrupted" as it has been copied and translated, so they do not accept the bible in its entirety.[39] They believe that the Israelites, or "chosen people" referenced in the bible, are Ethiopians. Therefore, they view Ethiopia as the promised land to which all Rastafarians will/should be repatriated.[40]

Rastafarians are, in many cases, very strict and conservative. They do not take in things that are deemed to be impure, unclean, or unnatural. Therefore, many Rastafarians are vegetarians or only eat certain types of seafood. Furthermore, alcohol and tobacco are typically forbidden.[41] Desecrating the body is also prohibited. This principle, which is based on several bible verses, bans shaving, tattooing, and cutting or trimming their hair and beards. Rastafarians generally allow their hair to naturally form in long strands known as "locs" or "dreadlocks."[42] This aspect of their religious practice has been particularly controversial, as dreadlocks, along with other natural Black hairstyles such as Afros, twists, and braids, represent a rejection of Western beauty or grooming norms.[43] Many people who wear dreadlocks regard them as a symbol of Africanness and liberation, as well as an opposition to European culture or identity and ideals about beauty.[44]

Rastafarians also utilize marijuana, or *ganja*, as a sacred herb that brings about revelations during religious ceremonies known as "reasoning sessions."[45] These reasoning sessions "are informal gatherings during which a small group of brethren sit in a circle to smoke marijuana (a sacred weed to the Rastafarians) and have 'lofty discussions.'"[46] This practice is based on bible verses referring to holy "herb."[47] Rastafarians believe that marijuana/ganja will bring them closer to god[48] and allow them to "free ... the mind from the snares of colonialism."[49]

Rastafarians have had conflicts with the law since the religion's inception, in part because they view the Western world and its governments as an exploitative system.[50] In 1932, one of the founders of the religion was arrested in Jamaica for sedition for placing his allegiance to Ethiopia/Africa and Haile Selassie over England.[51] Several other early devotees were imprisoned for encouraging others not to pay taxes to the British.[52]

Furthermore, Jamaica was at the height of unemployment, economic depression, and poor housing conditions when Rastafari developed in the 1930s.[53] It gained followers with the anti-colonial struggles of the mid-twentieth century.[54] Its popularity stemmed from the fact that it directly addressed issues of oppression, poverty, and racism. As Leonard Barrett succinctly explained, Rastafari "became an alternative to the vapid preachments of the established religious institutions, which ignored questions of social injustice, class, and color."[55]

CHAPTER 5

Headscarves, Dreadlocks, and Other "Disruptions"

African Diaspora Religions and the Right to Education

The past several years have seen rampant reports that African and African American children in the United States were being kicked out of classrooms for wearing natural Black hairstyles, such as braids, twists, and dreadlocks, and that adults of African descent were suffering employment discrimination over the same hairstyles. In response to these incidents, in July 2019, California became the first US state to ban natural hair discrimination.[1] The preamble of this law, which proponents dubbed the "CROWN Act," explains that physical traits associated with Blackness, including "kinky and curly hair," have long been seen as "a badge of inferiority." By contrast, the drafters continue, "professionalism was, and still is, closely linked to European features and mannerisms." They conclude that "in a society in which hair has historically been one of many determining factors of a person's race, and whether they were a second-class citizen, hair today remains a proxy for race." For this reason, the law classifies hair discrimination as a form of racial discrimination, the latter of which has been prohibited by law for decades.

Although this statute only classifies hair discrimination as a type of racial discrimination, analogous restrictions on visual representations of African diaspora faiths also represent a form of religious discrimination. Prohibitions of headscarves, dreadlocks, and other African diaspora religious symbols not only reflect a preference for European standards of professional appearance in schools, but many of these cases are deeply rooted in European gender norms—specifically, the notion that female children are "oppressed" by headscarves and male children are undisciplined if they wear long hair. Biases against African diaspora religious attire and hairstyles also revolve around the idea that adherents of these faiths can "contaminate" or influence other students—pressuring them to convert, encouraging illicit drug use, supporting "devil worship," behaving "disruptively," or promoting gang violence. Based on these racialized biases, numerous schools across the globe have imposed restrictions on African diaspora religious teachings or symbols, forcing devotees of these minority religions to choose between their faith and their education.

PART I: HEADSCARVES AND VEILS IN FRENCH SCHOOLS

Perhaps the most famous restrictions on the rights of devotees of African diaspora religions to attend school have occurred in France since the late twentieth century. France has dismissed all claims about religious discrimination against Muslims by proclaiming that bans on headscarves and veils in public spaces are derived from long-standing policies of secularism designed to prohibit any coercive or disruptive religious symbols. However, in many ways, French bans on headscarves and veils are a direct result of France's colonization of Africa and subsequent African immigration to France.[2] Because this controversy has been written about extensively elsewhere, this section provides only a brief overview and focuses on the role that the African diaspora played in it.

A. *The Headscarf Controversy*

The question of wearing headscarves in schools in France began in the fall of 1989. A public secondary school about sixty kilometers outside Paris suspended three North African students (two sisters from Morocco and one girl from Tunisia) because they refused to remove their headscarves.[3] Shortly thereafter, the families and the school reached an agreement that the students could return wearing their headscarves at the school but not inside the classroom.[4] However, the girls decided not to remove their headscarves in class, and they were once again suspended. The king of Morocco visited the two Moroccan girls and their families at the consulate in Paris and convinced the children to stop wearing their headscarves. The Tunisian student followed suit a month later.[5]

Five years later, in September 1994, the dispute about wearing headscarves in schools resumed when François Bayrou, France's new education minister, announced during an interview that he planned to prohibit students from wearing headscarves at school. He followed this up with a circular instructing schools to ban "ostentatious signs" of religion, averring that they were "elements of proselytism or discrimination" that could pose a threat to secularism and student safety as well as disrupt the school.[6] Of course, by banning only "ostentatious signs" but permitting students to wear "discreet" religious symbols, schools could allow Christians to wear crosses or Jews to wear a yarmulke, while barring Muslim girls from wearing a veil or hijab.[7]

Sixty-nine girls were expelled for wearing headscarves because of this rule.[8] Many of them successfully contested these policies in French courts.[9] However, the Conseil d'Etat, the highest administrative court in France, reviewed this rule and determined that such bans were appropriate if the symbols were "ostentatious or protesting" or if the way that they were worn "constituted an act of pressure, provocation, proselytism or propaganda, jeopardized the dignity or freedom of the students wearing the signs or of other students or staff, compromised health or safety, disrupted teaching activities or disturbed order and the normal operation of the school."[10] Still, with no explanation about what constitutes "ostentatious" or what might be considered a provocation or propaganda, the interpretation of this rule was a local decision that could vary from case to case, not a nationwide standard.

All this changed in March 2004, when the French parliament enacted a law that eliminated the schools' discretion and made a universal policy barring certain religious symbols.[11] This law says, "In public elementary, middle and high schools, the wearing of signs or clothing which conspicuously manifest students' religious affiliations is prohibited. Disciplinary procedures to implement this rule will be preceded by a discussion with the student. The clothing and religious signs prohibited are conspicuous signs such as a large cross, a veil or a skullcap. Not regarded as signs indicating religious affiliation are discreet signs, which can ... be medallions, small crosses, stars of David, hands of Fatima, or small Korans."[12] On the first day of the school year in 2004, the ban went into effect. Approximately 240 girls wore a headscarf to school in protest. Of these, 170 were forced to take it off. Between 50 and 60 students were expelled[13] and had to "turn to distance learning, private schools, or in some cases leave the country altogether and go to school abroad."[14]

In 2009, France began to take these bans on visible religious symbols a step further. Following a speech by President Nicolas Sarkozy condemning "the full-face or full-body veil ('voile intégral'), also known as the burqa or niqab," the French National Assembly formed a commission to explore whether the burqa should be permitted in France.[15] In 2010, the commission concluded that the burqa should be "condemned as contrary to Republican values and that discrimination and violence against women should also be condemned."[16] The commission also urged that "immigration and refugee laws should be amended to require would-be citizens and refugees to accept values such as equality of the sexes and the principle of secularism and to allow the refusal of residency status and citizenship to religious fundamentalists."[17] The parliament passed said law, which carries a fine of up to €150 or citizenship classes for anyone who conceals their face and a €30,000 fine plus up to one year of imprisonment for anyone who forces someone to conceal their face.[18] In 2011, France also banned the niqab ("the full-length burqa covering the face").[19] The European Court of Human Rights upheld this law in 2014. Therefore, in addition to bans on "ostentatious" religious symbols in schools, all Muslims are barred from wearing a burqa or niqab in France.

B. The African Diaspora and French "Secularism"

As one can see, there were no overt references to race or ethnicity in the laws or circulars delineating these policies. Instead, policy makers focused on "Republican values," citizenship, and "conspicuous" religious symbols. However, when one analyzes the broader context of these policies, there are at least three aspects of the bans on headscarves and veils in France that suggest that it was a direct attack on the presence of Africans and their religion in France.

First and foremost, France's headscarf bans can be directly traced to bitterness over the loss of its African colonies, particularly Algeria. In the nineteenth and twentieth centuries, France controlled more than a dozen colonies on the African continent. However, of its vast empire, Algeria was unique; it was geographically close to southern France and "was France's closest and largest trading partner, as well as the French colony with the largest European settler community."[20]

Because of France's special relationship with Algeria, it was particularly troubling to France when the Algerians rose up against them in 1954, and a very bloody war of independence ensued. At that time, the French "publicly and forcibly unveiled Muslim women" in an effort "to demonstrate the necessity of French colonial rule for the liberation of women."[21] The war ended eight years later in 1962, with each side suffering approximately four hundred thousand deaths.[22] When the headscarf controversies began in 1989, there were still at least three million French soldiers alive who had fought against Algeria in the war for independence and another one million French colonists who had been expelled from Algeria because of the war. These individuals were living with a constant, growing reminder of their bitter defeat, as more North African immigrants poured into France in the decades following independence.

Second, the beginning of the controversies over head coverings in schools was the result of a drastic shift in the racial and religious composition of France from the mid-to-late twentieth century as its African colonial subjects moved to the metropole. At the end of World War II, in 1946, Africans composed a negligible part of the immigrant population in France—North Africans were 2.3 percent and "Sub-Saharan" Africans were 0.8 percent.[23] However, following World War II, the French brought in North Africans to fill labor needs in areas such as construction and manufacturing cars. The French did not intend for these workers to stay; they viewed them as a "transient" labor force who would return when they were no longer needed.

In 1974, as France's labor needs shifted again, they prohibited unskilled foreign workers coming in as immigrants. After this time, the only permissible immigrants from North Africa were family reunifications—wives and children coming to be with the predominantly male immigrants who had previously entered as laborers. Judy Scales-Trent explains, "This has led not only to the increased percentage of women immigrants, but also to a major structural change in the African population in France. No longer primarily single male workers thinking of one day returning to their homelands and their families, these immigrant Africans are now families with children who were born in France and who are being educated in French schools: it appears that they might well stay. And it is this shift that troubles many French, leading to heightened racism and xenophobia."[24]

By 1990, the ratio of immigrants in France had changed drastically from 1946. Europeans, who had been nearly 90 percent of immigrants in the middle of the century, were now only 40.6 percent.[25] By contrast, Africans, who had been only a combined 3.1 percent of immigrants entering France in 1946, jumped to 50.5 percent of all immigrants (North Africans: 38.7 percent; other Africans: 11.8 percent). Perhaps most strikingly, in 1990, North Africans constituted over 36 percent of all foreign women residing in France, and Africans generally represented more than 40 percent of foreign women. In 1996, Milton Viorst estimated that there were approximately four to five million Muslims living in France, which equated to 10 percent of the population.[26] Despite the absence of specific statistics about the religion of the inhabitants of France, experts agreed that Islam had become the second-largest religion, surpassing Protestant Christianity and Judaism but following Catholicism.[27]

In the 1990s, studies showed that "only 10 or 15 percent of France's Muslims regularly practice their religion," yet polls revealed that "two-thirds of the French associate[d] Islam with religious fanaticism."[28] Furthermore, in 1992, shortly after the headscarf controversy began, a survey found that 65 percent of French people thought there were too many Arabs in the country and 38 percent thought there were too many Africans.[29] Therefore, one of the main concerns behind these policies was that Muslims would "take over" France and the large number of them seemed to threaten secularism (*laïcité*).[30]

Ironically, despite all the fearmongering about the destruction of "secularism," when the minister of education circulated the original headscarf ban in 1994, there were only somewhere between two thousand and fifteen thousand Muslim girls wearing a hijab out of three hundred thousand female Muslim students in French high schools. Similarly, when the national law was under review in 2003, a newspaper reported that the vast majority (76 percent) of teachers supported the ban, but 65 percent had never even seen a girl wearing a veil in school the entire time they had been teaching.[31]

Third, the debates about these laws have been rife with judgments about the supposedly oppressive nature of Islam and North African culture. The policy makers banning the hijab tried to position themselves as the liberators of women and the people who are defending gender equality.[32] In 2003, the year before the national law about headscarves, a commission composed of twenty white people (eighteen men and two women) drafted a report about juvenile delinquency in France. They averred that bilingualism was a major problem in French schools, which they must eradicate by convincing students' mothers to speak only French at home. The commission suggested that the mothers of these bilingual children "may be too weak to stand up to their husbands" and, according to Judith Ezekiel, essentially described the husbands as "exoticized, ignorant patriarchs" who "supposedly insist upon speaking patois."[33] Similarly, after the passage of the 2004 "ostentatious symbols" law, one of the members of the commission wrote a law review article arguing that the ban was necessary because Muslim girls were forced to wear the headscarves.[34] Even some protesters of the law based their arguments on negative perceptions of North African, Muslim immigrants. They argued "that the schools have a mission to neutralize religious differences between students while imbuing them with French civilization."[35] Therefore, some believed that it was better for these girls to stay in their classrooms because school would expose them to French culture and "could save these women from the tyranny of their fathers."[36]

As controversies over head coverings continue, it is important to remember that Africans remain the largest group of immigrants in France, and Muslim Africans dominate this population. According to the Institut national de la statisique et des études économiques, in 2014, there were 5,848,314 immigrants in France.[37] Africans constituted 44.36 percent of the immigrant population, or 2,594,286 people.[38] Approximately 34 percent of all immigrants in France, just shy of 2 million people, were from predominantly Muslim countries in Africa.[39] France's population was around 65.8 million in 2014, meaning that Muslim African immigrants made up approximately 3 percent of France's entire population. Of course, this does not account for the former immigrants who have become French citizens or the descendants of former immigrants who were born in France. The Pew Research Center estimated that in 2010, approximately 7.5 percent of France's population was Muslim and that this would increase to 9 percent by 2020.

PART II: GLOBAL BANS ON DREADLOCKS IN SCHOOLS

Rastafarians also experience severe discrimination in educational institutions. In at least six different countries—England, the Cayman Islands, Kenya, South Africa, Zimbabwe, and Malawi—schools have prohibited Rastafarians and other children from enrolling or attending classes because they had dreadlocks. These restrictions have taken two primary forms: (1) schools have implemented general restrictions on hair length for male children, which have been applied to Rastafarians because they do not cut their hair, or (2) schools have implemented direct prohibitions on particular hairstyles, including dreadlocks.

A. Cultural and Gender Discrimination

Many cases related to the right to wear dreadlocks in primary and secondary schools center on distinct policies for what are appropriate grooming standards for male and female students. Beginning at around ages four to six, as students are entering grade zero or kindergarten, schools enforce bans on male students wearing hair longer than their shirt collar or they require male children to shave their heads. School officials justify these bans by contending that permitting long hair or "unusual" hairstyles might lead to gang violence and drug use. They argue that uniform appearance cultivates better discipline. Disputes over these policies focus on two central issues—whether developing different hair policies for boys and girls constitutes gender discrimination and whether children whose hair reflects their "culture" deserve the same protections as those whose hair reflects their religious beliefs.

i. Zimbabwe

One of the first cases about hair length began in early March 2005, when two Rastafarians, Brighton Zengeni and Tambudzayi Chimedza, enrolled their child, Farai Benjamin Dzvova, in grade zero at Ruvheneko Government Primary School in Zimbabwe.[40] According to their religious beliefs, Zengeni and Chimedza had never cut Dzvova's hair, and they styled his hair in dreadlocks. Dzvova had attended the same institution for preschool, and during that time, the school administration had never raised any issues about Dzvova's hair. However, on January 25, 2006, about ten months after Dzvova was enrolled in grade zero, the teacher in charge sent a letter to Dzvova's father, stating that school regulations required that "hair has to be kept very short and well combed by all pupils attending [the school], regardless of sex, age, race or religion."[41] The school advised Zengeni that he needed to "abide by this regulation" immediately or withdraw Dzvova from Ruvheneko and transfer him to a different school.[42] By the time this letter went out, the school had already removed Dzvova from his regular classroom and placed him in a room separate from the other students. After another a series of unsuccessful attempts to resolve the issue directly with school officials, Zengeni filed an application with the courts to determine whether the exclusion of Dzvova from school was constitutional.

On January 10, 2007, the Supreme Court of Zimbabwe issued its ruling, finding in Zengeni and Dzvova's favor. The court determined that the school's application of the hair policy violated Dzvova's right to freedom of religion and violated Zimbabwe's Education Act, which provides every child with the fundamental right to school education and prohibits refusing to admit any student. The court noted that the only exception to the right to education under the Education Act is that schools have the power to discipline, suspend, and expel students. The court determined that the headmaster exceeded his authority because a child's hair is not related to obedience, indiscipline, or any other aspect of a child's conduct at school.[43] The court declared that "expulsion of a Rastafarian from school on the basis of his expression of his religious belief through his hairstyle is a contravention" of the constitution.[44] They barred the school from discriminating against Dzvova or separating him from his classmates and required the administrators to admit him. They also ordered the school to pay the costs of the litigation.

ii. England

From 2010 to 2011, St. Gregory's Catholic Science College in Harrow became embroiled in two cases related to their hair policy that introduced an argument that would become popular in other cases around the world—that dreadlocks and other "nontraditional" Black hairstyles posed a danger to school security. The first case began in 2009, when "G," an eleven-year-old boy with Afro-Caribbean heritage, was enrolled in classes and scheduled to begin school at St. Gregory's.[45] However, St. Gregory's dress code policy said that a boy's hair could not be longer than the collar of his shirt, and that boys could not wear braids. G had long hair, which, according to family tradition, had not been cut since birth and was worn in braids known as "cornrows." St. Gregory's refused to allow G to attend school unless he removed the cornrows and cut his hair above his collar. G's mother transferred him to another school and then filed a complaint alleging that St. Gregory's had practiced gender and racial discrimination against her son.

In 2011, the England and Wales High Court of Justice heard G's case. Although G was already enrolled in another school and his mother no longer sought his admission to St. Gregory's, both parties were interested in hearing a ruling on whether the policy to prohibit cornrows was lawful, so the court proceeded. Since the Department of Education had issued no national guideline about hair policies, this case turned on whether the policies at St. Gregory's constituted indirect discrimination based on gender, race, or other protected characteristics. If so, this would render the policy invalid.

In England, the test of indirect discrimination is whether someone has been subjected to a particular disadvantage or detriment. First, the court evaluated whether G had experienced indirect discrimination based on race. G's attorney explained that most of the students at St. Gregory's were nonwhite, and approximately 30 percent were students of Caribbean and African heritage. G's attorney argued that cornrows and similar hairstyles were rooted in Africa and common among Afro-Caribbean people and African Americans. They could signal things like status and kinship. In G's case, this was particularly true—all the men in his family wear their hair in cornrows. St. Gregory's responded that they were concerned about gang culture creeping into the school through hairstyles, bandanas, jewelry, and so on, so they have a no-tolerance policy on these appearance regulations.

The court found that G had been subjected to unjustified indirect discrimination because they saw no merit to the school's slippery-slope argument. The school officials conceded, and the court agreed that a student could refuse to comply with the policy for religious reasons. The court believed that "if there is a genuine cultural and family practice of not cutting males' hair and wearing cornrows," the school had no valid basis for not making a similar exception.[46] The judge stressed that allowing cultural hairstyles did not, as the school suggested, require them to allow hairstyles that indicated gang culture.

Then the court moved to the issue of gender. St. Gregory's dress code explicitly allows cornrows for girls but not for boys. The court determined that treating boys and girls differently does not necessarily mean that the school is discriminating against one gender or the other. With regard to dress codes, such differences could be lawfully based on "a conventional standard of appearance," which the court noted did not presently include cornrows and long hair for boys, although it might for girls.[47] Therefore, the court determined that the hair policy did not constitute gender discrimination. However, because the court had already found that the hair policy could result in indirect racial discrimination, G's right to wear cornrows was protected.

In September 2011, less than six months after the High Court's decision in G's case, St. Gregory's refused to enroll eleven-year-old Mahlei Simpson Miles unless he cut his dreadlocks.[48] Mahlei's mother, who is Rastafarian, withdrew her son's enrollment application and searched for a different school. St. Gregory's rejection of Mahlei's application runs directly contrary to the school's own statements in G's case, when they conceded that Rastafarians, Sikhs, and others who had a religious reason would be exempt from the hair policy.

Cases continue to arise in England regarding the right to wear dreadlocks in schools.[49] Twelve-year-old Chikayzea Flanders attended Fulham Boys School in London, which has a dress code policy prohibiting long hair for boys. His mother tied his hair up so that it would not touch his shoulders in an attempt to comply with the dress code. On the first day of school in 2017, officials put Chikayzea in isolation and called his mother demanding that she cut his hair or Chikayzea would be suspended. She refused, citing both cultural and religious (Rastafari) beliefs. According to the *Daily Mail Online*, the headteacher took an astonishing position that dreadlocks were not a required feature of Rastafari religious beliefs. The headteacher told Chikayzea's mother: "At the moment we are treating this as a social issue. I have seen no tenets that you have to have dreadlocks."[50] Chikayzea's mother began a petition on September 10, 2017, against Fulham Boys School.[51] By early November, Chikayzea had moved to Hurlingham Academy, but his mother continued to speak out against what she perceived as racial and cultural discrimination against her son.[52]

iii. Malawi

Schools in Malawi have also recently enforced hair length restrictions against Rastafarians. In September 2012, Makapwa Primary School sent home three Rastafari students who came to school in dreadlocks: eight-year-old Fadweck, eleven-year-old George, and thirteen-year-old Miriam.[53] Lindiwe Chide, spokesperson for the Ministry of Education, confirmed that the ministry backed this decision and explained that the reason for prohibiting dreadlocks was to promote uniform appearance. Ras Jah Vision, spokesperson for the Rastafari community, criticized this policy for suppressing Rastafari children's right to education.[54] Nearly a year later, the children's father, James Dinesi, told *The Nation* that his children were still staying home from school because of the dreadlocks controversy.[55]

The US Department of State's *International Religious Freedom Report* for 2012 noted of Malawi that "Rastafarian leaders continued to complain of an unofficial ban on long hair in some government-run schools. Although there is no law relating to hair length, some school dress codes prohibited long hair. In addition, according to the president of Rastafari for Unity (a Malawian organization), Rastafarians are only able to obtain employment in the private sector because the government does not employ Rastafarians."[56] The following year, the Rastafarian community continued to press for a change in the country's education policy. They conducted a street march in September 2013 and sent a petition to the government about the dreadlocks ban.[57] However, the US Department of State's *International Religious Freedom Report* for 2016 indicated that Rastafarian protests had not yielded any positive change. Rather, Rastafarians reported that most parents had given in to the schools' demands that they shave the children's heads in order to attend public school.[58]

The most recent development came in March 2017, when an unknown person circulated a letter on social media directed to managers and teaching schools that said that Muslim children wearing hijabs and Rastafari children wearing dreadlocks would be permitted in Malawian public schools. The letter bore the name of the secretary for education, science and technology, Ken Ndala.[59] Lindiwe Chide, the deputy director of inspection and advisory services for the Ministry of Education quickly denounced the letter as a fake during a radio interview later that month. Chide reported that the government was still discussing the right to wear dreadlocks and hijabs in schools with "relevant stakeholders."[60]

B. Direct Bans on Dreadlocks

In addition to the regulations on the length of a child's hair, which school officials have interpreted to ban dreadlocks for male children, there are several countries where schools have implemented more specific dress codes barring delineated hairstyles. Similar to the arguments that St. Gregory's made in G's case in England, school officials often justify these regulations based on theories that certain hairstyles promote illegal behavior such as drugs, gangs, and violence. In most cases, courts or other adjudicatory bodies have determined that schools may maintain these general grooming policies but must provide a religious accommodation to Rastafarian students. However, schools have often demeaned Rastafarians in the process of contesting these rights.

i. Cayman Islands

One of the earliest cases of a direct ban on dreadlocks began in the Cayman Islands in the 1990s. G, a Rastafarian, attempted to register his eight-year-old son, Shemiah, at a government primary school. However, the principal, E.C., refused to register Shemiah because he had dreadlocks and school rules prohibited this hairstyle.[61] G repeatedly sent Shemiah to school anyway, and each time the school turned him away. In December 1995, the Cayman Islands' Education Council approved E.C.'s decision to expel Shemiah.

The following year, G asked for judicial review of the expulsion, claiming that E.C. violated Shemiah's right to education and freedom of religion. E.C. responded that the school might be viewed as permitting illegal drugs if it admitted Shemiah because it is well known that Rastafarians use marijuana.[62] Ironically, E.C. also argued that the dress code was designed to prevent students from experiencing discrimination based on their hairstyle or clothing; he contended that exemptions to the dress code would undermine these antidiscrimination measures. In 1999, the Grand Court ruled in E.C.'s favor, finding that Shemiah would have to cut his hair to continue his schooling.[63]

In 2001, approximately six years after the start of the litigation, the Court of Appeal reversed the Grand Court's decision. It dismissed E.C.'s purported concerns about the correlations between admitting Rastafarians to the government school and the school's position on marijuana, which is banned in the

Cayman Islands. The Court of Appeal held that Rastafari is a religion, despite adherents' sacramental use of an illegal substance. (They also noted that there was no evidence that Shemiah or his family used marijuana.) Furthermore, the court discounted E.C.'s purported concerns about discrimination resulting from exemptions to the dress code, stating that "other students would not suffer prejudice because of his [Shemiah's] dress or appearance. However, [Shemiah] would be prejudiced if he was removed from school as he would be deprived of an education at the only primary school he could attend."[64] Therefore, they quashed the order to expel Shemiah and ordered that the school find a way to readmit him.

ii. South Africa

A few years after G filed the lawsuit contesting Shemiah's expulsion, a series of cases began in South Africa, commencing controversies over dreadlocks that continue to the present day. One of the first cases began in December 1999, when fifteen-year-old Danielle Antoine became a Rastafarian. Antoine and her mother repeatedly met with the headmaster of Settlers High School in Bellville, Western Cape, where Antoine was a tenth-grade student, to discuss the requirements of her religion. Although there was nothing in the school dress code addressing these issues, Antoine asked for permission to wear dreadlocks and a cap covering her hair.[65]

After a few months, Antoine grew tired of waiting while the headmaster failed to give permission. In April 2000, she began wearing a cap to school that she had made to match the school uniform. The headmaster summoned Antoine to a disciplinary hearing for violating the code of conduct regarding the school uniform. The school charged Antoine with serious misconduct, stating that her head covering and dreadlocks had violated school rules and had caused "disruption and uncertainty."[66] The governing body of the high school determined that she was guilty of serious misconduct and sentenced her to five days' suspension.

Antoine filed a case asking the Cape of Good Hope Provincial Division of the High Court of South Africa to review the governing body's decision. The court found in Antoine's favor for a variety of reasons. First, the court noted that there was absolutely nothing in the code of conduct prohibiting dreadlocks or any headgear analogous to what Antoine had worn. Even if such a prohibition had existed, the court stressed that Antoine's actions must be assessed to determine whether they constituted "serious misconduct" as defined by South African law.

"Serious misconduct" can be shown by a number of actions, such as possessing drugs or alcohol, repeatedly missing classes or school, committing a criminal offense, or behaving "in a disgraceful, improper or unbecoming manner."[67] The High Court determined that because Antoine's action was not even a violation of the code of conduct, it was "a blatant absurdity to categorise the growing of dreadlocks or wearing of a cap" as serious misconduct.[68] Therefore, the High Court set aside the governing body's decision finding Antoine guilty of serious misconduct and reversed her suspension. By the time the court reached its decision, Antoine had left Settlers High School, but the court's decision removed the disciplinary action from her permanent record.

Despite the High Court's ruling that dreadlocks were not "serious misconduct," South African schools have continued to ban them under the premise that they are disruptive and induce unlawful behavior. In 2013, a Rastafarian child named Lerato Radebe was an eighth-grade student at Leseding Technical School in Free State, South Africa.[69] The school's code of conduct prohibited "elaborate styles" "such as parting, shaven paths, steps, dyes, fizzes, dreadlocks and hairpieces."[70] Leseding authorities permitted Radebe to enter the school with dreadlocks but forced her to spend the day sitting alone in the staffroom, receiving no educational instruction.

After a few weeks of in-school isolation, Leseding authorities met with Radebe's parents. However, instead of addressing Radebe's dreadlocks as a simple dress code violation, Leseding officials told Radebe's parents that they could not permit her to attend their school because other children would find it "highly upsetting" to see their fellow student wearing dreadlocks, a symbol that she was practicing a religion that involved cannabis use. There was no evidence that Radebe was using marijuana.

Over the following months, Lerato's father, Lehlohonolo Radebe, met with various officials from the school, the Department of Education, and the South African Human Rights Commission to try to resolve his daughter's situation. Because he had missed so much work to address his daughter's schooling issues, Lehlohonolo lost his job. However, all his efforts were to little avail, as Lehlohonolo was unable to reach an adequate resolution with Leseding and the Department of Education. Therefore, Radebe, her parents, and an organization known as Equal Education filed an urgent application seeking an order from the Free State High Court declaring Radebe's suspension to be unlawful and discriminatory.

When the case proceeded before the High Court, Leseding officials sidestepped the question of the legitimacy of their own policies by asserting that

Radebe's rights were not violated because she could simply attend another institution that didn't have restrictions on hairstyles in their code of conduct. However, Judge Nkophane Phalatsi was not swayed by this argument. Phalatsi determined that Leseding violated Radebe's constitutional rights to education, dignity, equality, culture, and freedom of religion, belief, and association, among others. He ordered Leseding to readmit Radebe and barred them from harassing or discriminating against the child. Phalatsi gave Leseding five days to conduct an assessment to determine what materials Radebe had missed since she was suspended and to create a program to help Radebe catch up on the missed coursework. He also ordered Leseding, within one month of the order, to attend "an education and relationship building workshop" provided by the Human Rights Commission and to "explain their error in banishing [Radebe] from her classroom and their improved understanding of the religious and cultural rights of learners, to a full assembly of the learners and educators of the" high school.[71]

Despite these strong decisions in favor of Rastafarian students, the disciplinary actions over dreadlocks continue in South Africa. In the past five years, at least half a dozen students have missed days or weeks of classes because of controversies about their hair, and the schools continue to allege that Rastafarians will corrupt their institutions. For instance, in 2016, a teacher reportedly refused to hold class while seventeen-year-old Anathi Marhe was in the room and yelled at him, saying: "We don't teach Rastafarians in the school, you will bring bad influence."[72] That same year, when Nonkosi Stofile took her son Azania to the first day of eighth grade, the teacher said that the school prohibited boys from having long hair. When Nonkosi tried to explain that Azania's long dreadlocks were part of his religious beliefs, the teacher predicted that Azania would start selling cannabis to other students.[73] Nonkosi eventually sought the advice of an attorney, who discovered that the school had a history of refusing to admit Rastafarian students.

These controversies over dreadlocks also appear to be part of a larger culture of prohibiting natural Black hairstyles in South Africa. In September 2016, Prega Govender of the *Mail and Guardian* published an article alleging that a poll of schools had revealed that many banned hairstyles such as Afros, dreadlocks, braids, "bushy" hair, and related styles.[74] Others pressured, if not required, students to straighten their hair. Also writing about this problem, Thando Sipuye, member of the Africentrik Study Group at the University of Sobukwe, asked: "What is it about African hair, African hairstyles and African culture that breaks school 'rules' and 'codes of conduct'; do the kinks and knots in African hair bind and incapacitate Africans from thinking?"[75] Sipuye speculated that it was some kind of desire for whiteness and internalized self-hatred that caused many Black people to go along with these dress codes that classify natural Black hairstyles as "dirty" and unprofessional.

PART III: CANDOMBLÉ AND UMBANDA IN BRAZILIAN SCHOOLS

In contrast to the aforementioned cases that have centered on controversies over head coverings and hairstyles, Brazil's supposedly secular and progressive institutions are displaying a myriad of discriminatory policies limiting the rights of devotees of Afro-Brazilian religions. First, teachers have been suspended and transferred for using instructional materials referencing Afro-Brazilian faiths. Second, students of all faiths have been forced to recite Christian prayers and take courses on Christianity in public institutions. Finally, like Rastafari and Muslim students, those same public educational facilities have barred Afro-Brazilian adherents from entering while wearing symbols of their faith. These controversies in Brazil represent a very extreme intersection of racial and religious discrimination in schools, which are grounded in the same rhetoric about contamination and disruption as the cases discussed previously.

On paper, Brazilian schools are far advanced beyond most of their counterparts in the Western Hemisphere in terms of their policies regarding race and inclusion. In 2003, legislators amended the General Education Law to require instruction on Afro-Brazilian history and culture in elementary and secondary public schools.[76] However, in 2014, the Working Group of Experts on People of African Descent expressed concern "at reports from civil society about the obstacles faced in the implementation of this law, including the lack of suitable training for teachers, lack of relevant school materials and opposition from ultra-right, evangelical sects at the teaching of Afro-Brazilian cultural and religious traditions."[77] The Working Group noted that it had received reports that many teachers did not believe that Afro-Brazilian history and culture was important, so they refused to provide instruction in this area. Furthermore, the ICCRR's 2019 report on religious racism in Brazil documented more than two dozen cases of intolerance against Afro-Brazilian religions in educational institutions since the start of the twenty-first century.

These recent cases include several in which public school teachers who have incorporated Afro-Brazilian culture into their lectures and programming have been suspended or dismissed from their positions. For instance, in October 2009, Maria Cristina Marques, a literature professor at Municipal School Pedro Adami in Macaé, was banned from teaching after she utilized a book called *Legends of Exu*, which discusses the folklore of Afro-Brazilian deities, in her classes.[78] The mothers of some of her evangelical students accused Marques of sympathizing with the devil. They demanded that she stop teaching literature about Africa and about a religion that involved black magic and selling children's organs.[79] Marques, an Umbanda priest, explained that she used this book to teach grammatical tools and to stimulate students' imagination. She also stressed that the book was recommended by the Ministry of Education.[80] Marques filed a complaint of religious intolerance with the Public Prosecutor's Office against the school and its evangelical director, Mery Lice da Silva Oliveira.[81] In 2014, Marques also wrote her master's thesis on how teaching *Legends of Exu* fulfills the goal of Law 10.639 to develop a more inclusive model of education that engages with Afro-Brazilian worldviews and debunks negative stereotypes about Afro-Brazilian religions.[82] At the time she was completing her thesis, Marques was again teaching Portuguese language classes at Colégio Municipal Pedro Adami and used this institution as a case study for her thesis.

Only a month after Marques experienced serious backlash for teaching *Legends of Exu*, Francisco Albuquerque Santo Filho, a public school teacher in Brasilia, was removed from teaching at Centro Educacional nº 4 de Taguatinga under similar circumstances.[83] Santo Filho was organizing a program in honor of the National Day of Black Consciousness (November 20), which celebrates Afro-Brazilians' struggle against slavery and specifically honors Zumbi, a historic figure who led Quilombo dos Palmares, a fugitive slave community. Santo Filho scheduled a series of lectures as well as games and dances honoring Afro-Brazilian heritage for the holiday.[84] Santo Filho planned to have the students perform Candomblé dances as a part of this celebration; however, Catholic and evangelical students refused to participate, claiming that he was forcing them to practice Candomblé.

As a result of the students' protests, the school sent Santo Filho back to the Regional Board of Education, who reassigned him to a different school until the allegations could be resolved. They continued a celebration of Zumbi but removed the so-called religious practices from the program. Santo Filho filed a complaint of religious discrimination against the school with the federal public prosecutor. However, I have been unable to locate the results of the complaint.

In addition to the censorship and exclusion of educational content about Afro-Brazilian religions, scholars have recently documented numerous cases of religious racism in Brazil's supposedly secular schools. The US Department of State's *International Religious Freedom Report* from 2010 indicated that "according to media reports, some students who practiced Candomblé and other Afro-Brazilian religions in schools were discriminated against by teachers or other students, including being told to repeat prayers or face expulsion and forced by school authorities to attend Catholic or evangelical classes."[85] The *International Religious Freedom Report* from 2013 added that approximately half of schools in Brazil force students to take classes in Christian religious instruction despite the fact that pursuant to Brazilian law, public schools may only offer religious courses but may not require students to take them.[86] Marcelo Andrade and Pedro Teixeira's recent study on religious conflicts in Brazilian schools supports the US State Department's claims, indicating that Christians frequently harass non-Christian students in public schools, calling them devil-worshippers.[87] Andrade and Teixeira added that school officials often refuse to acknowledge these cases of discrimination and see no need for teachers to modify their behavior.[88]

Finally, multiple reports have emerged from Rio de Janeiro over the past few years where students were kicked out of public schools for wearing Afro-Brazilian religious symbols such as beaded necklaces known as *ilekes*, which serve as spiritual protection for the wearer. For example, in 2011, a Portuguese teacher observed a thirteen-year-old boy wearing ilekes under his school uniform.[89] The teacher, a Protestant, ordered the child out of the classroom, calling him "Satan." The teacher banned the boy from her classes and encouraged his classmates to ignore him. The boy's mother contacted the school administration, but they didn't help her, so she went to the police to file a discrimination complaint.

Three years later, in 2014, another male student at a public school in Zona Norte who had been recently initiated into Candomblé had a similar experience.[90] When the twelve-year-old arrived at school wearing ilekes underneath his shirt, the principal refused to allow him to enter, claiming that he was violating the dress code.[91] The boy's family spoke to the mayor, Eduardo Paes, who informed them that religious symbols are permitted in public schools so long as there is no conflict with the school uniform.[92] The boy's mother reported the case to a human rights center, noting that this seemed to be a case of religious discrimination because other children wore various kinds of jewelry to school without incident. The child ended up having to transfer to a different school after missing thirty days of classes.

PART IV: CONCLUSION

As the aforementioned cases and laws demonstrate, policy makers frequently try to ban African diaspora religions and their adherents from primary and secondary classrooms. They express concern that mere visible symbols or discussions about these faiths will infringe on other students' religious freedom, pressuring them to convert or encouraging illicit behavior such as drug use or gang violence. One cannot help but notice that this uneasiness with African diaspora faiths is directly connected to racial discrimination—specifically to the desire to maintain Eurocentric norms in the classroom environment and instructional materials.

African diaspora religions have a long history of serving as a rallying force against oppressive colonial forces and are constant reminders that twenty-first-century societies are more racially and religiously diverse than many would wish to envision their "modern" state. In the case of Islam and Rastafari in particular, these faiths often flout gender norms—the notions that "liberated" women cannot also cover themselves or the idea that "respectable" males must cut their hair above their shirt collar. Afro-Brazilian religions likewise offer students non-Western worldviews and underscore non-Western histories that evangelicals have contended promote devil worship and other kinds of disorder. In these ways, once more, these cases reflect the use of purported concerns about "contamination," "public health," and violence to limit the rights of devotees of African diaspora religions.

Perhaps as much as the existence of these cases and the racialized basis for the challenges to the presence of African diaspora religions in schools, the silences about them also demonstrate considerable bias in modern interpretations of religious liberty. Unlike the issues discussed in part I, religious attire and the role of religion in schools are at the core of debates about religious freedom both in scholarship and in policy. However, discussions of Rastafari and Candomblé adherents are almost never incorporated into the study and discussions about these matters. Furthermore, while Islamic head coverings are frequently, but not always, included in debates about religious attire and the presence of religions in schools, the centrality of race and the African diaspora in these disputes is rarely highlighted and does not often factor into analyses of potential bias in these supposedly secular policies. These omissions are another layer of religious racism because the lack of recognition of African diaspora faiths in scholarly, legislative, and judicial debates about these issues paves the way for discriminatory cases to continue unrestrained.

CHAPTER ◊ 6

Neither Litigant, nor Lawyer, nor Law Enforcement

Religious Barriers to the Justice System

Adherents of African diaspora religions have been restricted or denied access to justice systems across the globe because of their religious practices. First, and most disturbing, litigants have been denied access to courts unless they remove their religious head coverings or necklaces. Similarly, judges have found African diaspora religious adherents unfit to practice law because of their hairstyles or sacramental drug use. Courts and supervisors have restricted police and security officers from wearing headscarves and dreadlocks because it supposedly undermines uniformity of attire expected of persons in such positions. Correctional officers have been prevented from working in prisons because their hair or head covering allegedly poses a security risk or suggests that they might be prone to corruption. Furthermore, even when held in custody for a very brief period of time, police officers have forcibly removed religiously based dreadlocks and headscarves from bodies of people of African descent.

PART I: ACCESS TO COURTS

In at least three countries, and involving four different religions, judges and other court officials have limited the ability of devotees of African diaspora faiths to access courts. They have kicked people out of their courtrooms, refused to continue proceedings, and sent them to jail for contempt because they decided that the religious symbol a person was wearing was inappropriate.

Often while simultaneously admitting that they have little or no knowledge about the devotee's faith, court officers and judges provided racially and religiously biased explanations about how their hair or attire was disruptive, dangerous, or otherwise prevented the administration of justice. In doing so, they frequently belittled the person's appearance and/or questioned the validity of the faith itself.

A. Rastafarians in the United Kingdom

The earliest of these cases occurred in the United Kingdom during the same period as the controversies over Afro-Caribbean persons wearing dreadlocks and other natural Black hairstyles in schools. However, these cases involved hats, sometimes called "tams," that Rastafarian men often use to cover their dreadlocks. Ironically, the first controversy about Rastafari hats in English courtrooms began during a trial about racial discrimination in educational facilities.

In 1991, Donna Phillips, a Black woman, sued St. Mary's Church of England Primary School in South London for racial discrimination after they expelled her children.[1] During the trial at Westminster County Court, some of Phillips's Rastafarian relatives were sitting in the courtroom with their hats on. Judge Percy Harris announced that he would allow anyone who was Sikh to wear a head covering, but he demanded that Rastafarians remove their hats. Phillips's attorney repeatedly explained to Judge Harris that the Rastafarians were wearing religious headwear based on the same principle as Sikhs. Harris finally relented, stating that he had been "pushed into" allowing the hats. Phillips's lawyer asked the judge to recuse himself from the case following this exchange, and a group known as the Black Liaison Forum campaigned for Judge Harris's removal from the bench.

A similar case occurred in 2002 when a Rastafarian man, Terence Lynch, was sitting in the public gallery in Birmingham Crown Court wearing a tam.[2] Judge Robert Orme told Lynch to remove his hat or leave the courtroom.[3] Lynch refused, explaining that it was against his religion to remove the hat. The judge told Lynch to go outside if he wanted to practice his religion. When Lynch refused to remove the hat or exit, Orme arrested him for contempt of court and put him in a jail cell. After two hours, Orme let Lynch out of jail because someone told him that Lynch was a single father to a disabled child. However, Orme was initially unwilling to apologize for holding Lynch in contempt, stating that he was not sure if Rastafari was a religion or a way of life.[4]

The next day, the judge issued a statement expressing his regret and explaining that he had no intention of offending Rastafarians.

B. Muslims and "Voodoo" Practitioners in the United States

African American Muslims and self-proclaimed "Voodoo" adherents have experienced similar exchanges with judges in recent years in the United States. However, unlike their British counterparts, some of these individuals were the litigants in their cases, not mere observers. Furthermore, after judges questioned whether their faith truly required these religious symbols or queried whether their faith was a "religion" at all, they never issued an apology for these abuses or displayed any remorse for their actions.

Two of the most egregious US cases concerned Black American Muslim women and the right to wear religious head coverings in court. The first involved Ginnah Muhammad, an African American Muslim who wears a veil that covers her entire head except her eyes.[5] In 2006, Enterprise Leasing of Detroit and Muhammad filed small claims action against each other concerning a dispute as to whether Muhammad had caused damage to a vehicle she rented from Enterprise. Both cases were assigned to Judge Paul Paruk of the 31st District Court in the state of Michigan.

Small claims proceedings are simple; each side testifies about their claim and then the judge renders a verdict. However, Paruk refused to permit Muhammad to testify in her hearing unless she removed her veil. He claimed that he needed to be able to see Muhammad's face to judge from her "demeanor and temperament" whether she was telling the truth.[6] Muhammad explained that she wore the veil as a component of her religion and could not remove it before Judge Paruk but would be willing to do so for a female judge. Paruk dismissed her explanation, telling her that her decision to veil herself was not a "religious thing"; it was a "cultural thing."[7] Paruk also claimed that there was no female judge who could hear Muhammad's case and again instructed her to take her veil off to testify. Muhammad refused and Paruk dismissed her case against Enterprise.

A few weeks later, Muhammad was scheduled to appear before Paruk again regarding Enterprise's small claims case against her. She filed a motion asking Paruk to recuse himself because of the prior exchange about the veil in her case against Enterprise. Paruk denied her motion. About seven months later, he decided in favor of Enterprise, awarding them over $2,000 in damages.

Muhammad filed an appeal in Enterprise's case; however, I have been unable to find the outcome of the appeal. She also sued Paruk on the case that he dismissed, claiming that he had violated her rights to religious freedom and to access the courts. The United States District Court dismissed her appeal, finding that it would cause too much federal court interference into the way that Paruk (a state court judge) handled his courtroom if they were to evaluate whether he had a valid, neutral reason for requiring witnesses to show their face while testifying.

Shortly thereafter, a similar dispute arose in Georgia. Lisa Valentine is an African American Muslim[8] who wears a headscarf. On the morning of December 16, 2008, Valentine's nephew had a traffic hearing at Douglasville Courthouse, and Valentine wanted to accompany him. However, as Valentine attempted to enter the courthouse, Officer Mullis, who worked at the metal detector at the courthouse entrance, told Valentine that court policy prohibited headgear. Valentine explained that her religion required her to wear the headscarf, but Mullis repeatedly insisted that there were no religious exemptions to the policy. Valentine called the policy "bullshit," then tried to leave the courthouse.[9] Mullis refused to permit Valentine to leave; he grabbed her and called another police officer, Camp, to forcibly bring her to the judge.

Mullis and Camp handcuffed Valentine and took her to the booking area of the police department, where she waited for a few minutes before being taken to Judge Rollin's courtroom. Mullis and Camp told the judge that Valentine fought them in the hallway after Mullis informed her that she could not enter the courtroom with her "headdress on."[10] Valentine insisted that she was just trying to leave but the officers had blocked her path to the exit.

Judge Rollins signed an order holding Valentine in criminal contempt of court, claiming that she "created a disturbance in hallway adjacent to the courtroom by becoming boisterous and combative with [the] police officer at [the] metal detector."[11] Rollins sentenced Valentine to ten days in jail. A third officer told Valentine that she would have to remove her headscarf and then placed her in a holding cell, where she waited until she was transported to the county jail. During the transport, she was not permitted to wear her headscarf, and she was also chained to male prisoners—contact that violated another principle of her religious beliefs.

Later that day, Judge Rollins had a meeting with several senior staff members of the police department about Valentine's charge. Chief Whisenant convinced the judge to rescind his contempt order and release Valentine from jail. Subsequently, Judge Rollins and the City Police Department both issued statements clarifying that persons who wear hats or head coverings for medical or religious reasons should be granted accommodations and taken to specific court personnel who can assist with their case.[12] The Georgia Judicial Council also implemented a nonbinding rule permitting religious head coverings in courthouses.[13]

Valentine sued the city government alleging the courthouse security officers had caused her severe humiliation, mental anguish, and emotional distress as well as violated her religious beliefs, her right to freedom from unlawful detention, and her right to equal protection of the law.[14] In 2011, Valentine and the city settled the case for an undisclosed amount.[15] The city also agreed to implement a new policy where an officer of the same gender would privately screen persons with religious head coverings before they entered the courtroom.

A few years later, Abu-Bakr Abdur Rahman of Fayetteville, North Carolina, had a similarly tense exchange over his religious attire that resulted in his temporary confinement for contempt of court but did not yield analogous changes in courtroom policy. In July 2015, Rahman appeared before District Court Judge Talmage Baggett on charges of communicating a threat. On the first court date, Rahman appeared wearing five necklaces, including a "metal chain [that] had a decorated container that he said was a medicine bottle. The others were colorful beaded strings with items attached such as shells, a skull-shaped amulet and skull-shaped beads."[16] Rahman explained that these necklaces served as amulets, protecting him from evil. Judge Baggett told Rahman that he would have to put the necklaces inside his shirt while he was in court. Rahman complied.

Later that night, Rahman consulted his priest, who told him that putting his necklaces inside his shirt was disrespecting his own faith.[17] The next day, Rahman appeared before Baggett again, and he put the necklaces outside his shirt. In its "Courthouse Blog," the *Fayetteville Observer* published the short transcript between Rahman and the judge, which Rahman had recorded on his phone. Baggett lectured Rahman, "Sir, I told you now about that stuff around your neck," to which Rahman responded, "Yeah, and I told you this is my religion."[18] Baggett told Rahman that he could take the necklaces off, leave the courtroom, or go to the "prisoner's box."[19] When Rahman protested that Baggett was discriminating against his faith, Baggett replied: "I don't know of any religion that requires you to wear this kind of stuff around your neck. I'm not familiar with your religion." Then Baggett instructed the bailiffs to lock Rahman up and told Rahman, "I'll let you practice your religion right over here in the box."[20] As Baggett informed Rahman that he was going to hold him in contempt of court and warned him to "get ready to spend the night in jail," Baggett continued to taunt Rahman: "Well, you're not going to be able to wear that in the jail." He had Rahman handcuffed and sent him to the prisoner's box for contempt of court, where Rahman remained for two hours and forty minutes.[21]

The following week, Rahman returned to Baggett's courtroom on a charge of fraudulently obtaining a $27.84 refund from Walmart.[22] Baggett once again insisted that Rahman put his necklaces inside his shirt or leave the courtroom. Rahman also recorded this exchange on his phone. Baggett told Rahman, "I'm not going to put up with Voodoo in this courtroom. This is a problem."[23] He continued, "You may have a religion. But sir, this is a security problem. And I want you to go to another courtroom and have another judge handle your case. I'm not going to have you in here like this."[24] After some additional words were exchanged, Baggett transferred Rahman's case to another judge.[25] It does not appear that Rahman filed a lawsuit against Judge Baggett or sought any form of compensation for these violations of his religious freedom.

C. Candomblé Devotees in Brazil

The same year that Rahman was jailed for wearing his religious necklaces, a young man in Brazil was prevented from even entering a judicial building because of his religious attire. Twenty-year-old college student Heráclíton dos Santos Barbosa arrived at the court seeking to authenticate documents for a property lease.[26] A doorman stopped him, ordering him to remove his *eketé* (a type of hat that protects the wearer from negative energies), in accordance with posted signs that warned that T-shirts, shorts, hats, and other informal attire were forbidden in the building. Barbosa offered to demonstrate that he was not concealing a weapon or other illicit materials but explained that his cap was a religious symbol that protected his head so he could not leave it off the entire time he was in the building. He requested an opportunity to go before the judge who he was scheduled to meet about the property lease so he could explain the issue and request an accommodation. Instead of permitting him to seek an accommodation from the judge, a police officer forcibly removed him from the building, dragging him out by the arms and neck. Barbosa filed a complaint of religious discrimination at the local police station and the Court of Justice. Unfortunately, available records don't indicate the results of these complaints.

Matheus Maciel, an attorney in Salvador, Bahia, had a similar experience when he attempted to enter the João Mendes Forum (a courthouse) wearing an eketé. A police officer approached Matheus and said that he could not enter the forum wearing a "hat." Matheus explained that the eketé was religious attire, but the officer still insisted that he remove it. However, when Matheus called the Brazilian Bar Association (OAB) to file a complaint, the officer said that he would allow Matheus to enter but told him that he would "have to pay attention in the next few times." Matheus went to his hearing in the João Mendes Forum, then he went to the Ruy Barbosa Forum to file a complaint with the OAB. An official at this forum likewise told him that he had to take off his hat so that he could go in. When he left, the official began to sing a gospel song, which Matheus interpreted as an act of religious intolerance.

PART II: FITNESS TO PRACTICE LAW

Devotees of African diaspora religions have not only been barred from courtrooms as observers and litigants, but judges have repeatedly questioned whether aspiring attorneys are fit for the practice of law based simply on their central religious practices. In the neighboring nations of Zimbabwe and South Africa, two Rastafarian males fulfilled nearly all the requirements for admission as an attorney before a government official abruptly denied them the opportunity to complete perfunctory components of the process because the official believed that they were unfit to practice law. Although these cases reach very different conclusions and involve distinct aspects of Rastafari religious practice, they demonstrate the varied ways in which adherents of African diaspora faiths are disparately barred from legal systems all over the globe. As both cases occurred in African countries, they also illustrate how being a devotee of an African-derived religion can become a mechanism for stereotyping and discriminating in a predominantly Black nation.

A. Dreadlocks in Zimbabwe

On November 17, 1992, Enock Munyaradzi Chikweche, a Rastafarian, submitted an application to the High Court of Zimbabwe to be registered as a legal practitioner.[27] Chikweche had all the necessary paperwork and qualifications; the law society saw no impediment to his application. However, Chikweche had to appear before the High Court to take an oath of loyalty and of office before he could be registered. On July 29, 1993, Chikweche went to the High

Court to take this oath, but the judge refused to administer it because he considered Chikweche's dreadlocked hairstyle to be "unkempt" and argued that Chikweche was not properly "dressed" to take the oath. Chikweche immediately responded that the judge's refusal to allow him to take the oath violated his freedoms of conscience and expression, as well as his right to protection from discrimination. He asked to have the issue referred to the Supreme Court.

The Supreme Court of Zimbabwe observed that the constitution permits the government to infringe on a person's religion for certain purposes, such as to ensure public safety, order, morality, and health.[28] However, the court believed that lawmakers didn't intend for a person to be judged on their physical appearance, because a person's "appearance bears no rational connection" to their fitness to practice law. They determined that the judge's assessment that Chikweche was not "fit and proper" to practice law was "factually incorrect" and exceeded the judge's authority for administering the oaths. They directed the High Court to permit Chikweche to take the oaths.

Although the Supreme Court decision was unanimous, one of the justices, McNally, wrote an addendum stating that he agreed with the ruling but had "reservations about the classification of Rastafarianism as a religion" and viewed it more as a "philosophical and cultural belief."[29] One would see similar concerns echoed in later cases regarding the right to wear dreadlocks in school (discussed in chapter 5) as well as in the right to wear hats in the courtroom, discussed previously.

B. The Sacramental Use of Marijuana in South Africa

A few years after Chikweche's case, a similar dispute arose in South Africa. Garreth Anver Prince wanted to be admitted as an attorney, a process that required him to first perform a period of community service.[30] Before fulfilling this requirement, he had to register a contract of community service with the local law society. The Law Society of the Cape of Good Hope refused to register Prince's contract because he had two criminal convictions for possession of cannabis and he admitted that he is a Rastafari adherent who had used (and planned to continue to use) cannabis as a religious sacrament. Cannabis was a Schedule 2 substance under the Drugs Act in South Africa, meaning that it was considered a dangerous or undesirable, dependence-producing drug, the possession of which was criminalized outside certain medicinal contexts. The Medicines Act contained analogous provisions limiting the possession of cannabis to pharmacists, medicinal cultivators, and the like.

The Law Society reasoned that Prince was not fit to be an attorney because he admitted that he had broken the law by using marijuana and intended to continue breaking the law. Prince appealed the Law Society's decision not to register his contract to the Cape of Good Hope High Court; he also contested the constitutionality of the Drugs Act and Medicines Act, which do not allow exemptions for religious use. The minister of justice and the attorney general of the Cape of Good Hope intervened in the case, arguing that the situation would quickly get out of control if a religious exemption were given for marijuana laws.

The High Court and Supreme Court of Appeal ruled against Prince, finding that providing Rastafarians with an exemption from the Drugs Act would put too much pressure on the already overburdened police and the courts to monitor these exemptions.[31] Prince appealed the case again to the Constitutional Court, who issued a 5–4 decision against Prince in January 2002.[32] The majority hinged their verdict on the decentralized nature of the Rastafari faith. The judges expressed concern that there are no strict rules about where cannabis would be used—the information Prince provided said that it was used at any place where two or more adherents come together. They argued that Rastafarians shouldn't be permitted to self-regulate how much to use and how to use it without harming themselves. Furthermore, because cannabis is used privately and in ceremonies, it would be nearly impossible for the government to determine whether it was being used for religious or recreational purposes. Therefore, they believed the only solution was to cut off all users.

Four justices wrote a dissenting opinion, in which they argued that the laws of South Africa stigmatize Rastafarians because they criminalize the use of cannabis for any purpose except as medicine, thereby prohibiting Rastafarians from practicing their religion and placing them in the same category as drug abusers. The judges lamented that the lack of religious exemption also prohibited Prince from entering his profession of choice. They opined that "there can be no doubt that the existence of the law which effectively punishes the practice of the Rastafari religion degrades and devalues the followers of the Rastafari religion in our society. It is a palpable invasion of their dignity. It strikes at the very core of their human dignity. It says that their religion is not worthy of protection. The impact of the limitation is profound indeed."[33]

One of the dissenting judges, Sachs, also wrote an individual opinion strongly in favor of Prince and other Rastafarians. Sachs pointed out that Rastafarians are "easily identifiable, subject to prejudice and politically powerless, indeed, precisely the kind of discrete and insular minority whose interests courts abroad and in this country have come jealously to protect."[34] Sachs contended that Christians would be able to successfully litigate any attempt to prohibit the use of communion wine, but Rastafarians do not have that same political power. Therefore, he argued, "One must conclude that in the area of claims freely to exercise religion, it is not familiarity, but unfamiliarity, that breeds contempt."[35]

After the Constitutional Court, the last option for appeal within South Africa, found against him, Prince submitted a complaint to the African Commission on Human and Peoples' Rights. He alleged that South Africa had violated its obligations under the African Charter on Human and Peoples' Rights by infringing on his rights to dignity, to freely manifest his religion, to occupational choice, and to a cultural life.[36] The commission also ruled against Prince, finding that South Africa's limitations on the use of cannabis were reasonable and served a general purpose of protecting the rights of others. The commission explained, "Minorities like the Rastafari may freely choose to exercise their culture, yet, that should not grant them unfettered power to violate the norms that keep the whole nation together."[37] Furthermore, since Prince and other Rastafarians were not being singled out for their inability to use cannabis, the commission opined that they had "no grounds to feel devalued, marginalized, and ignored."[38]

After being rejected by this regional human rights body, Prince decided to move to a global forum. In October 2005, he submitted a complaint to the Human Rights Committee, the treaty body that oversees implementation of the International Covenant on Civil and Political Rights.[39] Prince alleged that South Africa violated his religious freedom, right to nondiscrimination, and his rights as a minority. Two years later, the committee ruled against Prince. They believed that South Africa's failure to provide a religious exemption to cannabis laws was justified because of the "threat" that such an exemption might pose to the public. The committee also determined that because the ban on cannabis was a blanket proscription not targeted at Rastafarians, it did not violate minority rights.[40] Accordingly, it found no breach of the ICCPR. This decision exhausted Prince's last option for claiming his right to be admitted as an attorney and use marijuana as a religious sacrament.

PART III: EMPLOYMENT AS POLICE AND PUBLIC SAFETY OFFICERS

Echoing these concerns about the fitness of Rastafari adherents to practice law in Zimbabwe and South Africa, some police departments and private companies in the United States have questioned the capability of Muslims and

Rastafarians to enforce the law. Citing purported concerns about uniformity, they have asked officers to choose between their employment and their religious head coverings or hair. Similar to the education controversies discussed in chapter 5, although rooted in seemingly neutral concepts about professionalism and uniform appearance, these cases reveal racially and religiously discriminatory standards about how a police officer should look, including the idea that dreadlocks and headscarves are not "professional," and that the people who wear them are not members of the communities they serve.

In 1995, an African American woman named Kimberlie Webb began working as a police officer for the Philadelphia police department.[41] Webb grew up as a Christian; however, after meeting a Muslim neighbor, she converted to Islam and began covering her hair in public. She filed a request with her department to wear a covering over her hair and the back of her neck that fit underneath her uniform hat. Webb's request was perfunctorily denied, because the department directive related to uniforms and equipment provided no accommodations for religious symbols.[42] However, Webb and another Muslim officer aver that Christian officers were permitted to use numerous religious symbols while they were on duty, such as wearing crosses and angels on their lapels or placing palm fronds in their cars on Palm Sunday.[43]

In February 2003, shortly after her accommodations request was denied, Webb filed a claim of religious discrimination with the Equal Employment Opportunity Commission. Approximately six months later, she began wearing her headscarf at work. For three straight days, her supervisor told her to remove the covering, Webb refused, and her supervisor sent her home. The department brought disciplinary charges against Webb for insubordination and neglect of duty. Webb was found guilty and suspended for thirteen days.[44] She returned to work without her covering. Nevertheless, in January 2004, the department penalized her by placing Webb on the "graveyard shift"—an unpopular work schedule lasting from midnight to 8 a.m.[45]

Webb hired an employment lawyer and sued the city, alleging, among other things, that the City's refusal to accommodate her head covering constituted religious discrimination. The City argued that "the police force is a para-military organization in which personal preferences must be subordinated to the overall policing mission."[46] They explained that uniformity of appearance promotes "cooperation, fosters esprit de corps, emphasizes the hierarchical nature of the police force, and portrays a sense of authority to the public."[47] The City even alleged that if they did not display uniformity, they could be seen as favoring or disfavoring a particular group. The District Court accepted these as nondiscriminatory reasons for denying Webb's accommodation and found in favor of the City.

Webb appealed, and when the case went before the District Court, the City continued to emphasize the importance of "the essential values of impartiality, religious neutrality, uniformity, and the subordination of personal preference" in the "proper functioning of the police department."[48] Unfortunately, Webb's claims that Christians were permitted to use religious symbols did not specify who or when, or indicate whether the department was aware of these actions. Therefore, they were not considered in the court's decision.[49] The Third District found in favor of the City, determining that accommodating Webb would cause an "undue hardship."

During the same period, a Rastafarian police officer fought a similar struggle in Pennsylvania over the right to wear dreadlocks. In 1999, Niles Dodd started working as a police officer with the Southeastern Pennsylvania Transportation Authority (SEPTA).[50] He became a Rastafarian around three to four years later and began to grow dreadlocks. Shortly thereafter, Dodd's colleagues started harassing him about his hairstyle. On November 30, 2004, the deputy police chief told Dodd to remove his dreadlocks.[51] Three days later, Dodd sent a memo to the police chief, asking for his intervention to stop the harassment from his coworkers and the deputy chief. Instead, the chief also insulted Dodd's dreadlocks and Rastafarians.[52]

In 2005, Dodd was subject to formal discipline for violating SEPTA's grooming code, which prohibits officers from wearing hair that extends beyond or "interferes with" their uniform hat. In February of that year, Dodd's supervisor, Captain Rowell, claimed that he had observed Dodd wearing a ponytail (which is expressly prohibited), so he suspended Dodd for five days and ordered him to cut his hair. An arbitrator reviewed the disciplinary action and upheld the violation but reduced the suspension to one day.

In December 2005, Captain Rowell claimed that he once again saw Dodd wearing a ponytail, and he fired him for neglect of duty, conduct unbecoming an officer, and failing to obey a direct order. Dodd disputes that he was wearing a ponytail on either occasion. Dodd sued the department for religious discrimination and creating a hostile work environment. He asked for lost wages and benefits, back pay, and compensatory damage for emotional pain and suffering.[53] In September 2008, the parties settled the case under undisclosed terms.[54]

These US cases questioning whether Rastafarians with dreadlocks are suitable law enforcement officers are not limited to state cases; private corporations have fired or refused to hire their security or public safety officers over disputes about their hair. For example, in 2004, Wackenhut Corporation refused to hire a Rastafarian security guard because he had dreadlocks.[55] A few years later, in 2009, Grand Central Partnership settled a lawsuit with four Rastafarian public safety officers who claimed that the company had refused to grant them religious accommodations to the grooming policy to allow them to wear dreadlocks and short beards.[56]

PART IV: CORRECTIONS OFFICERS

Over the past few years, South African and US courts have heard several cases related to whether Rastafarians should be permitted to wear dreadlocks and Muslims should be permitted to wear headscarves while working in prisons. In some instances, these cases center on the same questions as those of police officers—will religious hairstyles or attire impact the corrections officer's ability to perform their duties by destroying uniformity of appearance? In others, corrections officials went much further, suggesting that dreadlocks and headscarves posed a safety violation to prisons and could lead the officers to engage in illicit behavior. These cases, once again, resurrect the racialized notion that African diaspora religions pose a threat to public health and morality.

A. *South Africa*

For many years, Pollsmoor Prison in the Western Cape of South Africa has had a Corporate Identity Dress Code, which contains a clause about hairstyles.[57] The section on female officials says that hair must be neat, clean, combed, and have no unnatural colors or styles. The section on male officials says that hair must not be longer than the shirt collar and "may not be dyed in colours other than natural hair colours or cut in any punk style, including a 'Dreadlocks' hairstyle."[58] On January 19, 2007, the area commissioner of Pollsmoor Prison sent a written instruction to nine male correctional officers with dreadlocks that they had to comply with the hairstyle policies by January 25, 2007, or give reason why they could not comply. Four correctional officers cut their hair. Five men refused for religious and "cultural" reasons. These five men either knew of the dress code prior to receipt of this noncompliance letter but thought it was not being enforced or expressed confusion about whether there was a written dress code in place, and if so, when it had been finalized.

Two of the men, T. R. Ngqula and L. T. Kamlana, wore dreadlocks because they were undergoing training as traditional healers. Both had experienced a series of dreams in the early 2000s that they interpreted as a calling to become healers. At trial, a traditional healer, Mr. Toyo Khandekana, testified as an expert witness on behalf of Ngqula and Kamlana. Khandekana explained that dreadlocks were called "ivitane" in isiXhosa and that they are "a symbol in the realm of Xhosa spiritual healing that their wearer has heeded the call of his ancestors to become a traditional healer."[59] Unlike Rastafarians, who are barred from ever shaving their dreadlocks, the "ivitane" are only worn for a period of time and then "shaved off at a cleansing ceremony, a sacred, elaborate affair which includes the use of dagga, conducted at [the] completion of the process to signify the initiate's transition into a traditional healer."[60] Ngqula began growing dreadlocks in 2001, and his mentor required him to wear the dreadlocks until December 2007, at which time he shaved them off. Kamlana began working with the Department of Correctional Services in March 2000 and began growing dreadlocks the following year. At the time of the litigation, he continued to wear dreadlocks because he had not yet received a message from the ancestors that it was time to cut them. Neither men had problems with their supervisors during the five or six years they had been wearing dreadlocks prior to the 2007 warning letter.

The other three correctional officers who refused to cut their dreadlocks, E. J. Lebatlang, C. Jacobs, and M. W. Khubheka, were Rastafarians. All three had been working as correctional officers in South Africa since the 1990s and had begun wearing dreadlocks at least two years before the commissioner issued his warning. None of the men were subject to any discipline for their hair prior to 2007, although Jacobs reported that one supervisor had told him that his hair looked funny and another asked him why his hair was long and told him to keep it neat. Khubheka had begun wearing dreadlocks in 1994 and never received any negative feedback in the thirteen years that he had worked for the Department of Corrections while wearing dreadlocks.

On February 2, 2007, all five men were charged with violating the disciplinary code and dress code as well as failing to follow a routine order. They were suspended until their disciplinary hearing, which was held more than four months later, in June 2007. At the hearing, they were found guilty of failing to comply with the dress code and fired from their posts as correctional officers at Pollsmoor Prison. The men filed suit against the prison and the Department of Correctional Services. They demanded reinstatement to their jobs and an order declaring that the dress code policy regarding dreadlocks is unconstitutional. The men also claimed unlawful discrimination, arguing that the dress code was disparately applied between men and women, and focused on people with dreadlocks.

The department argued that the dress code applied equally to all people so there could not be any valid claim of discrimination. They depicted the enforcement of the dress code as part of the new policies under the new leadership. Mandla Jephtha Mkhabela became deputy commissioner of Pollsmoor in January 2007, shortly before sending out the letters demanding that the men cut their dreadlocks. He had previously worked in other positions in the department for twenty-two years. When he began at Pollsmoor, he noted the noncompliance with the dress code and feared a domino effect that would lead to "lawlessness."[61] There had been other problems at the institution, such as absenteeism, assaults, and officers smuggling dagga into the prison. He asserted that fixing the dress code violations was the first step in correcting the problems. The Department of Correctional Services claimed that Mkhabela's initiatives had been effective—assaults, absenteeism, and escapes had declined since he arrived.

The department also alleged that it was well known that Rastafarians use marijuana, so if a correctional officer wore a hairstyle that obviously signified that he was a Rastafarian, convicts might use that as a "soft spot" to "be able to manipulate him or her."[62] The court summarizes this argument as follows: "If dreadlocks are allowed, Rastafarian officials will stand out and undesirable associations between such officials and Rastafarian offenders are likely. This is likely to result in offenders finding ways to influence Rastafarian officials to bring dagga—central to the Rastafarian religion—into correctional centres. These officials will be manipulated. Discipline will also be adversely affected because officials will have to look the other way. This, in turn, will adversely affect the rehabilitation of offenders."[63] The department also expressed concern that an inmate could grab the dreadlocks and disarm a correctional officer.

The Labour Court found in favor of the Department of Correctional Services on the religious discrimination claim and in favor of the Rastafarians on the gender discrimination claim. The court found no intention to discriminate against the officers' religious beliefs because the area commissioner had just arrived at the department and would not have known why the five men were wearing dreadlocks. The men had never responded to his letter nor provided any religious or cultural explanations directly to him; therefore, the court believed that the commissioner had no knowledge of their religious beliefs. With regard to the claim for gender discrimination, the court believed that the department had clearly made a gender distinction in their dress code policies because female employees were not required to cut their dreadlocks but the men were. The department had not provided a nondiscriminatory reason for this distinction.

The Labour Court ordered the department to reinstate the officers (if the men wanted to be reinstated), effective on the date of their dismissal. They also ordered back pay with a deduction from any earnings from other employment. For those men who did not wish to be reinstated, the court ordered the department to pay them twenty months' salary from the date of their dismissal. The court gave the men thirty days to report for duty and gave the department one week to issue the back pay.

The department appealed the decision twice, first to the Labour Court of Appeal and then to the Supreme Court. Both upheld the lower court's decision that the termination was unlawful based on gender discrimination. They also found discrimination based on religion and culture. The Supreme Court's decision is worth mentioning because of the court's strong rhetoric about religious discrimination. The judges opined, "Without question, a policy that effectively punishes the practice of a religion and culture degrades and devalues the followers of that religion and culture in society; it is a palpable invasion of their dignity which says their religion or culture is not worthy of protection and the impact of the limitation is profound. That impact here was devastating because the respondents' refusal to yield to an instruction at odds with their sincerely held beliefs cost them their employment."[64] The court also criticized the department for unfairly changing its argument halfway through the case, suddenly asserting that there was a connection between the dress code and dagga. The Supreme Court dismissed the department's appeal and ordered the department to pay costs, including attorney's fees, for both parties.

B. The United States

Similar to South Africa, correctional institutions in the United States have fired Rastafarian corrections officers for having dreadlocks.[65] Most of these cases center on policies about hair length that resemble those in schools that prohibit males from having hair that extends beyond the collar of their shirt. The Rastafarian officers typically sue for racial, religious, and/or gender discrimination. These cases have frequently settled under undisclosed terms.[66]

While most of these disputes over dreadlocks centered on issues of uniformity of attire and gendered standards for hair length, a recent case regarding a Muslim female correctional officer more closely resembles the rhetoric about safety, security, and illicit behavior that purportedly motivated the Pollsmoor

Prison case in South Africa. In January 2019, twenty-five-year-old Jalanda Calhoun converted to Islam and began wearing a hijab.[67] She asked Rogers State Prison in Reidsville, Georgia, where she worked as a correctional officer, for ten-minute prayer breaks and the authorization to wear a hijab with her uniform. Less than a month later, the prison warden issued a memo stating that, pursuant to the prison's personal appearance standards for correctional officers, she could wear a cap issued by the Department of Corrections that would cover her hair. The warden rejected her request to wear a hijab, averring that the garment posed a security threat to Calhoun because she could not be recognized as prison personnel if she deviated from the standard uniform. He also claimed that it posed a security threat to the prison because "an alternative head covering could be used by an offender in his efforts to conceal his identity in conjunction with an attempt to escape," and contraband could more easily be hidden beneath her hijab because it covered her ears.[68] They also denied her request for prayer breaks.[69] In April 2019, the Council on American-Islamic Relations filed a discrimination complaint on Calhoun's behalf with the Georgia Commission on Equal Opportunity. This case was still pending at the time of publication.

PART V: PRISON ABUSES

In addition to the aforementioned cases about limitations on devotees' rights in the legal system prior to conviction of a crime, there are dozens of cases worldwide relating to the right to wear religious attire while incarcerated. While this vast and complex body of cases is beyond the scope of this book, there are some recent cases regarding short-term periods in custody that warrant mention here. In situations where adherents have merely been detained for a few hours on minor charges or mere suspicion of criminal activity, state officials have committed gross violations of religious freedom against these individuals. Like the cases discussed in chapter 1, these represent another form of unchecked violence against devotees that is likely motivated by a combination of racial and religious bias.

A. South Africa

In January 2012, police officers in the Western Cape conducted a 5 a.m. raid on the house where four Rastafarian men—Jonathan Daniels, Jonathan Constable, Evert Faro, and Adam Faro—were staying.[70] The police burst into the home, without a search warrant, and demanded to know where the drugs were located. They had multiple weapons and violently beat the Rastafarians—punching, kicking, and stomping on them. Two of the men also reported that the police cut off their hair.

Adam Faro claimed that the officers threw him to the ground, then kicked and trampled him; one even stood on his neck. The officers grabbed his head and pulled it up by his dreadlocks, then cut off some of his hair, which he had been growing for around fifteen years. Jonathan Daniels told an even more detailed story. He claimed the police asked him where to find the dagga (cannabis). When the police found no illegal substances, four officers held him down and started cutting his hair. After the scissors broke, two of the officers grabbed the blades of the scissors and used these to continue cutting his hair. Daniels recounted that he began to cry and his head burned as they attacked him. When they were done, the officers told him to get up and punched him in the face.

All four men sued the police for their misconduct during the raid. The High Court of Pretoria ordered the minister of police to pay the men damages of R90,000 each and awarded Adam Faro an additional R2,000 for loss of earnings because he could not work for two weeks due to pain.

B. The United States

In May 2015, an African American Muslim woman, Kirsty Powell, and her husband, were pulled over by Los Angeles police officers because they were driving a lowrider vehicle.[71] The officers asked for Powell's identification and checked her name in their database. They discovered that she had outstanding warrants—one for a petty theft charge against Powell and two for crimes of vehicle theft and resisting arrest that Powell's sister had committed using her name. The male officers arrested Powell, despite her husband's protests that she should not be touched by the male officers and requests that a female officer be called to complete the arrest. Once in custody and booked, the officers forcibly removed Powell's hijab. Powell was held for approximately twenty-four hours in a jail cell without her hijab before she was released and it was returned to her in a property bag.

In April 2016, Powell sued the City of Long Beach and the police department, asserting that they had violated her religious rights under the First Amendment of the US Constitution and the Religious Land Use and Institutionalized Persons Act (RLUIPA). The City settled the lawsuit for $85,000 and changed its policies to expressly require a female officer to be the one to remove an inmate's hijab and limit the circumstances of removal to when it is required for safety and when there are no male officers or inmates present.

PART VI: CONCLUSION

These cases about courts, law enforcement, and prisons describe some very troubling patterns in access and representation in justice systems around the world. Employers and courts are increasingly demanding that Rastafarians and Muslims choose between the tenets of their faith and careers in law or law enforcement. These cases often commence after the adherent has been employed for years or even decades without incident, before a supervisor decides that their hair or head covering is a problem. When they ask for accommodations, their request is often met with official and unofficial pressures to comply with the grooming policy, as well as changes in scheduling and employment location when adherents insist on following their faith. Furthermore, such controversies are often accompanied by racially discriminatory remarks or suggestions that the person might be involved in illicit behavior.

Adherents of these same faiths have suffered terrible abuses at the hands of law enforcement. Their basic access to observe or litigate claims has been limited. Devotees of African diaspora faiths have been banned from courtrooms because of their religious attire and jailed for standing up for their beliefs. Their physical bodies have also been violated as religious coverings or hairstyles have been forcibly torn or cut from their heads, often during these unjustified detentions.

Read together, it seems clear that these cases where litigants and private citizens have been mentally and physically abused in courtrooms, prisons, and even their own homes are closely linked to the cases where lawyers, police officers, and correctional officers have been deemed unfit to join or continue in their professions. Most of these incidents arise from ignorance about African diaspora faiths and their religious tenets (i.e., lack of understanding of the circumstances in which they can remove their religious attire) or strong bias against them. Greater representation of adherents in these professions might diminish the number of rights violations that followers of Islam, Rastafari, and other African diaspora faiths must endure as they try to enjoy basic access to justice systems in the United States, South Africa, and other countries worldwide. However, devotees are prevented from entering these professions due to the same discriminatory beliefs and policies that lead to abuses against them.

SECTION III

❖❖❖

The Boundaries of Religion
Obeah and Voodoo

This final section introduces two religions: Obeah and Voodoo. A key aspect of these faiths is that they are difficult to define and, since the late nineteenth century, have become broad terms that encompass much more than the actual religious practices of the African diaspora. Due to myths and misconceptions of these religions, they face several interrelated challenges—they are often not classified as religions, they sometimes remain legally proscribed in the twenty-first century, and devotees are accused of crimes that have nothing to do with actual religious practices of the communities to which they are attributed.

PART I: OBEAH

"Obeah" is a vague, broad term encompassing a variety of primarily African-derived, spiritual practices in the former British Caribbean.[1] Although specific ritual practices might vary greatly from country to country, this belief system is generally characterized by individualized relationships between Obeah practitioners and their clients. Caribbean persons consult and compensate Obeah practitioners for performing a wide range of services related to bodily health (healing or inducing physical ailments), financial well-being (finding employment, increasing the success of one's business, or getting money that was lost or is owed), family relationships (finding or keeping a lover), and the legal system (evading arrest or winning a court case) as well as conjuring and expelling spirits.[2]

Rituals are typically conducted through the manipulation of supernatural and natural forces, rather than by appealing to a god or pantheon of deities.[3] Obeah practitioners use herbal concoctions, develop prayers or incantations, create charms or other potent substances, perform rituals including animal sacrifice, and communicate with spirits of departed persons.[4] Practitioners can, and historically did, perform malevolent, individualistic rites as well as benevolent, community-oriented rituals.

Etymological studies of the term "Obeah" indicate that it likely originated from Akan or Ibibio societies in West Africa and originally meant either "wizard,"[5] "doctor," or "herbalist."[6] Kenneth Bilby and Jerome Handler's in-depth study on the early use of "Obeah" argues that the term had a positive, or at least neutral, connotation in Africa and may have signified something akin to "a man of knowledge and wisdom."[7] However, when British colonists in the Caribbean began utilizing this word in the early eighteenth century, they gave it a new, primarily negative, meaning.[8]

As discussed further in chapter 8, the British proscribed Obeah in 1760, after so-called Obeah practitioners aided in a major slave uprising known as Tacky's Rebellion.[9] In this law, they described Obeah as devil worship and suggested that the central purpose of Obeah was to try to harm others.[10] Later, after emancipation, the colonists placed a greater emphasis on the idea that Obeah rituals were fraud, designed for the practitioner to make money off the client for rituals that they knew could not work.[11] Obeah remains proscribed in most countries in the former British Caribbean today, and now, more than 250 years after its initial proscription, colonial perceptions of this faith as fraudulent practices based on witchcraft and devil worship dominate the public forum.[12]

PART II: VOODOO

Nathaniel Murrell explains that at the mere mention of "Voodoo," "the American mind conjures up any number of sensational images: deadly 'black' or evil magic, the sticking of poisonous pins in dolls, satanic rituals, gross sacrifices of humans, zombies, hex-casting witchcraft, demonic spells, infamous human-preying zombies, blood-sucking vampires, and African cannibalism."[13] The term "Voodoo" is derived from "Vaudoux," the word that the French used to describe African spiritual practices in their colonies. Scholars believe that the French based this term "Vaudoux" on a word in the Fon-Dahomey language in West Africa that meant "serving the spirits, sacred objects, a set of divinities, and 'an invisible force, terrible and mysterious.'"[14] However, after the United States took possession of New Orleans in the nineteenth century, the orthography changed from Vaudoux to Voodoo and the word took on a different, more derogatory and sinister meaning.

During the Civil War in the United States, the Union forces seized New Orleans and liberated the slaves there. Shortly thereafter, Confederate supporters began to speak about the blossoming "superstitions" or "Voodoo" practices among newly emancipated Black populations to underscore that African Americans were supposedly unprepared for self-governance.[15] This rhetoric became common across the US South after the North won the war, abolished slavery, and passed constitutional amendments that would allow Blacks to vote, hold government office, and enjoy other citizenship rights that had been denied them before the war.[16]

Later, at the end of the nineteenth century, "Voodoo" took on an even more negative meaning, as travelers and foreign officials increasingly began to claim that religious practices in Haiti had become extremely barbaric. In the 1880s, Spenser St. John, former British consul general in Haiti, wrote a best-selling account of the supposed atrocities occurring in Haiti since its independence from France. This book contained a fifty-page chapter titled "Vaudoux-Worship and Cannibalism," as well as a separate chapter on cannibalism.[17] As these titles suggest, St. John averred that cannibalism and other atrocities were central to "Voodoo" worship in Haiti, and that all classes of Haitians were not only aware of these practices but were also complicit in them. As is discussed in greater detail in chapter 9, over the next fifty years, as the last countries in the Americas abolished slavery and governments of former slaveholding societies debated whether Blacks were capable of political participation and self-governance, tall tales of primitive African "Voodoo" practices in Haiti abounded. Particularly when the United States Navy invaded and occupied Haiti from 1915 to 1934, travelers and marines penned graphic fables about the bloody rituals of cannibalism and human sacrifice that people of African descent would undertake when the white man wasn't looking.

By the mid-twentieth century, "Voodoo" and its accompanying stereotypes—zombies, pin-laden dolls, and black magic—had become a staple feature in popular horror films. This trend continues today. Additionally, virtually every crime show that has aired for more than a few seasons has included an episode about "Voodoo," typically where a murder investigation involves a "Voodoo–witch doctor" hybrid who wears bones around his neck and performs black magic in a dark, candlelit room full of skulls and pentagrams. Even Disney's first film featuring a Black princess, *The Princess and the Frog*, centered on these snake-loving, devil-worshipping, black magic stereotypes of "Voodoo."

Buried beneath all these stereotypes, what is "Voodoo"? The answer is somewhat elusive and changes depending on the time period in question. Ina Fandrich argues that the foundations of Louisiana Voodoo were rooted in Africans from Senegambia, who constituted approximately 80 percent of the enslaved population of Louisiana in the eighteenth century, and from the Kongolese, who constituted most of the other 20 percent of the population.[18] In the early nineteenth century, refugees from the Haitian Revolution arrived in Louisiana and brought with them enslaved persons who were from Dahomey and Yoruba communities.[19] These individuals added a new layer of beliefs and practices to the foundations that the Senegambians and Kongolese had established.

New Orleans Voodoo resembles Obeah in the sense that, unlike Santeria/Lucumi or Haitian Vodou, it is not primarily based on the collective worship of deities; in fact, there are very few deities in the religion at all.[20] However, there are a few recognizable beings who should be mentioned. First, Voodoo adherents believe(d) in the existence of God, who they called Li Grand Zombi, likely derived from the Kongo Bantu word for God, *nzambi*.[21] Certain Catholic saints were also important in New Orleans Voodoo, including St. Anthony, St. Michael, St. Paul, and St. Peter, who was also known as "Legba" or "Limba."[22] Finally, there are many records from the nineteenth century documenting that one of the main annual Voodoo celebrations centered on June 23, in honor of St. John's Eve (celebrating St. John the Baptist) and the summer solstice.[23] During this time, devotees engaged in ritual baths, made bonfires, as well as sang and drummed.[24]

One of the distinguishing features of the foundations of New Orleans Voodoo is that it centered on the leadership of powerful priestesses known as Voodoo "queens."[25] The most famous of these was Marie Laveau, a free-born mulatto woman who was the leader of the New Orleans Voodoo community for forty years in the mid-nineteenth century.[26] These priestesses became wealthy and influential by building a large clientele base who came to them for services such as charms, root work, and the manipulation of spiritual forces.[27] Priestesses would charge a fee to clients to create spiritual artifacts such as candles or to intercede on the clients' behalf with the spirit world.[28]

After Laveau's death, scholars argue that no other priestess was capable of holding the community together, and the religion became divided into a variety of sects led by different priests and priestesses. As a result of these divisions, organized public ceremonies became less common.[29] Dances and the "worship of African deities" also became less frequent. In its place, the practice of "hoodoo" became more prevalent. Historian Jessie Gaston argues that, in the twentieth century, "hoodoo" referred to the process by which "an individual was made to do something against his or her will," such as making someone fall in love or causing someone's death.[30] Male "hoodoo" practitioners or conjurers began to dominate the spiritual community in New Orleans. They sold "enormous quantities of charms, amulets, and magic powders" to people of all races.[31]

Unfortunately, most, if not all, studies on New Orleans "Voodoo" center on the nineteenth and early twentieth centuries. I am unaware of any published research focusing on present-day beliefs and practices. However, in the many trips that I have made to New Orleans in recent years, I have seen firsthand that African diaspora religious communities persist and continue to pass down their spiritual knowledge to new generations. Hidden behind a deep layer of commercialized tourist traps and Hollywood legends, there are genuine belief systems there that warrant the same legal protections as other faiths.

CHAPTER 7

Continued Proscription
The Rights of Western Versus African "Witches"

Obeah is the only African diaspora belief system that remains widely proscribed in the twenty-first century. At least fourteen countries in the former British Caribbean ban the practice of Obeah and/or the possession of Obeah instruments as a criminal offense.[1] These laws date back to the late nineteenth and early twentieth centuries, when virtually every colony in the British Empire prohibited "pretending" to use supernatural powers as a type of fraud, vagrancy, or a violation of public "morality" and order. These statutes were modeled on England's own legislation barring vagrancy and "pretending" to practice witchcraft.

In the mid-twentieth century, England repealed its witchcraft statute and the section of its vagrancy laws dealing with "occult" practices, citing concerns about infringing on religious freedom. In the twenty-first century, Canada and South Africa began repealing their witchcraft statutes based on complaints from Wiccans and related groups. However, most former British colonies in the Caribbean, where African diaspora and other minority rituals were targeted by these laws, are showing no signs of abolishing their provisions banning "witchcraft," "Obeah," and other types of "supernatural powers." This has created a disparity in the recognition of Spiritualists, Wiccans, and other white or European-derived "witches" and the proscription of similar African-based faiths.

PART I: HISTORY OF OBEAH AND WITCHCRAFT PROSCRIPTIONS

In order to understand the laws discussed in this chapter, it is necessary to start with the history of witchcraft and vagrancy legislation in England.[2] In the fourteenth and fifteenth centuries, the Great Plague caused population decline in England, leading to the implementation of compulsory labor laws.[3] These laws, known as vagrancy statutes, established specific parameters of lawful means of earning a living. Since at least 1597, they prohibited a person from claiming "to have knowledge in physiognomie [sic], palmistry, or other like crafty science, or pretending that they can tell destinies, fortunes, or such other like fantastical imagination."[4]

England also passed its first witchcraft legislation in the sixteenth century. In 1541, English law criminalized invoking or conjuring spirits, practicing witchcraft, or using enchantments or sorceries.[5] It likewise specifically banned using "non-natural means" to discover hidden treasure and stolen goods, or to provoke unlawful love. Persons contravening these laws were guilty of a felony, punishable by the death penalty. These laws were revised in 1563 and 1604 but retained the same premise of imposing harsh, often lethal, penalties for the exercise of supernatural power. Between the late sixteenth century and the late seventeenth century, the English executed hundreds of people for violating witchcraft statutes.[6]

The purpose of witchcraft legislation was twofold. For the majority of the English population at this time, witches were a significant threat to society who, through the use of malefic magic, could destroy property, as well as cause injury, sickness, and death to people or animals.[7] For church officials and theologians, every supernatural power had been obtained through a pact with the devil and his agents or "familiars."[8] They believed this was true of individuals who deployed their power to cause destruction and death, as well as diviners and healers known as "cunning folk," who used their powers for more benign or even beneficial purposes.[9]

Over time, judges grew skeptical about the evidence that was typically used in witchcraft cases, including the physical tests such as "swimming" and "scratching" or even the suspects' own confessions, which judges feared had been coerced.[10] Theologians also began to change their perceptions of witchcraft, arguing that God was the only one with the power to make someone fly, harm without touching a person, or cause one's crops to fail.[11] These concerns led to the passage of a new statute, the Witchcraft Act of 1735,[12] which repealed existing laws and abolished all "prosecution[s], suit[s], or proceeding[s]" for the actual practice of "witchcraft, sorcery, inchantment [sic], or conjuration."[13] Instead, this law prohibited any person from "pretend[ing] to exercise or use any kind of witchcraft, sorcery, inchantment [sic], or conjuration, or undertake to tell fortunes, or pretend from his or her skill or knowledge in any occult or crafty science to discover where or in what manner any goods or chattels, supposed to have been stolen or lost, may be found."[14] Any person who contravened this law could be sentenced to one year of imprisonment without bail, including one hour on the pillory every quarter. This law was rarely enforced in the decades after its passage;[15] however, in the late nineteenth and early twentieth centuries, it would form the basis for British laws in most of its colonies.

In the British Caribbean, English witchcraft beliefs helped formulate the laws that colonists passed following concerns that African ritual specialists assisted in slave rebellions. For instance, in 1760, Jamaican colonists accused African priests, who they referred to as "Obeah practitioners," of providing protective charms and administering sacred oaths to participants in a large uprising known as Tacky's Rebellion.[16] Later that year, legislators in Jamaica passed a law titled "An Act to Remedy the Evils Arising from Irregular Assemblies of Slaves, and to Prevent Their Possessing Arms and Ammunitions and Going from Place to Place Without Tickets, and for Preventing the Practice of Obeah, etc."[17] The preamble of this law lamented that persons going by the name "Obeah Men and Women" have "deluded" superstitious people by "pretending to have communication with the devil and other evil spirits."[18] The main section therefore prohibited "any negro or other slave" from "pretend[ing] to possess any supernatural power."[19] In the late eighteenth and early nineteenth centuries, similar laws were passed in some of Britain's other Caribbean colonies.[20] These laws somewhat resembled Britain's witchcraft laws and views, in the sense that they characterized supernatural powers as "pretended" and alleged that Obeah practitioners endeavored to communicate with "the devil and other evil spirits."[21]

As other scholars have discussed, legislators made several key corresponding changes to British and Caribbean laws regulating spiritual practices in the 1820s and 1830s that brought the two even closer together.[22] First, in 1824, British legislators revised the Vagrancy Act, maintaining the provisions prohibiting fortune-telling, palmistry and other "subtle crafts" but adding a section indicating that individuals who professed to use supernatural powers "deceive[d] or impose[d] on his majesty's subjects."[23] Analogous vagrancy laws were passed in the Caribbean in the 1840s (following the abolition of slavery), which added Obeah to the list of prohibited "subtle crafts."[24]

Legislators also modified Obeah statutes to more closely align with England's Witchcraft Act of 1735.[25] The Obeah Act of 1855 in Barbados copied language directly from the English law.[26] It prohibited the practice or pretended practice of witchcraft or Obeah, as well as using these practices to tell fortunes or discover stolen goods. Similarly, Jamaica's Obeah Act of 1857 prohibited any person from "pretend[ing] to the possession of supernatural power" for "false, crafty or unlawful purposes" or "falsely, cunningly, or unlawfully mak[ing] use of omens, spells, charms, incantations, or other preternatural devices."[27]

Although some colonies such as Jamaica and Guiana passed new Obeah laws in the middle of the nineteenth century, the bulk of them implemented their first or their modified statutes between the 1880s and the 1920s. These are the laws that remain in effect in fourteen Caribbean countries today, mostly or completely unchanged after approximately one hundred years. These laws typically contain a few basic components. They broadly prohibit "pretend[ing] to possess any supernatural power or knowledge" for "any fraudulent or unlawful purpose," "for the purpose of frightening any person," "for gain," to "restore any person to health," to "inflict any disease, loss, damage or personal injury upon any person," or to "cause or divert affection."[28] Some countries also passed statutes that prohibit Obeah and witchcraft as a type of fraud, using language from England's Witchcraft Act of 1735, prohibiting "pretending" to tell fortunes or using any kind of "witchcraft, sorcery, enchantment or conjuration" and/or prohibiting a person from professing to use Obeah to "discover lost or stolen things."[29] However, many of the laws added provisions not seen in English statutes, including consulting an Obeah practitioner, possessing any "instruments of Obeah," and/or having, producing, or distributing any "printed matter calculated to promote the superstition of Obeah."[30]

During this same period, the 1880s to the 1920s, legislators enacted analogous laws in some of Britain's African colonies. For instance, Bechuanaland's Witchcraft Proclamation of 1927 states: "Any person who for purposes of gain, pretends to exercise or use any kind of supernatural power, witchcraft, sorcery, enchantment or conjuration, or undertakes to tell fortunes, or pretends from his skill or knowledge in any occult science to discover where or in what manner anything supposed to have been stolen or lost may be found" can be sentenced to a fine of up to £100 or imprisonment for up to five years.[31] Even Basutoland's Native Medicine Men and Herbalists Proclamation of 1948, although passed decades after the majority of these laws and more than two hundred years after England's Witchcraft Act, contains similar language. Section 10 prohibits a person from practicing as a diviner or professing a knowledge of spells, charms, or witchcraft.[32] Punishment for violating the proclamation was up to one year of imprisonment and/or a fine of up to £50. Several African countries, such as Zambia, Tanzania, Botswana, Uganda, the Seychelles, and Malawi, maintain criminal laws barring any person from using or "pretending" to use supernatural powers.[33]

Although I have discussed some notable differences in the enforcement of these laws in other publications,[34] these regions also shared some important similarities. First and foremost, the vast majority of persons charged with contravening these laws between the mid-nineteenth and mid-twentieth centuries were not persons who sought to harm others. Instead, they were diviners (palmists, tea leaf readers, bone-throwers, fortune-tellers, etc.), spirit conjurers, persons who removed curses, and individuals who performed rituals to improve one's luck, secure love, or increase chances of employment.[35] Second, although the degree to which fraud had to be proven varied from region to region, concerns about charlatanism and debates about proof of deception always played a role in these cases. Magistrates and judges questioned whether these were offenses against public order because in "these days of advanced knowledge," people could/should no longer believe in astrology, fortune-telling, witchcraft, or conjuring spirits.[36] This was analogous to other parts of the world where similar laws about public health and morality regulated spiritual practices that were regarded as antiquated, or superstitious. As laws directly prohibiting certain types of supernatural rituals were nearly universal in the Anglophone world in the early twentieth century, the primary problem lies not in the fact that African diaspora religions were historically suppressed but rather in the continued existence of these laws in the twenty-first century.

PART II: REPEALING LEGISLATION

Over the past few years, scholars have increasingly examined the history of the proscription and prosecution of Obeah to understand why this Afro-diasporic belief system continues to be outlawed. One of the key interventions in this area came in 2008, when Diana Paton published an article, "Obeah Acts: Producing and Policing the Boundaries of Religion the Caribbean," that underscored how the language that British colonists used in the prohibition of Obeah during the colonial period created a dichotomy between Western "legitimate" religions and African "fraud" or "superstitions." In their book examining the history of the proscription of Obeah, Kenneth Bilby and Jerome Handler added that colonists' mischaracterization of Afro-Caribbean faiths also played an important role in their ability to distinguish these belief systems from legally protected religions. Bilby and Handler contend that the term "Obeah" never described a single belief system but rather was used as a catch-all term for spiritual forces that could be deployed for beneficial or harmful purposes, depending on the client's request. Colonial authorities established hierarchies between European and African religions, Handler and Bilby maintain, by focusing on the negative usages of the latter—equating Obeah with sorcery, witchcraft, and other "evil" practices.

Despite these and several other rich studies examining how the colonial period laid the foundations for twenty-first-century legal and popular understandings of Obeah to exclude it from the category of religion, researchers have largely ignored important shifts in the mid-to-late twentieth century that likewise contributed to this distinction. In the mid-twentieth century, a growing number of countries in the Global North began to recognize that witchcraft and vagrancy laws infringed on the religious freedom of white and/or Western astrologers, spirit conjurers, and soothsayers. Meanwhile, African and Caribbean nations resisted the move toward decriminalization of "witchcraft" and Obeah, unless white and/or Western "witches" and astrologers or adherents of theistic African diaspora religions contested the validity of this legislation. These conversations about who is protected by the repeal of witchcraft, Obeah, and vagrancy laws help elucidate the entrenched racial bias in these proscriptions.

A. England's Witchcraft Act of 1735 and Vagrancy Act of 1824

To truly understand the hypocrisy underlying the continued existence of Obeah and witchcraft legislation in the twenty-first century, one must begin with the rhetoric and rationale for the repeal of these laws in England. More than sixty years ago, English legislators determined that their witchcraft and vagrancy laws infringed on religious freedom and removed these laws from their statute books. The removal process began in the 1940s, when a spiritualist medium named Victoria Helen Duncan was convicted of violating the rarely enforced, antiquated Witchcraft Act of 1735.[37] The application of this two-hundred-year-old statute generated widespread discussion and criticism.[38] In November 1950, a member of the House of Commons introduced the Fraudulent Mediums Bill, which would repeal both the Witchcraft Act of 1735 and the sections of the Vagrancy Act of 1824 that pertained to spiritual practices, replacing them with provisions that would limit punishment to persons who committed intentional fraud. The legislators made several types of comments during the debates about this bill that are notable in comparison to later discussions about the repeal of Obeah and witchcraft statutes in Africa and the Caribbean.

First and foremost, they made it clear that this bill was introduced by Spiritualists and was primarily designed to ensure the religious freedom of Spiritualists. Numerous members of the House of Commons and the House of Lords explicitly spoke in favor of Spiritualists, explaining that while they may or may not believe in their mediumship or clairvoyance, Spiritualists had the right to practice their religion.[39] Second, they reiterated that no matter what faith a person might subscribe to, they had the right to enjoy religious freedom. The members of Parliament described the repeal of these laws as progressive and evidence of England's commitment to religious freedom, tolerance, and public decency. They expressed their desire that England should be a beacon of hope for other nations.[40] Third, they described the Witchcraft and Vagrancy Acts as outdated statutes that should have been abolished long ago and had no place in modern society.[41] The members agreed that despite the relatively rare enforcement of these laws in recent years, the mere presence of such statutes chilled the free exercise of religion because they could be invoked at any time.[42]

In June 1951, the Fraudulent Mediums Act became law. In addition to repealing the Witchcraft Act of 1735 and the sections of the Vagrancy Act of 1824 dealing with the purported exercise of supernatural powers, this law criminalized acting as a "spiritualistic medium" or purporting "to exercise any powers of telepathy, clairvoyance or other similar powers" for purposes of a reward and with the intent to deceive.[43] At the time of its passage, the only meaningful opposition to this law came from some members of Parliament who expressed concern that the Fraudulent Mediums Act did not go far enough to protect religious freedom. They opined that it was wrong to repeal the Witchcraft and Vagrancy Acts just to replace them with other crimes, even though the proscribed practices only included intentional fraud committed for financial gain. Nearly sixty years later, this notion reached a consensus. In 2008, the UK Parliament passed the Consumer Protection from Unfair Trading Regulations Act, which repealed the Fraudulent Mediums Act. There are no longer any laws in England that expressly target mediums, palmists, fortune-tellers, or other spiritual practitioners, whether committing intentional fraud or otherwise.

B. Jamaica's Obeah Law

In same period that Britain repealed its witchcraft and vagrancy legislation to protect religious freedom, Jamaican legislators and courts found no similar concerns with their own Obeah and vagrancy laws, which had been modeled on the rescinded English legislation. Just one year after England repealed its Witchcraft Act and the sections of the Vagrancy Act proscribing fortune-telling, palmistry, and other occult practices, the Jamaican Supreme Court reinforced its commitment to maintaining Obeah and vagrancy legislation. This case began when Molly Brodie was convicted of "pretending to deal in Obeah," in violation of Jamaica's Vagrancy Act, after the police witnessed Brodie and another woman performing a purported healing ritual on a sick baby, which involved sprinkling an unknown fluid on the child while speaking in an unidentified language.[44] Like all vagrancy laws in Britain's Caribbean colonies, Jamaica's statute was modeled on England's recently repealed Vagrancy Act of 1824, except that it added "pretending to deal in Obeah, myalism, duppy catching, or witchcraft" to the list of proscribed offenses.[45]

Brodie appealed her conviction, arguing for a very narrow interpretation of vagrancy and Obeah laws that only prohibited using supernatural powers for fraud, for gain, to frighten someone, or for an unlawful purpose—none of which would apply to Brodie's actions. The Jamaican Supreme Court examined an English case from 1921, *Stonehouse v. Masson*, to determine whether Brodie's interpretation of the vagrancy statute was correct. In *Stonehouse*, the court opined that in vagrancy cases, "the mens rea consists in [sic] the intention to do the act prohibited by the statute, which is to pretend or profess to tell fortunes."[46] The Jamaican Supreme Court explained: "If we substitute the words 'to tell fortunes' [with] the words 'to deal in Obeah' and apply the reasoning in that judgment to the facts of the present case, it becomes clear that the mere pretending to deal in Obeah is an offence under the Vagrancy Law."[47] The irony about the Jamaican Supreme Court using *Stonehouse v. Masson* as precedent to decide Brodie's case was that *Stonehouse* was no longer valid in England because the vagrancy law had been repealed the year before. Even though Jamaica was still a British colony and although their Obeah laws were modeled on legislation that the English determined violated religious freedom, Jamaica continued to follow these defunct metropolitan policies.

Sixty years later, in 2013 (five years after Britain repealed its last remaining provisions banning supernatural practices), the Jamaican government once again emphasized the stanchness of its stance against the practice of Obeah. At that time, Justice Minister Mark Golding introduced a bill that would remodel Obeah legislation, removing the sections about corporal punishment. Two legislators, Lambert Brown and Tom Tavares-Finson, vowed to implement legislation that would abolish the Obeah Act altogether, referring to it as an outdated colonial mechanism of controlling Black people. Diana Paton, one of the world's foremost researchers on the history of Obeah legislation, wrote an editorial in favor of the proposed changes, explaining: "The existence of the law was part of a broader stigmatisation of anything considered African. It made religious activities that would be legal in other countries or contexts, punishable by imprisonment and flogging. The law has hardly been used since the early 1960s, and its continued existence is anachronistic."[48] However, the Jamaican public's response to the law's proposed repeal was much less favorable and was rife with concerns about "witchcraft" and "evil" permeating Jamaica if these laws no longer existed.

For example, the following day after Paton's editorial was published, a person who identified themselves as "The Jamaican Watchman" or "Jamaica Opposed (to sin)" wrote: "My stomach churned as I read [Dr. Paton's letter] to think that yet again here is another overseas-based observer being published in our local newspaper seeking to support this 'evil' agenda."[49] The Jamaican Watchman opined that the Atlantic slave trade had been a "blessing in disguise" for Jamaicans because the "very reason we got sold into slavery out of the 'mother' country [sic] Africa, was because we were entrenched into this evil practice."[50] The Watchman warned that "neither the Church nor the Lord Jesus Christ will stand idle, while our legislators drag this nation to hell along with them."[51] Somewhat unsurprisingly, considering this and other negative feedback, Brown and Tavares-Finson never followed through with their promises to repeal Jamaica's Obeah legislation.

The dispute about Obeah legislation in Jamaica did not end there. In the years following the modification of the Obeah Act, there has been a sharp increase in debates on whether the proposed abolition of the law should take place. Many of these exchanges have been sparked by observations about a perceived rise in Indian astrologers and other spiritual workers in Jamaica; several editorials have questioned whether these individuals should also be charged with practicing Obeah and/or suggested that Obeah laws discriminate against African spiritual practices while permitting foreign ones. Public comments to these editorials have repeatedly stressed that Jamaica is a Christian nation, and that the practice of any kind of "witchcraft" is a threat to the nation.

For example, on June 2, 2016, a person who only wished to be identified as a "Concerned Citizen" wrote a letter to the editor of the *Jamaica Observer* expressing "great concern" regarding "the startling rise in the number of witchcraft and palm-reading services which are being increasingly advertised on television."[52] Concerned Citizen explained that they were writing to the

Observer "to question both the legality of the services and, more importantly, to warn all who consider using these services that any supernatural power which exists outside of God's power is from Satan."⁵³ The author explained that "the sudden thrust in the promotion of these services comes as an alarm as our country has been predominantly Christian" and asked: "As these spiritualists are now taking over the airwaves, what will stop Obeah men and other cults from using this platform to lure persons to their evils?"⁵⁴

The following year, on September 19, 2017, a Jamaican lawyer named Linton Gordon echoed these observations that "foreigners" had increasingly begun advertising and offering supernatural services in Jamaica.⁵⁵ However, unlike "Concerned Citizen," who had expressed fear that this was a sign of "evil forces" growing in Jamaica, Gordon lamented that Jamaican Obeah practitioners were "forced by the Obeah Act to carry out their activities clandestinately [*sic*]" while "foreigners are advertising their supernatural abilities on television and are therefore now in the open."⁵⁶ Gordon called upon the House of Representatives to repeal the Obeah Act and create a licensing scheme for "those who are indulging in the offer of supernatural power."⁵⁷

On December 17, 2017, staff reporter Jediael Carter rehashed the issue that Gordon had raised in September, reminding the public that Gordon had questioned why the Jamaican government was not pursuing astrologers when their services were comparable to that which was categorized as Obeah.⁵⁸ Carter also cited Dr. Ajamu Nangwaya, professor at the University of the West Indies, who questioned the continued proscription of African spiritual practices. The following day, an anonymous person wrote an editorial in response, contending that Brown and Tavares-Finson should follow through with their promises to repeal the Obeah Act.⁵⁹ Thirty-two people commented on the online version of the editorial, mostly expressing opposition to the repeal of the Obeah Act. A person with the handle "ChuckI3s" argued: "I think it would be better if the Obeah Act was kept in force. It's obvious that unscrupulous persons can use the vulnerabilities of others to ruthlessly exploit them for monetary gain. In fact, it could be amended to also include any nefarious activities, where claims of supernatural abilities are used purely for financial gain."⁶⁰ Another with the handle "Tyroneosborne" said: "Some countries in west Africa openly say they do Obeah, and even in the Caribbean, some say openly they use Voodoo. But what is the Christian take on the matter, since we are 97% Protestant Christians. Should Satan have a fair go on the innocent humans?"⁶¹

Most recently, in June 2019, Minister of Justice Delroy Chuck made headlines when he reportedly vowed to repeal Jamaica's Obeah Act, referring to it as a "pointless" and "archaic" law.⁶² He allegedly made this statement during a House of Representatives debate about increasing the fine for the practice of Obeah to $1 million. However, Chuck later claimed that his comments had been taken out of context, and that "the government considered repealing the Obeah Act only to replace it with a broader law that banned Obeah and addressed 'fraudulent activities' related to people's belief systems."⁶³

Jamaica's continued strong stance against Obeah cannot be viewed out of its historical and present-day contexts. It is significant that in the most opportune moment, the year following the repeal of England's Vagrancy and Witchcraft Acts while Jamaica was still a British colony, the Supreme Court did not regard African diviners and conjurers as enjoying the same religious freedom as white and/or Western astrologers and mediums. Years later, after England has abolished all remnants of these laws, the Jamaican public seems to still hold fast to the idea that Obeah practitioners are frauds or persons who are in league with the devil. Whether legislators actually share these concerns is unclear; however, their refusal to abolish Obeah laws certainly sends that message.

C. Trinidad and Tobago's Obeah Law

Trinidad and Tobago is one of only four countries in the former British Caribbean to have repealed its Obeah statutes. The repeal of these laws came in 2000, following a series of legislative and policy changes that granted more rights and recognition to certain religious minorities, including the members of the Spiritual Baptists and Orisa faiths. The process of repealing these laws further highlights the biases in the persistence of anti-Obeah legislation.

Trinidad and Tobago's Obeah legislation closely resembled England's Witchcraft Act of 1735. Under a section of the Summary Offenses Acts titled "Superstitious Devices," this law prohibited any person from pretending to "discover any treasure or any lost or stolen goods, or the person who stole the same," as well as using such purported power to "obtain any chattel, money or valuable security from any other person," or "to inflict any disease, loss, damage, personal injury to or upon any other person, or to restore any other person to health, and any person who procures, counsels, induces, or persuades or endeavours to persuade any other person to commit any such offence ... by the practice of Obeah or by any occult means or by any assumption of supernatural power or knowledge."⁶⁴ In 2000, the Parliament of Trinidad and Tobago began reviewing a law that would modify the Summary Offenses Act and two other statutes, to "remove certain discriminatory religious references."[65] The relevant edit to the Summary Offenses Act maintained the language about pretending to discover lost or stolen goods, injuring or restoring any person to health, and so on, but deleted the phrase about Obeah and supernatural powers, replacing it with the phrase "by any fraudulent means."[66] These modifications somewhat mirror England's Fraudulent Mediums Act of 1951, limiting the proscribed activities to those that were proven fraudulent.

Parliamentary debates clearly reveal that this bill came about as a direct response to the lobbying of Orisa worshippers. In 1999, the Parliament reviewed the Orisa Marriage Bill, which would give priests of this faith the ability to perform marriage ceremonies. During the debate of this law, several members of the House indicated that a bill repealing Obeah legislation was forthcoming and was designed to further enhance the recognition of Orisa adherents.[67] When the Orisa Marriage Bill reached the Senate the following month, the then minister of legal affairs, Hon. Kamla Persad-Bissessar, lamented that it had taken until "the last year of the twentieth century" to recognize Orisa marriages and, referencing the Obeah law, reminded the Senate that other discriminatory comments remained on the books that "have been retained since the days of colonialism and which interfere with the exercise of religious freedoms of" Orisa devotees and other faiths.[68]

When the bill to repeal the Obeah provisions came before the Parliament the following year, Ramesh Lawrence Maharaj, attorney general and minister of legal affairs for the House of Representatives, reemphasized that "the laws which we are trying to reform today, are laws which impact tremendously on the right of worship of certain of the religions and, in particular, the Baptists and Orisas."[69] Others likewise stressed that the purpose of the modification of the Summary Offenses Act was to enhance religious freedom for Orisa devotees who had sent in letters lobbying for the repeal.[70] One member of the House of Representatives, C. Robinson-Regis, even incorrectly asserted that the term "Obeah" was designed to target Orisa worshippers because the word "comes from the very seed, the obi seed, which is used in their process of divination."[71]

However, even with this clarification that they were taking these measures to protect Orisa devotees (and to a lesser extent Spiritual Baptists), there was still some opposition to the repeal of Trinidad and Tobago's Obeah laws. Representative Colm Imbert explained that his "Christian principles" were causing him concern over the modification of the provisions about "superstitious devices" because it would involve the removal of the prohibition of the practice of "witchcraft" and "occult" practices.[72] Imbert said that he had looked up the terms "witch" and "occult" in the dictionary. They were defined as involving the practice of magic or sorcery, "engaging with mystical or supernatural phenomena" or having a relationship with the devil. Imbert explained, "This is why I am saying that I am having some difficulty with this legislation. From my Christian background, I am totally against any dealings with the devil. If we have legislation which makes it an offence to practice worship of the devil or something like that and one is now taking that out of legislation, I have a little problem."[73] He continued, "I would hate to be involved in anything in this Parliament where we are weakening the laws that deal with devil worship in this country. I cannot subscribe to any legislation that is going to promote and support the worship of the devil in this country."[74]

Later during the meeting, after several other members had spoken, Attorney General Maharaj and Imbert engaged in a rather heated exchange as the former tried to explain to the latter that the Miscellaneous Laws Bill was not about legalizing "witchcraft." Maharaj opined that the opposition to the bill was rooted in prejudices from the colonial era, when these laws were passed. In that time, "the whole society here was dominated by a certain established Christian church, therefore every other religion was regarded as heathen in those days," and these laws "were there as part and parcel of the package to discriminate against non-Christians in that context, and everything was regarded as Obeah, occult, heathen and so forth."[75] Maharaj explained that even Spiritual Baptists were accused of worshipping the devil, and Mr. Imbert interrupted, "Nonsense! Were you there?"[76] Without acknowledging this interruption, Maharaj continued to explain that Orisa practitioners were subject to this law as well. In fact, he averred that because "Obeah" encompassed "every pretended assumption of supernatural power," any person could be charged with this offense. He explained, "Every pundit who gets up to talk could be guilty of Obeah, every Swami, every Imam." Maharaj argued that this bill was designed to end the country's past discrimination against Baptists, Orisas, and other faiths. Mr. Imbert, however, interjected again: "You are a devil worshipper!" Maharaj cited further information to support his argument and told the opposition that they owed Baptists, Orisas, and Rastafarians an apology for stalling these reforms, then he yielded the floor. The bill passed both houses of Parliament, despite Imbert's objections.

The debates about the repeal of Obeah laws in Trinidad and Tobago create a sharp contrast to those in England fifty years earlier. One will recall that members of Parliament in England had expressed their embarrassment that laws regarding witchcraft remained in effect in the early 1950s and lamented that such antiquated ideas could be reflected in their statutes. They made clear that while they may not personally believe in spirit-conjuring or divination, they had an obligation to guarantee religious freedom for all persons and expressed hope that other nations would follow their example.

Trinidad and Tobago, on the other hand, emphasized that their intention was not to protect spirit conjurers or diviners but rather to guarantee the rights of Orisa adherents and other "legitimate religions" that might be discriminated against using these laws. Like the public comments about the possibility of repealing Obeah legislation in Jamaica, Imbert expressed anxieties that legalizing Obeah might condone "witchcraft" or devil worship. Maharaj's response did not contest the propriety of Imbert's apprehensions about "witchcraft" but rather alleged that Orisa adherents and Spiritual Baptists had been miscategorized as Obeah practitioners. These Caribbean responses seem far removed from English legislators' assertions that these laws were antiquated and embarrassing limitations on religious freedom.

D. South Africa's Witchcraft Legislation

A comparison between England and the Caribbean does not provide a complete picture of the trends in the repeal of legislation barring "pretending" to possess supernatural powers. As mentioned previously, witchcraft laws in Britain's African colonies mirrored those in England and the Caribbean. Most of these colonial statutes remain in effect in the twenty-first century. To my knowledge, South Africa alone has repealed these provisions as the result of concerns that they violated religious freedom. These legislative changes were brought about to protect European-derived "witches," specifically Wiccans, in South Africa.

The proscription on pretending to possess supernatural powers in South Africa dates back to the late nineteenth and early twentieth centuries, when South Africa comprised several different territories and was not yet one unified dominion or nation. The "Native Territories" annexed to the Cape Colony were first in passing witchcraft legislation; in 1879, legislators broadly proscribed "practicing or pretending to practice witchcraft."[77] Seven years later, in 1886, a more elaborate statute went into effect that prohibited a number of specific acts, including "professing to a knowledge of so-called witchcraft or the use of charms."[78] In 1904, another territory in southern Africa, the Transvaal, passed a statute that more closely mirrored England's Witchcraft Act of 1735, which stated that "any person who for purposes of gain pretends to exercise or use any kind of supernatural power, witchcraft, sorcery, enchantment, or conjuration, or undertakes to tell fortunes or pretends from his skill or knowledge in any occult science to discover where or in what manner anything supposed to have been stolen or lost may be found" could be subject to imprisonment at hard labor for up to one year.[79]

Decades later, the unified (apartheid) government of South Africa passed the Witchcraft Suppression Act of 1957, which consolidated all the ordinances that had previously been applied to various regions of the nation.[80] Most of this statute, including the final section on the "pretended" practice of witchcraft, was identical to the Transvaal's Ordinance of 1904, except the penalty for contravening it increased to two years' imprisonment or a fine of up to R200. Therefore, this section was very similar to England's Witchcraft Act of 1735. The irony, however, was that South Africa's Witchcraft Suppression Act was implemented six years after England's statute had been repealed and replaced with the Fraudulent Mediums Act amid concerns about religious freedom.

Although other parts of the Witchcraft Act were later modified (to prohibit corporal punishment and create harsher punishments for witchcraft-related murder), these sections about pretending to practice witchcraft for gain remained intact, unaltered into the twenty-first century. In July 2008, 50 years after the passage of this consolidated statute and nearly 120 years after the first witchcraft proscriptions were passed in the Cape, the South African Pagan Rights Alliance requested that the South African Law Reform Commission (SALRC) review the constitutionality of the Witchcraft Suppression Act.[81] They asked the commission to explore whether the act violated constitutional guarantees of freedom of religion with an emphasis on the rights of individuals who self-identified as "witches." About four months later, after the SALRC had already held a preliminary meeting to discuss the request, the Traditional Healers Organisation (THO) asked to be included in the investigation. Rather than calling for the complete decriminalization of "witchcraft," the THO asked for the implementation of a new statute that would better control harmful practices that they labeled as *busakatsi* and protect innocent people who were assaulted for suspected witchcraft practices.[82] On August 1, 2009, the commission agreed to review the act, focusing on thirteen issues such as whether witchcraft should be acknowledged, whether distinctions should be made between good and bad "witches," and whether the existing witchcraft legislation was constitutional.[83]

In 2014, the SALRC published their preliminary findings and opened up their solutions for public comment.[84] Two years later, after receiving comments and conducting further investigation, the commission released Discussion Paper 139.[85] The commission raised several concerns about the Witchcraft Act, but for purposes of this chapter, I focus on the section about "pretending" to practice witchcraft. The commission concluded that this section should be repealed, in large part because there is a need "to separate the practice of Pagan witchcraft from practices associated with harmful witchcraft."[86] Even though the commission appears to have received no reports that Wiccans had actually been prosecuted for violating the Witchcraft Suppression Act, they noted that the law encouraged "uninformed people" to link Wiccans with Satanism. The commission explained that the "constant challenge in convincing the wider public that they are not involved in sinister practices" made Wiccans "somewhat hypersensitive to perceived prejudices and unfair treatment against them."[87] Even though the commission did not observe any actual discrimination against Wiccans and referred to their claims as "somewhat hypersensitive," they concluded: "The practice of witchcraft can no longer be seen only through the lens of indigenous communities, where it is necessarily associated with evil. There are other sections of the community that now practice what they term 'witchcraft,' which is alleged to be an exercise of the right to religion. The religious rights of this small group cannot be ignored, especially in light of the constitutional jurisprudence, which emphasizes the protection of religious minorities."[88] The commission suggested that a new law be implemented that protected the constitutional rights of Pagans and traditional healers but still dealt with harmful practices. Specifically, the commission opined that the section about pretending to practice witchcraft for gain might limit the constitutional right to pick one's occupation or trade. The state might claim that it is trying to prevent fraud, but "the problem then relates to how to determine who is pretending and who is genuine, with regard to supernatural powers, since by definition this cannot be scientifically established."[89] They opined that the law was "clearly paternalistic" and "judgmental" about "supernatural powers and fortune-telling," without a clear rationale for limiting these practices.[90] For these reasons, the commission submitted their paper to the minister of justice and correctional services, suggesting that the minister propose new legislation to Parliament.

Therefore, South Africa, the only country in Africa to stress that these provisions about professing to have supernatural powers violate religious freedom, began the process of reviewing and repealing these provisions in response to complaints from Wiccans. Although these self-proclaimed "witches" had not been prosecuted for violating these laws, the commission still found that these laws infringed on religious freedom. They stressed that this small religious minority should not be depicted as evil as the result of this act. This is a striking contrast to the Caribbean, where the public and some legislators continue to associate African-descended diviners, healers, and spirit conjurers with devil worship and strongly oppose the repeal of Obeah laws.

E. Canada's Witchcraft Law

The most recent legislative debates about provisions banning the "pretended" use of supernatural powers began in Canada in 2017. The discussions of the repeal of Canada's witchcraft law were part of a bill to eradicate "obsolete" statutes. The response of Canadian legislators to this bill aligns with the repeal of England's statutes sixty years earlier and once again creates a sharp contrast to the response to the (attempted) repeal of Obeah laws in the Caribbean.

Section 365 of Canada's Criminal Code was virtually identical to England's Witchcraft Act of 1735 and comparable to many of the Obeah laws in the Caribbean and witchcraft laws in Africa. It banned "(a) pretend[ing] to exercise or to use any kind of witchcraft, sorcery, enchantment or conjuration, (b) undertak[ing], for a consideration, to tell fortunes, or (c) pretend[ing] from his skill in or knowledge of an occult or crafty science to discover where or in what manner anything that is supposed to have been stolen or lost may be found."[91] The penalty for violating this law was a maximum of six months' imprisonment and a fine of up to $2,000. Pretending to practice witchcraft had been an offense under Canadian criminal law since at least 1892, the same period that witchcraft and Obeah legislation was implemented in Britain's Caribbean and African colonies.[92]

In 2017, the Canadian parliament began reviewing Bill C-51, titled "An Act to Amend the Criminal Code and the Department of Justice Act and to Make Consequential Amendments to Another Act." The delineated goals of this bill were to clarify sexual assault legislation, to repeal Criminal Code provisions that courts have found unconstitutional, and to repeal several "obsolete" offenses that "were enacted many years ago, but that are no longer relevant or required today." There were six "obsolete offenses" listed in the bill, including provisions that banned challenging someone to a duel, publishing crime comics, publishing blasphemous libel, and fraudulently pretending to practice witchcraft. The bill became law on December 13, 2018.

The legislative debates about these provisions revealed no controversies about permitting "superstition"; instead, legislators almost universally remarked that these laws were useless and outdated. For example, Hon. Rob Nicholson lamented that the House had not addressed a sex offender law, but someone "has introduced a bill that ensures that individuals do not pretend to practice witchcraft."[93] Misunderstanding that the bill decriminalized witchcraft and dueling, Nicholson asserted: "I do not know about other members, but the last time I checked my neighbourhood, fake witchcraft and duelling in the streets were not an issue."[94] He later slightly rephrased this point, stating that he agreed with the removal of the witchcraft and dueling provisions from the law because they "no longer have any bearing on our society today."[95]

Similarly, Ali Ehsassi said, "In a modern Criminal Code, there is no need for an obsolete provision such as the offence of fraudulently pretending to practice witchcraft."[96] Wayne Stetski asserted, "One must wonder about the existing laws regarding the practice of witchcraft, sorcery, enchantment, or conjuration."[97] He mused, "In addition to the fact that it impinges on the rights of some religions, and would confuse the U.S. President who is certain that he is the target of a witch hunt, this might also hurt Harry Potter cosplayers; Dungeons and Dragons 'larpers', which I do not know much about but which my staff assure me is a thing; and others for whom sorcery is an entertainment. This is a good law to be rid of."[98] Christine Moore similarly exclaimed, "It is not hard to see that these measures are no longer of any real use."[99]

The sole objection came from Peter Van Loan, who demurred:

> The concern is, and we have all heard stories like this, that people use these kinds of fraudulent witchcraft powers to persuade people that, for example, if they put $10,000 in an envelope, which they say will be burned but they slide it under the table instead, he or she will be saved from whatever curse they say the person is under. These things really happen in our society, even in this day and age. Does that provision, as it exists right now, cause any harm? No. Does it give the police an avenue or resource in the case of those particular unusual offences? Yes, it does. This is why I ask why we need to look around for things to change, in the name of modernization, for the sake of changing.[100]

No one else echoed Van Loan's sentiments.

Furthermore, while there were seventeen briefs filed by various organizations such as the Canadian Civil Liberties Union and the Canadian Bar

Association in support of or in opposition to this bill, none of them addressed the repeal of the witchcraft provisions.

PART III: CONCLUSION

These examples of the disparities in the dialogue about legislative reform illustrate a continuing trend to discriminate against African diaspora and other minority faiths. While Spiritualists, Wiccans, and other Western faiths have been recognized and have slowly gained legal protection since the middle of the twentieth century, similar recognition of Obeah and related belief systems has yet to come. Analogous to Europeans during the witchcraft craze of the sixteenth and seventeenth centuries, Africans who practice divination, use charms, conjure spirits, and engage in other manipulations of supernatural powers continue to be characterized as evil persons in league with the devil. Furthermore, while Christian megachurches solicit millions of dollars from their followers, Obeah remains criminalized out of purported fears of fraudulent spiritual profits.

Unfortunately, the tide does not appear to be turning in favor of the recognition of Obeah as a religion. As I explore in the next chapter, judges and courts in the Americas are increasingly finding that African diaspora faiths do not meet the definition of "religion" and do not warrant the same protections guaranteed to other faiths. This, coupled with the outright proscription of "Obeah" and other supernatural practices, demonstrates a deeply concerning and growing trend to restrict religious freedom to mainstream and/or Western faiths.

CHAPTER ◊ 8

"Fragmentary," "Dangerous," and "Unethical" Belief Systems
African Diaspora Faiths and the "Accoutrements" of Religion

Except for the statutes discussed in chapter 7, the practice of African diaspora religions is generally legal in the Americas. However, over the past ten years, courts have repeatedly asserted that these faiths are somehow less than "religions" and have denied adherents the protections guaranteed to other belief systems. In the United States, prisoners have been denied religious accommodations after an expert testified that Obeah is not a religion and that its devotees practice human sacrifice. In Canada, the Court of Appeal for Ontario has adamantly proclaimed that it recognizes Obeah as a religion; however, the court still opined that some of its practices or rituals are not "religious" and not governed by guarantees of religious freedom. In Brazil, a judge refused to order Google to remove discriminatory videos from one of its online platforms because he did not believe that Afro-Brazilian faiths met the required characteristics to be protected by statutes banning discrimination against religions. These cases demonstrate the shifting boundaries of modern definitions of "religion" and the concerning trend to exclude African diaspora faiths from this category.

PART I: THE UNITED STATES

Appellate courts in the United States have heard at least two cases in the twenty-first century where they have been asked to consider whether African diaspora faiths such as Obeah and Santeria/Lucumi are legally categorized as "religions," and whether their adherents are protected by statutory or constitutional guarantees of free exercise. Both cases centered on whether devotees were legitimately practicing their religions or using them to hide criminal activities or cause harm to others. In one case, the court determined that African diaspora religions can be too "dangerous" to receive legal protection; in another, procedural problems resulted in a decision that sent an adherent to prison for years for possession of religious implements.

A. Miller and Taylor (2008)

In 2007, Omar Miller and Taekwon Taylor were housed in a correctional facility in Connecticut.[1] Each separately filed an application for a temporary injunction against the director of religious services for the Department of Corrections, Anthony Bruno, complaining that he had refused to give them the materials they needed to practice their religion. These materials consisted of honeysuckle, Hawaiian ginger oils, parchment paper, and incense sticks. Both men claimed that they were Santeria adherents; Miller alleged that he was also a practitioner of Obeah, which he suggested was a component of Santeria. Bruno responded that the items that Miller and Taylor requested would pose a danger to the safety and security of the prison; however, regarding the Hawaiian ginger oils, he noted that other alcohol-free oils were available for purchase in the commissary.

To support their requests for religious accommodations, Miller and Taylor employed Yale professor Lillian Guerra to provide expert testimony regarding their faiths. However, Professor Guerra's testimony ended up backfiring against them, as she opined that the items that Miller and Taylor requested were not used in Santeria, and that the men seemed to be "quite ignorant" of the faiths they professed. Furthermore, regarding Obeah, the court summarized Guerra's testimony as follows: "Professor Guerra noted that Mr. Miller's representations regarding Obeah, which he implied was a part of the Santeria faith, was not a religion at all, nor was it associated in any way with Santeria. Rather, Obeah was a form of black magic which originated in Jamaica and is a highly secretive practice which aims to harm others. Professor Guerra also noted that the practice of Obeah is criminalized in Jamaica, as its purpose is to bring irreparable harm to others."[2] Despite Guerra's testimony that Miller's and Taylor's practices were not associated with Santeria, the court could not use this as the sole basis to deny their requests. The US Supreme Court has determined that it is impermissible for judges to evaluate the truth or accuracy of a person's religious beliefs. Therefore, the court sidestepped these inconsistencies between Guerra's depictions and the plaintiffs' beliefs, stating that "the plaintiffs present with sincere, if not misguided, beliefs that their religious practices are in fact religion."[3]

Once the court determined that their beliefs seemed genuine and thus protected by the First Amendment's guarantees of free exercise of religion, the next step was to balance their religious freedom against the safety and security of the prison. Their request for accommodations failed this test, as the court determined that both parties' requests posed a danger to the security of the prison. In the case of Miller, the court's reasoning was as follows:

> The testimony of Professor Guerra [is] compelling, as she testified that Obeah, a practice which Mr. Miller has asserted is a part of his religion, is a doctrine which seeks to cause harm to others. As a form of dark magic, Obeah is understood and recognized to have as its primary purpose the poisoning and murder of another. Professor Guerra testified that practitioners of Obeah generally carry medicine bags around their neck containing the human remains of others, and ideally murderers, in order to exercise the full power of Obeah. Although Mr. Miller does not appear to engage in authentic Obeah practices, his belief and attempt to engage in what he believes are Obeah practices is itself inherently dangerous and threatening to the prison community because of what Obeah might objectively represent to others.[4]

It is clear that Guerra's testimony depicting Obeah as "dark magic" and a belief system focused on poisoning others is a carryover from the European stereotypes and superstitions discussed in chapter 7. Thus, these colonial biases against African religions were deployed in this case to determine that Miller should not receive religious accommodations because the belief system that he claimed to belong to was "inherently dangerous." The court reached the decision based entirely on Guerra's testimony, even though the items that Miller requested did not, in and of themselves, show a clear correlation to "evil" or "dangerous" practices. This rhetoric gets repeated again and again by courts in North America that cannot outright deny that Obeah is a religion but that do not wish to guarantee adherents the same protections enjoyed by other faiths.

B. Alberto Duncan (2008–2009)

The same year that the Superior Court of Connecticut denied Miller's and Taylor's requests for accommodations because Obeah is an "inherently dangerous" religion, United States Attorney (federal prosecutor) R. Alexander Acosta and other members of his office expressed similar questions about whether adherents of Santeria/Lucumi were guaranteed religious freedom. On January 29, 2008, police officers knocked on Alberto Duncan's door in southwestern Miami-Dade County in Florida.[5] When Duncan opened the door, between six and eight armed officers entered, advising Duncan that they had received information that he was selling narcotics and they were not leaving until he consented to a search of his home. According to Duncan, he complied out of fear, signing a waiver permitting the officers to search his residence. According to the police, Duncan calmly agreed to the search after maintaining his innocence and reporting that the complaints were probably due to the unusual traffic in and out of his residence at strange hours as devotees arrived to consult him in his capacity as a Santeria priest.[6]

When the officers searched the residence, they found $755 cash hidden in the bottom of a vase, small amounts of cocaine inside an aerosol can stuck between two pipes beneath the kitchen sink, and two handguns (a loaded .22-caliber Beretta and a replica gun) inside a "black kettle" near the doorway.[7] Duncan was charged with three serious offenses: being a felon in possession of a firearm (maximum penalty: ten years' imprisonment), possession of cocaine with intent to distribute (maximum penalty: twenty years' imprisonment), and possession of a firearm in furtherance of a drug-trafficking offense (maximum penalty: life in prison).[8]

Duncan contested these charges on several grounds. First, he alleged that the search had been coerced by the presence of multiple armed officers in his home. He also claimed that even if the search was consensual, the officers exceeded the scope of consent by searching the can underneath the sink and by bringing in drug-sniffing dogs. Additionally, while Duncan admitted that the gun was in his home, he claimed that it was not there for purposes of drug trafficking. Rather, he maintained that it was an offering to the orisha Ogun, and that the officers had removed it from a religious shrine knowing full well that it was a spiritual talisman.

Ogun is one of four orishas who make up a group known as "warriors," whose shrines Santeria/Lucumi adherents usually place near the entrance to their homes.[9] As an orisha who represents blacksmiths and "owns" everything that is metal, Ogun typically resides in a metal pot with a set of metal tools (often a mixture of replica and real) such as knives, railroad spikes, and hammers, among other things.[10] Over time, through divination sessions where a priest consults the orishas using special shells, seeds, or other tools, the orishas will ask the devotee to add new "tools" to their shrine. Throughout the arrest and subsequent criminal proceedings, Duncan maintained that Ogun, who is the avatar of war and a strong protector, had required the offering of a gun to his shrine. Therefore, Duncan's counsel contended he should not be convicted of the most serious offense of which he was accused, possession of a weapon in furtherance of drug trafficking, because the weapon was for religious purposes.[11]

The testimony from both sides was replete with evidence that Duncan had the gun as part of a religious practice and that the police immediately knew that the gun was inside a Santeria shrine. Detective Borrego with the Miami-Dade Police Department testified that the first thing he noticed in Duncan's foyer was "a black kettle" with "railroad spikes, feathers, obviously some blood had been sprinkled over it, there was a machete next to it, and there was two guns inside of it. I think it is a .25 caliber Beretta, and then another toy gun."[12] He admitted, "I can obviously tell it is a Santeria shrine."[13] Furthermore, several officers testified that Duncan said nothing during the search until Borrego seized the handgun. At that time, Duncan asked the officers why they were taking the weapon. When they responded that it was evidence, he contested the seizure and proclaimed that it was part of his religion.

Although criminal defendants are not required to testify in the United States, Duncan decided to take the stand at trial and explained that the "kettle" where the officers found the gun was one of the many shrines that he had to his orishas. He added to the detective's description, admitting that he had a railroad spike, an arrow, a knife, a lance, and an eighteen-inch machete inside the shrine as well as the gun.[14] He explained that the feathers and blood found on the gun and the other items in the shrine were from animals that had been sacrificed to Ogun. When his attorney asked him whether the gun had anything to do with the cocaine that the police found in his house, Duncan replied: "Of course not. That weapon has been there for 22 years now. It is even rusted and it doesn't even work."[15] His attorney later helped Duncan clarify to the jury that in his view, he did not personally possess the firearm, that once it had been placed in Ogun's shrine, it belonged to Ogun.[16]

During closing arguments, the United States attorney accused Duncan of using his religion as a "shield against the law"[17] and claimed that Duncan kept the weapon by the door for dual purposes—religion and "protecting his criminal enterprise."[18] Duncan's attorney, on the other hand, reinforced the idea that the only reason that Duncan possessed the weapon was for religious purposes. He emphasized this "tiny rusted 20-year-old .22 caliber gun that was in that kettle with all that other stuff and the blood" was not shown to have "in any way helped, furthered, promoted or advanced the drugs."[19] He asked the jury in closing: "Do you really think this is what [Duncan] would rely on to protect his house?"[20] The jury deliberated for less than three hours and then found Duncan guilty of possession of the weapon and intent to traffic but not guilty of possession of the weapon in furtherance of trafficking.[21] The judge sentenced Duncan to eighty-seven months' (a little over seven years) imprisonment on each count (sentences to be served concurrently), followed by three years' supervised release.

Duncan appealed his conviction for possession of the gun and possession of cocaine with intent to distribute. One of the bases for Duncan's appeal was that during trial, his counsel had filed a motion asking the court to provide instructions to the jury about the relationship between the possession of a firearm charge and his religious freedom. Florida has a state law called the Religious Freedom Restoration Act (RFRA), which requires the government to show that any restriction on religion must further a compelling government interest and must be the least restrictive means of furthering that interest. This is a very high standard for the government to meet and often results in the invalidation of government action. Duncan's counsel had asked the court to instruct the jury that they could only find Duncan guilty of possessing the weapon if the government showed beyond a reasonable doubt that it had "an interest of the highest order" in limiting Duncan's possession of the weapon in his religious practice. However, the judge rejected the motion.

On appeal, Duncan's counsel resurrected the argument about RFRA as a defense to the possession charge, contending that the judge should have instructed the jury that if the government had substantially burdened his religion without a compelling interest or failed to use the least restrictive means of burdening his religion, then Duncan was not criminally liable for possessing the weapon. However, the government argued that RFRA did not apply because Santeria was not a religion.

In its appeal brief, the government wrote: "The record is bereft of any evidence, save for Duncan's own musings, that Santaria [sic] is an organized religion within the aegis of RFRA's protection. There was no evidence to demonstrate that the cult was suitably concerned with 'ultimate ideas, metaphysical beliefs and moral or ethical standards' or that it held out 'comprehensive beliefs on all aspects of life' and possessed the accouterments of religion such as foundational writings, organizational structure and holidays" (components of the definition of religion, set out by a prior court case).

The government further argued that Duncan's "fragmentary and disjoined description of the Santaria [sic] sect made it seem more akin to voodoo then to an organized religion."[22] Duncan's counsel, naturally, responded that in the *City of Hialeah* case (discussed in chapter 2) "the Supreme Court recognized Santeria as an organized religion entitled to First Amendment protection."[23] The defense also pointed out that Duncan had testified that the gun was a religious item and that the government's own witnesses had testified that they had recognized the "black kettle" as a Santeria shrine.[24] The Eleventh Circuit did not weigh in on the disputes about whether Duncan's religion required him to possess a weapon or whether Santeria was a religion protected by RFRA. Rather, they focused on the fact that where RFRA applies is a question of law to be determined by a judge, and therefore the District Court was within its rights to refuse to submit the issue to the jury.[25] On these procedural grounds, Duncan lost his appeal of this issue.

PART II: CANADA

The US cases just discussed have already demonstrated the beginning of a concerning trend. However, these are not isolated rulings. Around this same time, Canadian courts were wrestling with similar questions of whether Obeah practices were too dangerous to be protected by principles of religious freedom. In the late twentieth and early twenty-first centuries, amid widespread allegations that Jamaicans were disproportionately perpetrating violent crime, persons of Caribbean descent in Toronto developed elaborate ruses involving "Obeah" to trick suspected criminals into confessing to murder and robbery. As the defendants appealed their convictions, Canadian courts were asked to determine whether "Obeah" was a religion and, if so, whether the police violated the religious freedoms of Obeah practitioners by deploying spiritually based ruses. Canadian courts reached similar conclusions to those espoused by the Connecticut Superior Court in response to Taylor's and Miller's accommodations—they would not go so far as to opine that Obeah was not a religion, but they would declare that some of its practices were not protected by religious freedom.

A. *The* Queen v. Rowe *Case*

This case began in January 1999, when Jamaican-born cousins Marlin Rowe and Dwayne Lawes, along with their accomplices Dain Campbell and

"Brownman," robbed a Toronto bank. During the process of the robbery, Rowe shot and killed a bank teller named Nancy Kidd. Rowe and his accomplices were apprehended after another Caribbean immigrant, Rhyll Carty, pretended to be their spiritual advisor and then reported their confidential communications to the police. The litigation that ensued over the admissibility of Carty's evidence revealed the limitations of the protection of Jamaican spiritual practices in Canada.[26]

In 1998, prior to the bank robbery, Rowe and Lawes solicited Carty's assistance in circumventing arrest and prosecution for their planned criminal activities. Carty was a self-described "spiritualist" and "psychic counsellor" who had a reputation in the Toronto Jamaican community as an Obeah practitioner.[27] He owned a shop in Toronto called O'Shanti's Herbal Store, the sign for which advertised it as a location that provided counseling services as well as sold religious articles, candles, and herbs. Carty's primary source of income came from "performing 'psychic' or 'spiritual' readings for clients from the Caribbean community."[28]

Rowe and Lawes became aware of Carty's reputation as an Obeah practitioner through Rowe's friend, Jacqueline Thompson, and Rowe's aunt, Sonia Gallimore, both of whom were Carty's regular clients. The latter introduced Rowe and Lawes to Carty, and they quickly inquired about his services. They told Carty that they were bank robbers and promised to pay him a substantial sum of money if he could help them evade the authorities.

Over the following weeks, Rowe and Lawes met with Carty twice, first at his shop and then at Gallimore's home. They detailed their plans for the robbery and renewed their requests for spiritual protection for their illegal activities. Whether Carty provided them with any "protection" services at this time is unclear, but he reportedly admonished Rowe and Lawes not to do anything "crazy or stupid" and threatened to turn them in to the police if anyone got hurt as a result of their crimes.[29]

On January 11, 1999, Rowe, Lawes, and their accomplices carried out their plans to rob a Toronto bank. Within forty-eight hours, Carty learned of the robbery and reported his knowledge about the crime to the police. In exchange for payment as a police agent and a $200,000 reward, Carty agreed to help the authorities in their investigation. He allowed the police to set up equipment to record his phone conversations and the activities in his shop, then he contacted Rowe and arranged a meeting to discuss how he could help them. Lawes and "Brownman" had already fled to Jamaica,[30] but Carty convinced Rowe and Campbell that he could assist them in evading the authorities.

Carty instructed Rowe and Campbell to each place an egg inside a black sock, knot it twice, and then bring the socks with them to Carty's shop later that evening. When they arrived, Carty, who had donned a bulletproof vest under priestly robes for the ceremony, explained that for him to properly "protect" them, Rowe and Campbell would have to divulge all the details of their participation in the crime. Rowe described the guns they had used in the robbery and confessed that he, not realizing the safety on his weapon was off, had accidentally shot the bank teller, Nancy Kidd. Additionally, Rowe described the stolen minivan that they had used as a getaway car and informed Carty where they had stashed it. He and Campbell also paid Carty a fee of $3,000 for his spiritual services, taken out of the proceeds of the robbery.[31]

After Carty helped them build a case against his "clients," the police arrested Rowe and Campbell and charged them with bank robbery. Carty was called as a witness for the prosecution, and he testified about what Rowe and Campbell had admitted to him during the Obeah rituals. As the police had collected little other evidence against the defendants, Carty's testimony was a central part of the prosecution's case.[32] Rowe was particularly aggrieved by Carty's subterfuge because, prior to his admission to Carty, the police had not known which of the four had shot the bank teller. Based on his confession, Rowe was also charged with first-degree murder.

Rowe objected to Carty's evidence against him at trial, arguing that the statements he made to Carty were inadmissible for two interrelated reasons. First and foremost, Rowe claimed that his communications with Carty were part of a religious exchange that should be protected by the special privilege that often safeguards confidential communications with spiritual advisors. If not shielded by religious privilege, then Rowe argued that Carty's ruse constituted a "dirty trick"—that it transgressed the boundaries of permissible deceptions that the police and their agents may employ in solving a crime. The trial and appellate courts found against Rowe on both challenges, determining that the defendants' interactions with Carty represented "a corrupt criminal relationship, not a legitimate relationship between a religious practitioner and a penitent."[33] Ultimately, based largely on the introduction of Carty's evidence, Rowe was found guilty of first-degree murder, and both men were convicted of robbery.

B. The Queen v. Welsh Case

As Rowe's case was making its way through appellate courts, Canadian police officers decided to employ similar tactics to solve a series of homicides that occurred in 2003 and 2004, and that were suspected to have involved Jamaican immigrants. These murders began in December 2003, when a man named Adrian Baptiste was found dead in Youhan Oraha's car.[34] Several months later, Shemaul Cunningham was killed, and police suspected that Oraha had committed this murder in retaliation against those who had shot Baptiste. When Oraha himself was gunned down by multiple assailants about one month after Cunningham's death, police believed that the individuals who murdered Oraha were part of this cycle of violence. They suspected that two Jamaican-Canadian brothers, Evol Robinson and Jahmar Welsh, were involved because Cunningham had been the latter's best friend.

Lacking sufficient evidence to prosecute anyone for Oraha's murder, a Jamaican-Canadian police officer named Andrew Cooper employed an elaborate scheme to obtain Robinson's and Welsh's confessions. After the authorities learned that their mother, Colette Robinson, believed in spirits and thought the ghost of Cunningham was still around her, Cooper posed as an Obeah practitioner and befriended her. Going by the name "Leon," Cooper convinced Ms. Robinson that she and her sons were being haunted by an evil spirit (Oraha), who was in conflict with a good spirit (Cunningham). Cooper insisted that he could protect them, but only if they confessed what they had done to anger the malevolent ghost. To this purported end, he met with Ms. Robinson over the course of four months and had ten meetings with her son Evol and two with Welsh's friend Reuben Pinnock. The police secretly taped these sessions, as well as Cooper's phone calls with Ms. Robinson and the suspects, to be presented as evidence against them at trial.[35]

From their first meeting, Cooper's interactions with Ms. Robinson, Evol Robinson, and Reuben Pinnock were infused with detailed deceptions meant to convince the suspects of his powers and thus encourage the disclosure of their involvement in Oraha's murder. Cooper initiated his relationship with Ms. Robinson by staging an accident between his car and hers. When he introduced himself, he claimed he felt a "vibe" from her and offered to pay for the damage to her vehicle. Several meetings followed the accident, and Cooper warned Ms. Robinson that a vengeful spirit surrounded her and this spirit was capable of manipulating police officers and judges.[36]

After Cooper began performing rituals for Ms. Robinson, he had his fellow officers place a dead crow on Ms. Robinson's doorstep. Cooper told her that the crow died because of the protection spell he had performed for her. Later, Cooper asked another police officer to pull Ms. Robinson over for a traffic stop. To illustrate the purported power of a handkerchief he had provided to keep her out of trouble with the police, Cooper arranged for this officer to pretend to become ill when he approached her and release Ms. Robinson without citation.

Once he finally convinced Ms. Robinson and the suspects of his powers, Cooper persuaded Evol Robinson and Reuben Pinnock to take him to the scene of the crime, claiming that in order to protect them from the evil spirit, he needed to go where it was created. They took him to where Oraha was murdered and confessed to being present at the time of his death but insisted that was the extent of their involvement. Frustrated by the limited confessions, Cooper had Ms. Robinson arrested and convinced her son Evol that her detention was brought about by Oraha's spirit. Cooper insisted that the spirit was escalating, and that Evol needed to be more forthcoming about what he had done to anger it so that Cooper could protect him from being arrested as well. Under this pressure, Evol admitted his involvement in Oraha's death and also implicated his brother Welsh and several other accomplices.

Soon thereafter, Welsh, Robinson, and Pinnock were arrested and charged with first-degree murder. At trial, Robinson and Pinnock raised similar arguments about the inadmissibility of the statements they made to Cooper as Rowe had made about his interactions with Carty. They contended that they had viewed Cooper as a religious advisor; therefore, their statements to him were protected by common law privilege and his deception violated their charter rights to freedom of religion. They further asserted that Cooper's actions constituted obtaining evidence through a "dirty trick." The Court of Appeal for Ontario once again determined that the Obeah exchanges were not protected by religious privilege and that the police's interest in catching criminals outweighed any harm caused by their deception.

C. Rowe, Welsh, and Freedom of Religion in Canada

When read together, these cases provide important insights into the boundaries of religious freedom for devotees of African diaspora religions in Canada. The problems began with the statements that Carty and the officers made to justify these ruses. Although Carty had been operating as a self-described "spiritualist" and had been profiting off his reputation as an Obeah practitioner, he denigrated his own practice as a nonreligious ruse. According to the appellate court, Carty "conceded that he had no genuine spiritual powers and that he could be described as a 'con man and a charlatan' because he misled his clients into believing otherwise."[37] The police used similar language when they laid out their plan to have Cooper pose as an Obeah practitioner to gain more evidence against Welsh and Robinson. Detective Sergeant Jarvis, who had worked on the *Rowe* case and, based on this experience, had constructed the Obeah ruse used in *Welsh*, explained "that he thought that Obeah was not a religion but a form of witchcraft or voodoo and that he would not use a similar operation for an established religion."[38] Cooper, the Jamaican-Canadian police officer who carried out Jarvis's scheme, also indicated that he regarded Obeah as a type of "voodoo and witchcraft."[39] Even in official police records, the officers noted that the *Merriam-Webster* dictionary definition of Obeah was "the use of sorcery and magic ritual" in the Caribbean and described their plan, stating "the undercover officer will explore the named person's willingness to use *sorcery* to fight the police and the judiciary."[40] By contrast, the trial and appellate court rulings did not categorically deny African diaspora belief systems the status of "religion"; however, they determined that certain practices were essentially secular and not entitled to the constitutional and statutory protections that shield religious actors from excessive governmental intrusions.

Rowe appears to have been the first case in which Canadian courts were asked to determine whether the Afro-Caribbean spiritual practices known as "Obeah" satisfied the legal definition of "religion." Therefore, the defense hired a Catholic priest, Father Thomas Lynch, as well as two professors of religious studies, Dr. Abrahim Khan and Dr. Frederick Case, who testified as to the religious nature of the Obeah sessions. On cross-examination, however, the prosecution forced the experts to admit several significant distinctions between recognized religions and these Obeah rites, including the offering of protection from arrest, charging a fee for spiritual services (particularly one collected from the proceeds of a crime), and the absence of repentance. Therefore, the trial judge determined, and the Court of Appeal agreed, that while Obeah might be a recognized religion, these specific exchanges were not "religious." As such, the defendants' sessions with Carty were not confidential religious exchanges.

Unlike *Rowe*, where the judges' rulings centered on the inconsistencies in the experts' arguments that Obeah was comparable to recognized religions, the trial judge in *Welsh* analyzed the defendants' exchanges with Cooper under a four-prong test used to determine whether religious communications are protected by privilege. The first two elements pertained to the confidentiality of the exchanges; the third was that the relationship is one that "in the opinion of the community ought to be sedulously *fostered*," and fourth was that the injury to the relationship from disclosing the communications must be greater than the benefit derived from "the correct disposal of litigation."[41] While the trial judge did not dispute the centrality of confidentiality between an Obeah practitioner and their client, he found that it failed the third prong of the test because their purpose in consulting "Leon" (Cooper) was to "obstruct law enforcement officials and the judiciary from prosecuting them," and the judge believed there was no community interest in allowing them to avoid penalties for their crimes.[42] This same reasoning also led the judge to find that the fourth prong was not satisfied; he believed that the harm in excluding the evidence and letting the defendants go free was greater than any damage to the relationship between Obeah practitioners and their clients.[43] Therefore in *Welsh*, as in *Rowe*, the determination that Obeah rituals were not privileged religious exchanges hinged on the fact that, unlike practitioners of mainstream religions, the defendants had not consulted a spiritual advisor to cleanse them of their "sins" but rather to avoid the legal consequences of their actions. In each case, the courts ruled that these communications were not "religious" or were not the type of spiritual interactions that were intended to be shielded when the concept of religious privilege was established.

The courts' determination that police agents and officers posing as Obeah practitioners was a valid method of obtaining evidence followed the same line of reasoning. The analysis was based on *Rothman*, a 1981 case in which the Supreme Court of Canada determined that police were entitled to use some deceit to further their investigation but that evidence obtained through "dirty tricks" was not admissible at trial. The justices had explained that "conduct on their part that shocks the community" would render a police tactic a "dirty trick."[44] They provided a series of examples of such "shocking" behavior, including "a police officer pretend[ing] to be a lock-up chaplain and hear a suspect's confession."[45] The defendants in *Rowe* and *Welsh* argued that employing a police officer or agent to pretend to perform Obeah rituals on their behalf was analogous to pretending to be a chaplain to take a suspect's confession, and thus constituted a "dirty trick."

In both cases, the Court of Appeal for Ontario disagreed. The judges determined that while these situations shared some superficial similarities to the example cited in *Rothman* of pretending to be a lock-up priest to take a suspect's confession, the defendants' purpose in consulting an Obeah practitioner rendered an otherwise religious exchange secular. The court explained that the *Rothman* example "presumes the sincerity of the religious belief of the penitent" who intends "the use of the confessional as a means of helping people overcome their errors by forgiving their sins."[46] As with the question of the applicability of religious privilege, the ruling hinged on the fact that the court viewed consulting a spiritual advisor to get away with a crime or rid oneself of an evil spirit as a secular activity that was significantly different from confessing one's "sins" to seek absolution from god.[47]

The Court of Appeal also emphasized that their determination that police could pretend to be an Obeah practitioner had no bearing on other circumstances where an officer posed as a religious advisor. The judges indicated that these Obeah ruses were the only case of this kind that they were aware of, and that "the police must proceed with the utmost caution" when dealing with religious freedom. They explained that the *Welsh* ruling does not mean "that the police are entitled to pose as religious advisers and expect that statements obtained from religiously-motivated suspects will be admitted."[48] They clarified that "in cases where suspects have sincere religious beliefs and seek counselling from a supposed religious adviser for non-corrupt religious reasons, the result could well be different."[49]

The courts' decisions in *Rowe* and *Welsh* demonstrate a very limited protection of African diaspora religions. The judges assumed that a religion must be centered on a belief in a dichotomy between good and evil, as well as grounded in the idea that a faithful adherent would only use religion for ethical purposes such as confession and absolution. Obeah, on the other hand, is based on the African-derived premise that supernatural forces and beings, as well as the priests or adepts who interact with them, are neither exclusively good nor evil and can be appealed to for any desired end.[50] One of the most common functions of Obeah practitioners is to assist their clients with their legal woes, including preventing arrest and impeding prosecution.[51] Thus, in ruling that some of the most central Obeah rituals were not protected by religious privilege or shielded from police intervention, the Court of Appeal carved out a very narrow definition of "religion" and left practitioners of this African diaspora faith more vulnerable to state infringements on their rights than adherents of other belief systems.

These Obeah cases therefore represent similar patterns to those heard in the United States about whether Obeah and Santeria were religions. The police officers and prosecutors have contended that African diaspora religions are all "Voodoo" or "witchcraft," which they regard as the antithesis of religion. Additionally, courts have focused on the issue of morality—how the religion is used and what its central function is. In the case of African diaspora faiths, spirits and spiritual power are neither entirely "good" nor "evil"; therefore, they can be deployed in circumstances that are meant to protect criminal activity and harm others as well as to protect a community and promote positive change. The potential (or perceived prevalence) of harmful or dangerous rituals has led courts to deny their protection as religious practices.

PART III: BRAZIL

A judge in Brazil also recently declared that African diaspora faiths are not religions. This case emerged under slightly different circumstances than those in Canada and the United States, centering on a civil rather than criminal controversy. However, the rationale that the judge gave resembled those in Duncan's case because he dissected the components of Afro-Brazilian faiths and singled out certain aspects that undermined their recognition as religions. Furthermore, this case, when set in its broader context, reflects once more on the relationship between criminality, race, and religious freedom.

The case began in 2009, when the Universal Church of the Kingdom of God (a Pentecostal Church founded in Rio de Janeiro more than forty years ago) posted videos on YouTube that associated Afro-Brazilian religions with witchcraft and criminal activity, and encouraged their followers to join together to help shut down Afro-Brazilian temples.[52] The Associação Nacional de Mídia Afro (an organization dedicated to freedom of expression and the dissemination of information about Afro-Brazilian culture and traditions) went to the Federal Public Prosecutor (Ministério Público Federal) to report that these videos were discriminatory against African-derived religions and violated Brazilian law. After a public hearing to evaluate the claims, the federal prosecutor demanded that Google Brasil, the owner of YouTube, remove the intolerant and discriminatory videos.[53] Google Brasil responded that they would not remove the videos because they did not violate any company policies. The federal prosecutor then filed a lawsuit pursuant to a 2014 statute that allows them to seek an injunction on an activity to avoid harm to the dignity of a racial, ethnic, or religious group.[54] The federal prosecutor demanded that the videos be removed from the internet within seventy-two hours, and that Google be fined R$500,000 per day if it didn't comply.[55] They also asked that Google provide the IP address of the computers that were used to upload the videos as well as the date, time, and place that they were posted.

On April 28, 2014, Eugenio Rosa de Araujo, a federal court judge in Rio de Janeiro, rejected the ministry's request to remove the videos.[56] He explained that, in theory, the case before him involved a dispute between three fundamental rights—freedom of religion, freedom of assembly, and freedom of expression. However, De Araujo opined that freedom of religion was not at issue in this case because Afro-Brazilian faiths such as Candomblé and Umbanda were not "religions," as they have no central text analogous to the bible or Qur'an, no hierarchal structure, and no singular concept of god.[57] In terms of the right to assemble, De Araujo argued that there was no evidence that Afro-Brazilian "cultural practices," which are centuries old and "deeply rooted in Brazilian collective culture," would be put in jeopardy because of the videos.[58] Therefore, he saw no reason to order the removal of videos denigrating them.

Numerous Brazilian newspapers and several international presses picked up the story about Judge De Araujo's decision, many of whom criticized his opinion that Candomblé and Umbanda were not "religions" deserving of protection under Brazilian law. The following month, on May 20, 2014, De Araujo issued a clarification in which he backpedaled slightly on his assessment that Afro-Brazilian faiths were not religions but reaffirmed his ruling.[59] He averred that the strong backlash to his decision clearly demonstrated that there is no real threat that these "cults" would become extinct because of the Universal Church's videos. He emphasized that this case was really about the freedom of expression of the Universal Church and their right to post these videos.

The following week, the National Committee on Respect for Religious Diversity (O Comitê Nacional de Respeito à Diversidade Religiosa) issued a public notice criticizing De Araujo's decision.[60] They argued that, despite the partial retraction of De Araujo's decision that Afro-Brazilian faiths are not religions, his assessments of these belief systems showed the necessity for further work in the area of religious freedom and diversity. The committee also stressed that, contrary to De Araujo's decision, hate speech is not protected under the right to free expression.

The federal prosecutor appealed De Araujo's decision to the Second Region Federal Tribunal. Like De Araujo, the tribunal also held that this case was about a conflict between freedom of religion and freedom of expression. However, rather than finding that Afro-Brazilian faiths did not fall within the boundaries of "religion," the tribunal determined that the Universal Church's recordings were hate speech and did not fall within the boundaries of protectable speech.[61] They explained that the right to freedom of expression is restricted and does not permit the rightholder to denigrate, insult, and defame others.[62] The tribunal opined that the same principle holds true for the Universal Church's right to freedom of religion, which does not include the right to offend persons of other religions. On the contrary, the tribunal ruled, the right to freedom of religion in a plural society such as Brazil requires a broad, encompassing definition of religion and requires that all belief systems be respected. In addition to the constitutional principles of freedom of expression and freedom of religion, the tribunal discussed Articles 24 and 26 of Law No. 12,288 of July 20, 2010, which guarantee Afro-Brazilian religions the right to free exercise and provide the Public Prosecutor's Office with the authority to take necessary measures to curb intolerance against these faiths, including restricting media that expresses hatred toward Afro-Brazilian religions.

Based on these constitutional principles and Law No. 12,288, the tribunal reversed De Araujo's decision. The tribunal ordered the immediate removal of the videos from YouTube, noting that every day they remained posted, they promoted discrimination, violence, and intolerance among the unlimited number of people who had access to view them.[63] However, it reduced the fine for noncompliance from the R$500,000 per day demanded by the prosecutor to R$50,000 per day, finding that the latter was more proportionate to the offense while still being sufficiently coercive to ensure compliance.[64] They also ordered Google Brasil to maintain the data on the date, time, location, and IP numbers of the computers used to post the videos until a future decision was reached about whether they were obligated to disclose this information.

Although this case ultimately had a positive result, it is important to acknowledge that Afro-Brazilian religions were doubly victimized in these proceedings—first by the posting of the offensive materials on YouTube and second by Judge De Araujo's declaration that these faiths were not religions.[65] Such statements by a judge cannot help but destroy confidence in the legal system and further discourage devotees from reporting violations of their rights. This decision would have been particularly harmful in the midst of evangelicals committing exactly the kinds of physical violence against Afro-Brazilian religions that the videos in question promoted.

As discussed in chapter 1, by 2014, when De Araujo issued his decision finding that Afro-Brazilian "cults" were not "religions," intolerance against these faiths had already become a serious problem. In September 2013, media reports surfaced that drug traffickers had expelled forty Candomblé priests from their communities in Rio de Janeiro, and that they had prohibited other followers from wearing attire associated with Afro-Brazilian religions.[66] Additionally, the UN Working Group of Experts on People of African Descent's visit to Brazil in December 2013—just five months before De Araujo's decision—led them to "voice ... concern about the racism, persecution and violations of cultural rights and the right to religious freedom suffered by the religious communities of African origin, such as *Candomblé* and *Umbanda*."[67] In 2014, the year that De Araujo determined that Afro-Brazilian religions were under no threat, "the Secretariat of Human Rights received 42 complaints of discrimination, ranging from discrimination to physical violence, against adherents of African-originated religions."[68]

Due to a series of well-known court cases that preceded the one that came before him, De Araujo almost certainly would have known that evangelical churches were motivating the intolerance against Afro-Brazilian faiths by posting discriminatory videos about them and encouraging their followers to attack devotees. In 2008, four evangelicals from the Geração Jesus Cristo Church invaded and vandalized an Umbanda Center in Catete, Rio de Janeiro, screaming that this Afro-Brazilian temple belonged to the devil.[69] They caused R$20,000 in damages. Shortly thereafter, the leader of the church, Tupirani da Hora Lores, was charged with religious intolerance, insult, and incitement to crime after he authorized one of those same congregants to post videos of Tupirani using similar language to disparage Afro-Brazilian religions and other faiths.[70] Tupirani's highly publicized trial was the first prosecution for religious intolerance in the nation.

Similarly, in March 2014, just one month before De Araujo's decision, the Supreme Federal Tribunal of Brazil opened an investigation into whether Marco Feliciano, an evangelical pastor and then-president of the Federal Human Rights and Minorities Commission, had incited religious intolerance in derogatory videos about Afro-Brazilian faiths.[71] In a televised broadcast of a church service, Feliciano predicted or prophesied the "burial" ("sepultamento") of Afro-Brazilian priests ("pais de santo") and the closure ("fechamento") of Afro-Brazilian temples (which he derogatorily referred to as "macumba" [sorcery] terreiros).[72] Despite these well-known controversies, De Araujo not only ruled that Afro-Brazilian "matrixes" were not protected by laws barring discrimination against "religions," but he also explicitly asserted that these "belief systems" were not threatened by videos depicting devotees as sorcerers and criminals and encouraging attacks against them.

PART IV: CONCLUSION

Each of these decisions about whether Africana faiths are "religions" is grounded in complicated and intersecting debates about the boundaries of religious freedom. For instance, the Canadian decisions finding that Obeah rituals were not legally protected because they were for "corrupt" purposes is rooted in long-standing disputes about whether and to what degree a state can limit the free exercise of religion in the interest of public order. The Brazilian and US debates about whether "religions" must have certain "accoutrements," such as a sacred text and a centralized hierarchy, are an extension of the complex discussions about racial bias in Western notions of the definition of "religion." Similarly, all of these decisions are in conversation with the immense body of global debates, both in scholarship and case law, about the boundaries between "religion" and practices that are secular, "non-religious," or "spiritual but not religious," and whether the same rights extend to beliefs or practices in all of these categories.

While much could be said about how each of these individual cases fit within these conversations, perhaps the most significant trend is revealed when they are read as a whole. When one compares each case in this chapter to the others, it becomes clear that they are different in nearly every way. The type of proceedings vary from a civil dispute about defamatory videos to a petition for religious accommodations in prison. The rituals at issue also range greatly, from the right to communicate with spirits of departed persons to the freedom to make certain offerings to a spirit or deity. Even the official status of the faiths in question is significantly different, extending from Obeah, which remains prohibited by law in many countries, to Santeria/Lucumi, which has been recognized as a religion by the US Supreme Court.

Amid all these vast distinctions, there is at least one common thread between all five cases that helps elucidate why police, prosecutors, judges, and other officials keep returning to the same idea that African diaspora faiths are not protected religions. That shared element is the lingering biases and presumptions about the purported special links between African-derived religions and criminality. The idea that Africana religions are inherently dangerous led a US court to deny inmates even seemingly benign accommodations such as parchment paper or incense. Similar notions led US prosecutors to argue that a Santeria devotee would use the twenty-year-old rusted gun from a religious shrine to further his drug trade and led a Canadian police officer to pose as an Obeah practitioner to perform fraudulent ceremonies even when courts have expressly forbidden pretending to be a Catholic priest and taking confession.

In part, these biased perceptions about the relationship between criminality and African-derived religions are concerning because they resemble ideas from the turn of the twentieth century—the height of the proscription and prosecution of African-derived faiths. However, De Araujo's ruling reminds us that much more is at stake than just the legal rights of devotees when they have been accused of a crime or are already in prison. The presumption that African-derived and other minority religions are "narco-cults" and have a particular predisposition to criminal behavior leads to the inverse assumption that more mainstream religions do not have these tendencies. Therefore, as one can see in this case of De Araujo's decision to uphold the "religious freedom" of an evangelical church to denigrate and encourage violence against Afro-Brazilian faiths, these biases also severely undermine the ability to recognize Evangelized drug traffickers and other Christian extremists as the meaningful threat that they represent to devotees of African-derived religions.

CHAPTER 9

Myths of African Diaspora Religions
Rumors and Religious Freedom

In October 2017, thirty-one-year-old Brandon Evans of Hollywood, Florida, stabbed his pit bull, Ollie, thirty-seven times, then stuffed in him a suitcase and left him to die.[1] After police received a 911 tip, they located the dog and rushed him to an animal hospital, but Ollie did not survive. When the officers searched Evans's apartment, they discovered animal blood and body parts from rats and cats throughout the residence. When police arrested Evans for animal cruelty, he responded that he was a "voodoo priest" who "had a right to kill animals in the name of voodoo."[2]

Evans, who is described on his booking sheet as a five-foot, ten-inch white male with brown hair and blue eyes, had no known affiliation with any Vodou or Voodoo communities. Authorities did not mention any shrines or other religious paraphernalia in or around Evans's home in their reports that would support his claims to be a "voodoo priest." Moreover, Evans's brutal stabbing and dismembering of rats, cats, and dogs is inconsistent with animal sacrifice in African diaspora religions, as the latter is done swiftly, is designed to limit the animal's suffering, and is typically restricted to farm animals. However, like Robert Harris's insane ravings about killing his tenant as a sacrifice to Allah in the 1930s, media reports of Evans's case often identified him as a "voodoo priest" and/or a practitioner of Afro-Caribbean religions.[3]

Evans's case is not unique. In the past twenty years, there have been countless instances in which a person or group of people have committed a (often violent) crime and attributed it to an African diaspora faith. After the perpetrators or investigators allege some ritual motive, facts often arise that quickly contradict these theories. However, the media generally ignores these revelations and continues to attribute the crimes to Afro-diaspora religious beliefs. At times, when such sensationalized cases surface, it is difficult to dismiss the crimes as completely unrelated to the cultures and religions to which they are attributed. When defendants originate from a nation or region where belief in certain supernatural practices is common, sometimes mental illness can lead that individual to distort or abuse principles or practices that exist in African diaspora religions. However, when the reports of these isolated or unusual practices reach the authorities and the media, they conflate it with an entire religious community or belief system. These cases contribute to prejudice against African diaspora belief systems and often lead to vocal backlash against actual devotees.

PART I: PAULA ALBRITTON AND JIMMIE LEE CLARK

In June 1997, a seventy-year-old African American man named Willie Sutton died of natural causes in Bradenton, Florida.[4] After the county medical examiner conducted an autopsy to determine the cause of death, Sutton's body was sent to Green's Funeral Home through a county-run program that assisted with the burial or cremation costs of deceased persons who had no representative or next of kin.[5] Five months later, Sutton's severed hand was discovered near the Manatee River, lying next to "a bag containing two clay pots and some decorative rocks."[6]

Once fingerprint analysis revealed that the hand belonged to Sutton, local authorities exhumed his body from the cemetery.[7] They discovered that his left hand was missing and that there were twelve "Voodoo" dolls inside his chest cavity.[8] There were pieces of paper pinned to the back of each of the dolls, some of which contained the names of local funeral directors as well as the soon-to-be ex-husband of Paula Albritton, the owner of Green's Funeral Home.[9]

On June 26 and 27, 1998, the police conducted videotaped interviews of Albritton, wherein she admitted to placing the dolls inside Sutton's body. She explained that each doll "represented a matter that was troubling to" her.[10] She referred to herself as a "Voodooist" and claimed that she had placed the names of her competitors on these dolls inside the body based on the belief that as the body decomposed, her competitors' businesses would likewise crumble.[11] She asked Sutton's spirit for assistance with these issues as a method of "bringing peace to Mr. Sutton's spirit," who, Albritton averred, "protected the business because his spirit had nowhere to go."[12] Albritton also confessed that she, with the assistance of her adult son, used a scalpel to sever Sutton's left hand. The pair said an "incantation," then threw the hand in the river in a ritual that Albritton described as "religious voodoo."[13]

Immediately after making these confessions, detectives arrested Albritton and charged her with mutilating or "grossly abusing" a dead human body—a second-degree felony punishable by up to fifteen years' imprisonment and a fine of $10,000. The following day, police also issued an arrest warrant for Albritton's son, Jimmie Lee Clark III, for the same offense. On November 25, 1998, Clark plead nolo contendere to the charges (a plea where the defendant neither admits guilt nor asserts innocence but states that they will not contest the charges and will accept the punishment for the offense). The judge sentenced him to eleven months and twenty-nine days in county jail and ordered him to pay $451.00 in court costs and fees.[14]

Paula Albritton's trial commenced on March 2, 1999. Albritton changed her story at trial, testifying that she invented the account about the religious ritual to protect her son, who had actually placed the dolls inside Sutton's body and cut off Sutton's hand. Albritton contended that an investigating officer had given her the idea to attribute the ritual to "Voodoo" when he told her that if she had performed these acts as a component of a religious practice, then her constitutional rights would protect her from prosecution.[15] Her son, Jimmie Lee Clark, corroborated her testimony. He claimed that he had been hearing voices since he was a young teenager, and that the voices told him to perform these acts.

Albritton's attorney also filed a motion to suppress the videotapes of her confessions, on the grounds that they were involuntary statements induced by the detective's promises that she would not be prosecuted if her actions were part of a religious practice. Albritton characterized her confession as involuntary (and thus inadmissible at trial), claiming that she only confessed "because she thought that what she was confessing to was legal and she could not be prosecuted."[16] She reported that she would not have made the statements she had if the detective had not told her that such rituals, if done for religious reasons, would be shielded by the constitution.

The trial court denied Albritton's motion and the prosecution proceeded to play these videos for the jury. The jury found Albritton guilty, and Judge Marc Gilner sentenced her to eleven months and twenty-nine days in county jail and five years on probation. He also fined Albritton $2,205—$1,319 in restitution to the City of Bradenton, $475 in restitution to Shannon Funeral Home (presumably the facility responsible for Sutton's second burial), $261 to cover court costs, and a $150 court facility fee.[17]

Albritton appealed her conviction, focusing on the argument that the videotaped confession was inadmissible. The District Court of Appeals agreed, finding that the detective had made an implied promise that Albritton would not be prosecuted if she confessed that her actions were part of a religious ritual, and that Albritton would not have confessed if the detective had not made this promise. For these reasons, the District Court reversed her conviction and remanded the case for a new trial without the videotaped confessions. On November 3, 2000, the trial court received the appellate court's decision and instructions; within a month, the prosecutor filed a nolle prosequi, or a notice that the state no longer planned to prosecute the case.[18]

Ultimately, Albritton was successful in escaping prosecution for abuse of a corpse because of the prosecutor's promise of religious freedom and due to her lie that her actions were part of her "Voodoo" beliefs. However, in the public eye, Voodoo adherents would continue to take the fall for her nonreligious crimes. For example, shortly after Albritton's arrest, the *Sarasota Herald-Tribune* published a story titled "Funeral Home Investigation; Expert's Report Confirms Ritual Was Voodoo Practice."[19] The author, Kellie McMaster, claimed that "the Bradenton Police Department received a 2 1/2-page report from Rafael Martinez, a Miami anthropologist who wrote his doctoral thesis on 'Voodooism' and who often works with the Miami-Dade Medical Examiner's Office on body desecration cases."[20] McMaster quotes Martinez, who allegedly reported that Albritton "was performing some type of black or malevolent magic based on the Voodoo religion."[21]

Even after Albritton confessed to fabricating her claims to be a Voodoo devotee, newspapers across the country continued to cover this story as if Albritton was engaging in rituals common among practitioners. For example, at the end of Albritton's trial, wherein her defense was that she made up the entire account, the *Los Angeles Times* published an article under the title "Mortician Guilty of Abusing Body," in which the author reported that Albittron had been found "guilty of abusing a human body after she cut the hand from a corpse as part of a voodoo ritual."[22] Shortly thereafter, in 1999, the HBO series *Autopsy* featured a story about Albritton titled "The Case of the Severed Hand," which depicted her actions as "black magic" and "Voodoo."[23] Even as late as 2004, the *Herald-Tribune* of Sarasota, Florida, ran a story titled "Revisiting a Bizarre Case," in which the staff writers merely recounted that Albritton had been convicted of putting Voodoo dolls, "apparently effigies of other funeral home owners and her ex-husband" inside Sutton's chest.[24] The writers noted that her conviction was overturned on appeal but never mentioned that the entire claim was fabricated to protect her son, who heard "voices."

PART II: MARIE LAURADIN (2011)

In 2011, Marie Lauradin, a Haitian-American woman living in New York, severely disfigured her six-year-old daughter, Frantzcia Saintil, in an act that authorities and the media unquestionably depicted as "Voodoo."[25] Lauradin believed that her child was possessed by demons. Therefore, she took off the child's clothes, poured accelerants over her head, and set her on fire. Although the child suffered severe burns, Lauradin waited twenty-four hours before seeking medical assistance.

When authorities arrested Lauradin, she changed her story three times. Initially, Lauradin reported that she had accidentally spilled boiling water on the child. Later, she claimed that she had been applying rubbing alcohol to ease her daughter's fever and that a poorly placed candle had fallen, igniting the alcohol.[26] Finally, when she was brought before the Supreme Court judge, Lauradin reported that her daughter was burned during a "Voodoo"ritual known as "loa."[27]

After hearing Lauradin's admission that the burns happened during a supposed Voodoo cleansing ritual, Judge Richard Buchter sentenced Lauradin to seventeen years' imprisonment. He referred to the purported Voodoo ritual as "an unspeakable act of savagery" that he did not believe was accidental.[28] He also sentenced Lauradin's mother, who knew about the burns but did not immediately take her granddaughter to the hospital, to one to three years' imprisonment for reckless assault.[29] The media stressed that both women could be deported once their prison terms had been served.[30]

The story was picked up by domestic media as well as newspapers across the globe, such as *Dominica News Online*, the *Sydney Morning Herald* (Australia), and the *Daily Mail* (UK), and was featured with titles like "Voodoo Child-Burning Grandma Going to Prison," "Mother Admits to Burning Child in Voodoo Ritual," and "'Voodoo Mum' Sentenced to 17 Years Behind Bars for Setting Fire to Six-Year-Old Daughter in Exorcism Ritual."[31] An article appearing in the *Queens Chronicle* titled "Voodoo Child-Burning Grandma Going to Prison" seemed to even suggest that a religious defense had been raised in the case, beginning "Voodoo ritual or not, standing by and watching a child burn is a crime."[32]

However, there are multiple indications that Lauradin's actions were completely unrelated to Haitian Vodou or New Orleans Voodoo. The simplest red flag in her story was that Lauradin claimed that she performed a ritual known as "loa," but this term refers to a category of spirit or divine entity, not a type of ritual. Furthermore, Lauradin claimed that the cleansing ceremony was to rid her child of "demons"; however, neither Vodou nor any of the non-Abrahamic faiths discussed in this book have devils or demons in their cosmology. Moreover, while Vodou devotees believe that spirits can possess followers, this typically takes place during religious ceremonies, occurs as the result of devotees performing rituals to call down the spirits, and it is viewed as a blessing because the spirits bring messages to enlighten adherents. Finally, there are no cleansing rituals in Vodou that involve pouring an accelerant on a follower and causing severe, permanent burns.

Despite these glaring inconsistencies, because Lauradin was from Haiti and her confession referenced actual Vodou terminology such as "loa," her crime had a negative impact on the local Vodou community. Around the time of the convictions, reporter Dan Bilefsky of the *New York Times* noted that these allegations of child abuse, as well as a recent incident where authorities claimed that a five-alarm fire in Brooklyn was caused by a "Voodoo priest" who was burning candles near a bed, "have shaken the tight-knit and largely secretive voodoo community in New York, and practitioners say they were aberrant acts perpetrated by ignorant people who were abusing the religion."[33] He quoted Dowoti Desir (Vodou priestess and former professor at Brooklyn College), who reported that although "voodoo has been a source of empowerment for generations of Haitians," following these incidents, "Voodoo practitioners are in the closet for fear of being hounded or suffering reprisals."[34]

PART III: THE MASSACHUSETTS CASES (2018)

Two other cases emerged several years later and led to a similar backlash against local devotees of African diaspora religions. In January 2018, two Haitian women in East Bridgewater, Massachusetts, fifty-one-year-old Peggy LaBossiere and forty-year-old Rachel Hilaire, were arrested for mayhem, assault, and other charges for tying up and burning a five-year-old child and threatening to decapitate the child's eight-year-old brother with a machete.[35] The children reported that the accused women blew fire into or across the girl's face and cut her arm and collarbone.[36] The girl was taken to the hospital and treated for third-degree burns that will permanently scar her face.[37]

LaBossiere and Hilaire appear to have defended themselves by stating that they did not cause the injuries or that the injuries were an accident. The sisters reported that they had performed "cleansing baths" that included prayers and rubbing a mixture of oils and sea salts on the children's bodies, something they had done for other friends and family members on previous occasions.[38] In this case, they performed this cleansing bath because the children's mother had taken her daughter to LaBossiere for spiritual treatments to exorcise a "demon" that she believed caused her to misbehave.[39] They claimed that the baths occasionally burned children as the spirits left the child's body.[40]

Although it is not clear whether the women themselves or anyone other than the mother (who was committed to a mental hospital) used the terminology "Voodoo," newspapers reported the story about the actions of these Haitian women with titles such as "East Bridgewater Women Disfigure Child in Voodoo Ritual, Say Police,"[41] "A Child Was Taken to a Voodoo Practitioner for Discipline. Police Say She Will Be Permanently Disfigured,"[42] and "Police: Child Burned in Voodoo Ritual in Massachusetts, 2 Women Charged."[43] This case even made international headlines, being picked up by several UK newspapers such as the *Business Insider* and the *Mirror*, who also referenced "Voodoo rituals" in the titles.[44]

Reporters not only used the ambiguous language "Voodoo" but specifically referenced spiritual practices in Haiti. For example, some journalists explained that "voodoo is an Afro-Caribbean religion" that has long been "a popular horror movie trope."[45] The *Washington Post* quoted former US president Bill Clinton's sensationalized description of a staged Vodou ceremony he had witnessed in Port-au-Prince, where a woman in a "frenzied state" allegedly bit the head off a live chicken.[46] The *VOA News* explained that "Voodoo is a religion that evolved in the seventeenth century when colonists brought slaves to Haiti from West Africa" and featured a photo of a skull and crossbones.[47]

Later that month, while the media was still reporting on LaBossiere and Hilaire's case, forty-three-year-old Latarsha Sanders stabbed her two sons, Edson and Lason Brito, with a kitchen knife as part of a supposed "Voodoo ritual."[48] She wrapped the boys, who were only eight and five years old, respectively, in a sheet and then left them in their beds for two days before telling a neighbor to call the police. When police investigators determined that Sanders was the murderer, she explained that she had attempted to conduct a "Voodoo ritual" with Edson, and when this ritual failed, she began stabbing Lason. The autopsy revealed that Edson had around fifty stab wounds.

It should need no explanation that stabbing children to death is not a part of Haitian Vodou nor a ritual practice in any other religion in the African diaspora. Rather, family members informed the police that Sanders suffered from mental problems and was fixated on "Voodoo" as well as the Illuminati.[49] However, the local community ignored the family's public statements about Sanders's real motive. Following this second crime, a Christian bishop held a candlelight vigil where he denounced "Voodoo" before hundreds of cheering people.[50] Local Haitian Vodou adherents gave statements to the media expressing concern about being "targeted" because of these crimes and emphasizing that the acts that these women committed were not reflective of their religious beliefs and practices.[51]

PART IV: VOODOO OATHS AND SEX TRAFFICKING (1990S–PRESENT)

These cases giving false depictions of Afro-diaspora religions are not limited to the United States. One of the most widespread false attributions of horrendous criminal acts to African diaspora religious practices has been in relation to cases of human trafficking in Western Europe. At least since the early 1990s, criminal networks have transported Nigerian women to Spain, Italy, the Netherlands, and other parts of Europe.[52] The women and the traffickers form a contract before they leave that the women will be indebted to the trafficker for the cost of the voyage and for assistance with finding employment once they arrive in Europe. Some understand that they will be working as prostitutes but do not comprehend the oppressive nature of this structure nor the full amount of their debt, which is typically about the equivalent of US$50,000.[53] The organizers of at least one major trafficking ring have administered ritual oaths to trafficking victims to bind them to their traffickers before they leave for Europe and to convince them that they will die a painful death if they abandon their service before repaying the trafficker. Then once they arrive in Europe, the madams reinforce this oath with threats of spiritual retribution.

These ritual oaths have been a common process in Nigeria, Ghana, Cameroon, and among persons of African descent in the Americas for centuries.[54] They have been used for a variety of purposes, such as swearing fidelity to a new ruler, solidifying loyalty in a war or uprising, or testing the veracity of a person's statement. However, in recent years, scholars, reporters, and human rights experts have glossed these oaths as "Voodoo" and depicted them as an unquestionably harmful practice that needs to be eradicated.[55] For instance, in October 2013, Ana Dols Garcia published a research paper for the UN High Commissioner for Refugees titled "Voodoo, Witchcraft and Human Trafficking in Europe," in which Garcia purports to examine "the misuse of voodoo to enslave women for sexual purposes."[56] Garcia describes "Voodoo" as a religion that is widespread in West Africa and explains that "ritual oaths are a practice derived from this religion."[57] Similarly, in 2014, the special rapporteur on trafficking in persons expressed the following concerns in her report about her mission to Italy: "Victims are also psychologically and spiritually coerced through voodoo oaths which make it difficult for them to denounce or give away the madams, even when they are approached by social workers or the police."[58]

The abuse of trafficked women is, of course, not a central part of any African-derived religion, including New Orleans Voodoo, Haitian Vodou, or West African Vodun. The police in the Netherlands were apparently the first ones to adopt the term "Voodoo" to describe these ritual oaths. Rijk Van Dijk explains that when the police intervened to assist the trafficked girls/women, the victims enquired about their ritual "packets" (the parcels containing cuttings of their hair, fingernails, toenails, underwear, and other items), wondering whether the police had gotten them back from the madams and traffickers. According to Van Dijk, "Almost immediately the term 'voodoo' was coined as a way of referring to the anxieties of supernatural origin the police recorded, the rituals that had supposedly taken place in relation to the girls' travel and the packets that one way or another seemed to keep them in bondage to their work as prostitutes."[59] Van Dijk averred that the term was used to "denote ... a kind of 'inauthentic' ritual, not performed on the girls' behalf, not with their own but solely with the operators' commercial interests in mind, and not performed by ritual specialists who would want to safeguard their public status and prestige. 'Voodoo' became synonymous with spiritual entrapment and with being policed through occult means by their madams and pimps in every move they made."[60]

Later, scholars made similar decisions to deploy this language of "Voodoo," although it does not appear to be the terminology used by the women and traffickers themselves. For example, in C. S. Baarda's 2016 article "Human Trafficking for Sexual Exploitation from Nigeria into Western Europe: The Role of Voodoo Rituals in the Functioning of a Criminal Network," Baarda repeatedly refers to the oaths as a "Voodoo contract" and to the place where the oaths are taken as a "Voodoo temple." However, when Baarda describes and partially transcribes a phone call between a trafficked woman and her father, they do not reference "Voodoo" but rather a place called the Ayelala shrine.[61] According to Nigerian professor Matthias Olufemi Dada Ojo, Ayelala is a "popular deity among the Yoruba people" who is known for serving a criminal justice function of "detecting and punishing offenders."[62] Ojo was exploring whether "traditional" methods of handling criminal justice, such as seeking the help of indigenous deities like Ayelala, could supplant the corrupt and foreign system presently in Nigeria.[63] Ojo describes how "Ayelala can be invoked to sanction an oath made between two parties," and that "anyone who has taken such [an] oath will not escape the punishment or sanction of a particular supernatural force or deity if the oath is broken."[64] Although Ojo mentions that the "cults of Ayelala have been infected with corrupt priests," some of whom had assisted human traffickers, nowhere in the article does Ojo connect the shrine to "Voodoo" or "Vodun," or even mention these terms to describe these oaths.[65]

Van der Watt and Kruger's recent study of the role of "juju" in human trafficking of Nigerians to South Africa further explains the problem with dubbing these oaths a type of "Voodoo." Between 2013 and 2016, these researchers conducted interviews of NGO representatives, shelter workers, victims, law enforcement officers, and even a trafficker to attempt to better understand the process by which individuals were being trafficked to South Africa for sexual exploitation.[66] They found that "the term 'juju' resonated with most of the participants, but included interchangeable references to 'witchcraft', 'voodoo', 'spirits', 'muti', 'black magic', 'demons', 'satanism' and 'curses.'"[67] They remind the reader of the ambiguity of such terms, stressing that "various sources and actors use the same concept with different interpretations of the meaning thereof."[68] They explain that the "current study has confirmed that Nigerian traffickers distort these practices and abuse the juju ceremony to effect human trafficking successfully," but stress that "cultural and religious practices are an invaluable part of the Nigerian society."[69]

PART V: CONCLUSION

This chapter has focused on the myths of brutal practices among adherents of African diaspora faiths, ranging from child abuse to sex trafficking to the meaningless mutilation of animals and corpses. All these cases share a striking similarity—isolated, bizarre incidents are characterized as central practices shared among all devotees of an African-derived faith. As the public protests of "Voodoo" in Boston and the calls for the banning of "Voodoo" in West Africa demonstrate, the atrocities of a few individuals have negative consequences for the religious freedom of many.

This book ends with this chapter on myths and misconceptions because it reveals much about the general climate of religious (in)tolerance in the African diaspora at this moment and how closely it resembles historical periods of heightened suppression. In the nineteenth and early twentieth centuries, the widespread myths about African diaspora religions were part and parcel of the continued subjugation of Black people following emancipation, and they usually preceded or accompanied official suppression of these faiths. In the twenty-first century, one cannot view the physical attacks on African diaspora religious devotees, the increasing restrictions on animal sacrifice, the continued proscription of Obeah, and bans on religious attire as separate from the rumors and misattributions that link these faiths to gruesome crimes. These continuing pervasive allegations distort the perceptions of legislators, lawyers, judges, and other decision makers, and make them more likely to regard African diaspora religions as threats to public morality and safety that need to be surveilled, suppressed, and otherwise restricted.

Conclusion
The Future of Religious Racism

As these nine chapters have illustrated, there has been a wide range of attempts to limit African diaspora religious freedom in the twenty-first century, from outright physical assaults on devotees to banning their central practices and religious attire to declaring that they are not religions. As discussed in the introduction, the first wave of attacks on African diaspora religious freedom in the eighteenth and nineteenth centuries was a product of the racialized political agendas of the time—namely, the protection/preservation of African slavery and post-emancipation efforts to whiten and "civilize" racially diverse American societies. Likewise, the new forms of discrimination against African diaspora religions cannot be viewed outside the context of racial politics in the twenty-first century.

Britain's recent disputes regarding Rastafarians and their right to wear dreadlocks in schools and other public places, for example, must be understood in the context of a wave of growing discrimination against racial minorities in the United Kingdom. In 2016, Britain voted to exit the European Union amid widespread debates and concerns about immigration. Although the vast majority of immigrants entering the United Kingdom were Eastern Europeans, the Independence Party's "Vote Leave" campaign gained support by featuring images of long lines of racial minorities waiting to enter Britain.[1] As Kehinde Andrews, a professor at Birmingham City University, explains, this imagery "was a reminder that 'immigration' is always a code word for 'race.'"[2] Andrews argued that Brexit, as this vote to leave the European Union has been dubbed, "has triggered a racial fault line that has unleashed racist violence and abuse."[3] The United Nations special rapporteur on contemporary forms of racism agreed, stating that following Brexit, there has been "growth in the acceptability of explicit racial, ethnic, and religious intolerance."[4] She reports that England and Wales recorded more than eighty thousand hate crimes between 2016 and 2017, the period leading up to and following Brexit, which was a 29 percent increase from the prior year.[5] Over 78 percent of these hate crimes were racially motivated.[6]

Brexit and the swell of hate crimes in the United Kingdom against racial and religious minorities should be viewed as an essential component of discrimination against African diaspora religions. Unlike the Americas, where people of African descent arrived hundreds of years ago through the Atlantic slave trade, most of Britain's racial diversity stems from immigration from Africa, the Caribbean, and other parts of the world over the past fifty to sixty years. While Syrian refugees may be the overt "threat" that fueled conversations about Brexit, the subtext of these concerns is about race, religion, and belonging in Britain. As the special rapporteur on contemporary forms of racism explains, both private citizens and civil servants have targeted racial and religious minorities, many of whom were regular immigrants or even British-born citizens, because of the perception that these individuals did not appear to be British nationals.[7] African diaspora religious minorities, with their dreadlocks, religious hats, and other customs that differ from mainstream British practices, are also challenging ideals about what it means to be British, and thus become targets of this nationalist, anti-foreigner political moment.

Brazil's multifaceted attacks on African diaspora religions can also be viewed as part of the changing political climate. In 2017, the famous city of Rio de Janeiro elected its first evangelical bishop as mayor, Marcelo Crivella. Within a year of his taking office, the public prosecutor filed a civil action against Crivella for administrative misconduct, on the grounds that he had already violated principles of separation of religion and state by allegedly giving excessive favors to evangelicals.[8] More significantly, in late October 2018, conservative candidate Jair Bolsonaro rather easily found a presidential victory in Brazil. Critics have described Bolsonaro as misogynistic, racist, and homophobic; he has a strong support base among the far-right and staunch evangelicals.[9] Bolsonaro has been quoted as saying that he does not have to "risk" his sons falling in love with a Black woman because they were well educated.[10] He has opposed the legally protected status of *quilombas* (communities of descendants of runaway/rebel slaves), stating that they are lazy and "do nothing";

they "don't even manage to procreate anymore."¹¹ Bolsonaro also famously said that he would prefer that his sons die rather than be homosexual.¹²

The election of these religious conservatives can be seen as central to the growing violence against devotees of Afro-Brazilian religions. It illustrates the increasing power of conservative, especially evangelical, Christians. It also increases the likelihood that the government will continue to turn a blind eye to this discrimination because their electoral base is not clamoring for religious pluralism or even tolerance.

It is also important to place discrimination against African diaspora religions within the global rise in the use of religious intolerance as a vehicle for expressing racial and national bias. For instance, over the past several years, many European nations have expressed concern about the growing number of Muslim immigrants in the region. Since the late 2000s, several European nations, including the Netherlands, Denmark, Poland, and Belgium, have introduced laws that would limit or eliminate halal slaughter of animals, thus cutting off Muslims from a key source of food.¹³ Animal sacrifice controversies in the United States, Brazil, and Venezuela should be viewed as part of this broader trend to suppress the ritual slaughter of animals as a mechanism of racial or national discrimination.

Likewise, one should understand the physical violence against African diaspora religious communities within the context of racially motivated attacks on minority religious communities, which have become an epidemic in the past five years. For instance, in 2015, a white supremacist murdered nine congregants praying at the Emanuel African Methodist Episcopal Church in Charleston, South Carolina. Two years later, in 2017, a white supremacist invaded the Islamic Cultural Centre of Quebec City, Canada, killing six people and wounding nineteen others. The following year, a white nationalist opened fire in the Tree of Life Synagogue in Pittsburgh, Pennsylvania, murdering eleven people and injuring six more. In 2019, white supremacists carried out devastating attacks on two mosques in Christchurch, New Zealand, and burned three historically Black churches in St. Landry Parish, Louisiana.

As the groundswell of conservative, racist, and nationalist sentiments sweeps across the globe, we can expect restrictions on African diaspora religions to increase. Religious racism appears in waves that coincide with more commonly recognized forms of discrimination, such as police brutality, overincarceration, housing discrimination, and voter suppression. Religious racism is arguably even more important to document and combat than other forms of racism, because religion is often at the heart of a person's identity, and suppression of religion is frequently intertwined with other issues, such as racism in the criminal justice system (chapter 6) and disparities in education (chapter 5). Like any other facet of racism, there can be no hope that discrimination against African-derived religions can be eradicated anytime soon, particularly given the current political climate in many parts of the globe. However, the first steps to improving religious freedom for devotees of African diaspora faiths are to identify, acknowledge, and study religious racism with the same fervor and frequency that we attack other forms of racial discrimination.

Notes

INTRODUCTION

1. *Queen v. Welsh*, 2013 ONCA 190.
2. Murrell, *Afro-Caribbean Religions*, 61–62; Murphy, *Working the Spirit*, 46–47; Houk, *Spirits, Blood, and Drums*, 70.
3. Murrell, *Afro-Caribbean Religions*, 62; Murphy, *Santería*, 27; Houk, *Spirits, Blood, and Drums*, 68.
4. Ramsey, *Spirits and the Law*, 58–67.
5. Murrell, *Afro-Caribbean Religions*, 66.
6. Prichard, *Where Black Rules White*, 74–101.
7. Ibid., 75.
8. Ibid., 284.
9. Ramsey, *Spirits and the Law*, 121.
10. Ibid., 148.
11. Ibid., 131.
12. Ibid., 148–49.
13. Ibid., 153.
14. Ibid., 184.
15. Murrell, *Afro-Caribbean Religions*, 66; Ramsey, *Spirits and the Law*, 200–202.
16. Johnson, "Law, Religion and 'Public Health,'" 18–19.
17. Ibid., 19.
18. Ibid., 22–23.
19. Johnson, *Secrets, Gossip, and Gods*, 84.
20. Ibid., 104.
21. Roman, *Governing Spirits*, 82–106.
22. Ibid., 83–85.
23. Ibid., 6.
24. Murrell, *Afro-Caribbean Religions*, 103–4.
25. Ibid., 105.
26. "Cult Leader Says Victim Gave Consent," *Daily Mail* (Hagerstown, MD), November 22, 1932.
27. "Called by Allah to Kill, Negro Slays Neighbor," *Nevada State Journal*, November 22, 1932; "Cult Leader Says Victim Gave Consent."
28. "Leader of Cult Called Insane," *Detroit News*, November 22, 1932.
29. "Police Guard Woman, Girl," *Daily Hawk-Eye Gazette* (Burlington, IA), January 19, 1937.
30. Boaz, "Voodoo Cult of Detroit," 25.
31. Sandoval, *Worldview, the Orichas, and Santería*, 327–29; Murrell, *Afro-Caribbean Religions*, 66.

SECTION I

1. Olmos and Paravisini-Gebert, *Creole Religions*, 117.
2. Ibid.
3. Murrell, *Afro-Caribbean Religions*, 58–59; also refer to the introduction to part III for a more detailed discussion of the concepts of "Voodoo" vs. Vodou.
4. McCarthy-Brown, "Afro-Caribbean Spirituality," 4.
5. Murrell, *Afro-Caribbean Religions*, 74.
6. Ibid., 74.
7. Ibid., 74–121.
8. McCarthy-Brown, "Afro-Caribbean Spirituality," 19.
9. Murrell, *Afro-Caribbean Religions*, 84.
10. McCarthy-Brown, "Afro-Caribbean Spirituality," 6; Olmos and Paravisini-Gebert, *Creole Religions*, 118–19.
11. Olmos and Paravisini-Gebert, *Creole Religions*, 121.
12. Ibid., 117.
13. Murrell, *Afro-Caribbean Religions*, 89; McCarthy-Brown, "Afro-Caribbean Spirituality," 11; Olmos and Paravisini-Gebert, *Creole Religions*, 117.
14. Olmos and Paravisini-Gebert, *Creole Religions*, 118–19.
15. Ibid., 159.

16. Johnson, *Secrets, Gossip, and Gods*, 12.
17. Murrell, *Afro-Caribbean Religions*, 167.
18. Ibid., 170; Voeks, "African Medicine and Magic," 54.
19. Murrell, *Afro-Caribbean Religions*, 170; Voeks, "African Medicine and Magic," 56.
20. Voeks, "African Medicine and Magic," 54.
21. Murrell, *Afro-Caribbean Religions*, 174; Voeks, "African Medicine and Magic," 63.
22. Voeks, "African Medicine and Magic," 67.
23. Johnson, *Secrets, Gossip, and Gods*, 48.
24. Hale, *Hearing the Mermaid's Song*, 3.
25. Ibid., 5.
26. Johnson, *Secrets, Gossip, and Gods*, 52.
27. Ibid., 53.
28. Ibid.
29. Ortiz, "Ogum and Umbandista Religion," 95.
30. Johnson, *Secrets, Gossip, and Gods*, 53; Murrell, *Afro-Caribbean Religions*, 188; Ortiz, "Ogum and Umbandista Religion," 91; Hale, *Hearing the Mermaid's Song*, 1.
31. Murrell, *Afro-Caribbean Religions*, 189.
32. Ibid., 97.
33. Ibid.
34. Ibid., 107–8.
35. Olmos and Paravisini-Gebert, *Creole Religions*, 70–71.
36. Ibid., 42.
37. Sandoval, *Worldview, the Orichas, and Santería*, 113.
38. Ibid., 111.
39. Murrell, *Afro-Caribbean Religions*, 136.
40. The Trans-Atlantic Slave Trade Database, "Estimates," http://www.slavevoyages.org/assessment/estimates.
41. Dodson, *Sacred Spaces*, 90.
42. Ibid., 85.
43. Ibid., 82; Olmos and Paravisini-Gebert, *Creole Religions*, 88–89.
44. Dodson, *Sacred Spaces*, 85.
45. Murrell, *Afro-Caribbean Religions*, 136.
46. Dodson, *Sacred Spaces*, 93.
47. Ibid.
48. Murrell, *Afro-Caribbean Religions*, 141.
49. Dodson, *Sacred Spaces*, 92; Olmos and Paravisini-Gebert, *Creole Religions*, 95.
50. Dodson, *Sacred Spaces*, 89.
51. Ibid., 145–46; Olmos and Paravisini-Gebert, *Creole Religions*, 85.
52. Murrell, *Afro-Caribbean Religions*, 146; Dodson, *Sacred Spaces*, 95.
53. Dodson, *Sacred Spaces*, 96.
54. Ibid., 100.
55. Murrell, *Afro-Caribbean Religions*, 147.
56. Ibid., 145.
57. Ibid. 147.
58. Ibid.
59. Olmos and Paravisini-Gebert, *Creole Religions*, 84.
60. Ibid., 84–85.
61. Report or Affidavit of Michael Atwood Mason, PhD, *Merced v. City of Euless*, No. 06CV00891 (November 27, 2007).

CHAPTER 1

1. "Líder de centro de umbanda se diz vítima de intolerância após ataque com bomba e agressão em SP," *Globo*, February 8, 2020, https://g1.globo.com/sp/ribeirao-preto-franca/noticia/2020/02/08/dona-de-centro-de-umbanda-se-diz-vitima-de-intolerancia-apos-ataque-com-bomba-e-agressao-em-sp.ghtml.
2. United Nations General Assembly, "Report of the Chair of the Working Group," ¶ 7. At that time, 43.1 percent described themselves as *pardo* (brown), 7.6 percent as *preto* (Black); 47.3 percent as *branco* (white), 2.1 percent as *amarelo* (Asian or "yellow"), and 0.3 percent as *indígenas* (indigenous).
3. Pew Research Center, "A Closer Look at How Religious Restrictions Have Risen Around the World," July 15, 2019, https://www.pewforum.org/wp-content/uploads/sites/7/2019/07/Restrictions_X_WEB_7-15_FULL-VERSION-1.pdf.
4. Ibid., 91.
5. Ibid., 5.
6. Ibid., 39.
7. Ibid.
8. Ibid.
9. Ministry of Human Rights, "Balanço–Disque 100."

10. Comitê Nacional de Respeito à Diversidade Religiosa (CNRDR), "Relatório sobre Intolerância e Violência Religiosa," 58–59.

11. Ibid., 59.

12. Ibid., 69. The committee indicates that Afro-Brazilian religions were 27 percent of all cases on which they received specific information.

13. "Preocupam-nos profundamente os recentes casos de agressão de lideranças e depredação de espaços de culto de religiões de matriz africana." CNRDR, "Recentes casos de agressão."

14. United States Department of State, "2015 International Religious Freedom Report—Brazil," 1–2.

15. Gabriele Roza, "The Persecuted Faiths," Rio on Watch, November 18, 2017, https://www.rioonwatch.org/?p=4011.

16. Ibid.

17. United Nations General Assembly, "Report of the Chair of the Working Group," ¶ 17.

18. Izsák, "Report of the Special Rapporteur," 1.

19. Disque 100 does not record the religion of the aggressor.

20. United States Department of State, "2015 International Religious Freedom Report—Brazil," 1–2.

21. CNRDR, "Relatório sobre Intolerância e Violência Religiosa," 70–71. The Committee provides contradictory information in the summary titled "Data on the Aggressors," in which it asserts that the religion of the aggressor was available in only 84 cases, and Graph 28, which shows that data on the religion of the aggressor was available in 73 percent of cases, which would equal approximately 106 cases. The figure of 63 percent of known aggressors is based on the data shown in the graph. However, if data on the religion of the aggressor was indeed only received in 84 cases, evangelicals would actually be nearly 80 percent of known aggressors.

22. International Commission to Combat Religious Racism, "Twenty Years of Religious Racism," 37.

23. United States Department of State, "2015 International Religious Freedom Report—Brazil," 4.

24. Mario Monken, "Tráfico é acusado de vetar umbanda no Rio," *Folha de Sao Paulo*, February 4, 2006, https://www1.folha.uol.com.br/fsp/cotidian/ff0402200614.htm.

25. Ibid.

26. "Crime e preconceito: Mães e filhos de santo são expulsos de favelas por traficantes evangélicos," *Geledes*, January 19, 2015, https://www.geledes.org.br/crime-e-preconceito-maes-e-filhos-de-santo-sao-expulsos-de-favelas-por-traficantes-evangelicos/.

27. Andre Coelho, "Criminals Force an Iyalorixa to Destroy Her Own Terreiro in Nova Iguassu, Rio de Janeiro," trans. Melissa Oliver, *Candomble in the USA*, September 16, 2017.

28. Roza, "Persecuted Faiths."

29. Coelho, "Criminals Force an Iyalorixa."

30. Robert Muggah, "In Brazil Religious Gang Leaders Say They're Waging a Holy War," *The Conversation*, November 2, 2017.

31. Roberta Jansen, "Traficantes evangélicos causam terror a religiões africanas," *Terra*, August 18, 2019, https://www.terra.com.br/noticias/brasil/cidades/traficantes-evangelicos-causam-terror-a-religioesafricanas-1780cd9c3e66e3685264918be080ac4db4ddw64t.html.

32. "RJ tem primeiro local de atendimento para vítimas de intolerância religiosa," *UOL Notícias*, February 27, 2020, https://noticias.uol.com.br/cotidiano/ultimas-noticias/2020/02/27/atendimento-intolerancia-religiosa.htm.

33. Jaline Santos, "Traficante que destruiu terreiro de macumba no Rio vai preso," *Buxixo Gospel*, August 5, 2019, https://www.obuxixogospel.com.br/2019/08/foi-preso-um-dos-autores-por-destruir-terreiro-na-baixada-fluminense/.

34. Roza, "Persecuted Faiths."

35. "Centro de Umbanda em Piatã é Atacado Durante Festa e Três Pessoas Ficam Feridas," *Dossiê Intolerância Religiosa*, February 13, 2017, http://intoleranciareligiosadossie.blogspot.com/2017/02/centro-de-umbanda-em-piata-e-atacado.html.

36. "Terreiros de Candomblé são incendiados em Goiás," *Extra Globo*, December 9, 2015, https://extra.globo.com/noticias/brasil/terreiros-de-candomble-sao-incendiados-em-goias

-encontrei-uma-biblia-diz-dono-de-um-dos-locais-17476382.html.

37. "Polícia investiga vandalismo em terreiro de candomblé em Lauro de Freitas," *Correio*, August 12, 2017, https://www.correio24horas.com.br/noticia/nid/policia-investiga-vandalismo-em-terreiro-de-candomble-em-lauro-de-freitas/.

38. Júlia Vigné, "Terreiro Oxumarê, em Salvador, é alvo de intolerância religiosa," *Correio*, October 31, 2018, https://www.correio24horas.com.br/noticia/nid/terreiro-oxumare-em-salvador-e-alvo-de-intolerancia-religiosa/.

39. Bruno Alfano, Luã Marinatto, Pedro Zuazo, and Rafael Soares, "Um Rio de ódio: Terreiro de candomblé é atacado com pedras, ovos e legumes podres," *Globo*, July 29, 2017, https://extra.globo.com/casos-de-policia/um-rio-de-odio-terreiro-de-candomble-atacado-com-pedras-ovos-legumes-podres-21645654.html.

40. "Casa de Religião de Matriz Africana é Atacada em Maceió," *Dossiê Intolerância Religiosa*, March 6, 2017, http://intoleranciareligiosadossie.blogspot.com/2018/03/casa-de-religiao-de-matriz-africana-e.html.

41. "Terreiro de Candomblé é Destruído em Nova Iguaçu," *Dossiê Intolerância Religiosa*, August 9, 2017, https://intoleranciareligiosadossie.blogspot.com/2018/08/terreiro-de-candomble-e-destruido-em.html.

42. Denise Menchen, "Evangélicos são acusados de quebrar centro de umbanda no rio," *Dossiê Intolerância Religiosa*, May 3, 2008, http://intoleranciareligiosadossie.blogspot.com/2011/07/evangelicos-sao-acusados-de-quebrar.html.

43. Emilio Azevedo, "Homem invade e quebra tudo em terreiro no Maranhão," *Teia*, September 10, 2018, https://teiapopular.org/homem-invade-e-quebra-tudo-em-terreiro-no-maranhao/.

44. Jane Santos, "Evangélicos são presos por intolerância religiosa," *A Tarde* (Salvador, Bahia), March 18, 2006.

45. Larissa Baltazar, "Jovem de 14 anos praticante de candomblé denuncia ter sido agredida por intolerância religiosa em Curitiba," *Geledes*, October 1, 2015, https://www.geledes.org.br/jovem-de-14-anos-praticante-de-candomble-denuncia-ter-sido-agredida-por-intolerancia-religiosa-em-curitiba/.

46. Ariana Lobo, "Violência em nome de Deus," *Dossiê Intolerância Religiosa*, April 8, 2016, http://intoleranciareligiosadossie.blogspot.com/2016/04/violencia-em-nome-de-deus.html.

47. Conte, "Umbanda," 55.

48. James Hider, "Rio Drug Gangs Use Religion as Weapon to Drive Out Opponents," *The Times* (London), June 18, 2015; "Hate Crimes Shake Brazil's Religious Melting Pot," *Bangladesh Government News*, June 28, 2015; "Religious Intolerance Leads to Death of 90-Year Old Priestess and Stoning in Head of 11-Year Old Girl," *Black Women of Brazil*, June 28, 2015.

49. "Ogã é morto com tiro na cabeça por vizinho de terreiro de candomblé em Itaparica," *Dossiê Intolerância Religiosa*, September 25, 2012, http://intoleranciareligiosadossie.blogspot.com/2012/09/oga-e-morto-com-tiro-na-cabeca-por.html.

50. International Commission to Combat Religious Racism, "Twenty Years of Religious Racism," 19.

51. "Polícia prende 'Bonde de Jesus' que atacava terreiros de umbanda e candomblé," *Estado de Minas*, August 18, 2019, https://www.em.com.br/app/noticia/nacional/2019/08/18/interna_nacional,1078089/policia-prende-bonde-de-jesus-que-atacava-terreiros-de-umbanda-e-can.shtml.

52. Izsák, "Report of the Special Rapporteur," 18.

53. Ibid., 20.

54. United States Department of State, "2017 International Religious Freedom Report—Brazil," 6.

55. Brazil, "Combating Intolerance, Negative Stereotyping," 1–5.

56. Izsák, "Report of the Special Rapporteur," ¶ 86.

57. Following the September 2017 attacks, the government in Rio de Janeiro did create a Joint Commission to Support Victims of Attacks on Religious Temples, which was tasked with mapping the violence and ending this type of crime. Governo do Rio de Janeiro, "Secretário de Direitos Humanos cria Comissão." However, it did not actually begin operations until 2020. "RJ

tem primeiro local de atendimento para vítimas de intolerância religiosa," *UOL*, February 27, 2020, https://noticias.uol.com.br/cotidiano/ultimas-noticias/2020/02/27/atendimento-intolerancia-religiosa.htm?cmpid=copiaecola.

58. Bellegarde-Smith, "Man-Made Disaster," 264–65.

59. Frerichs, *Deadly River*, 1; Agence France-Presse, "45 People Lynched Amid Haiti Cholera Fears: Officials," December 23, 2010.

60. "45 Lynchings Over Cholera," *Sunshine Coast Daily* (Maroochydore, Queensland, Australia), December 24, 2010.

61. "45 People Lynched Amid Haiti Cholera Fears."

62. Frerichs, *Deadly River*, 1.

63. Bellegarde-Smith, "Man-Made Disaster," 266.

64. Carelock, "Leaky House," 2.

65. Ibid., 90.

66. Ibid., 88.

67. Ibid., 66.

68. Ibid., 66.

69. Miranda Blue, "Trump's Christian Liaison Threatened to Withhold Food from Haitians Who Don't Give Up Voodoo," *Right Wing Watch*, May 20, 2016.

70. Paisley Dodds, "Haiti Earthquake Leads to Increased Tensions Among Religions," *Associated Press*, February 13, 2010, http://www.nola.com/religion/index.ssf/2010/02/haiti_earthquake_leads_to_increased_tensions_among_religions.html.

71. Germain, "The Earthquake, the Missionaries," 257.

72. Ibid. at 250.

73. Ibid.

74. Dodds, "Haiti Earthquake Leads to Increased Tensions."

75. Carelock, "Leaky House," 47.

76. Ibid., 94–95.

77. Grimaud and Legagneur, "Community Beliefs and Fears," 27.

78. "45 People Lynched Amid Haiti Cholera Fears."

79. Cornelio Sotelo, "Witch Hunters in Haiti Kill 12 Accused of Spreading Cholera," *El Paso Examiner*, December 4, 2010; Johnathan M. Katz, "Cholera Panic Sparks Haiti Witch-Hunt; 12 Killed," *Associated Press News Service*, December 3, 2010.

80. "HAITI-CHOLERA-Voodoo Leader Says 45 People Lynched Amid Cholera Fears," *CANANews* (Barbados), December 24, 2010.

81. "45 Lynchings Over Cholera"; Grimaud and Legagneur, "Community Beliefs and Fears," 28. Additional murders took place in other parts of the country. Human Rights Council, "Report of the Independent Expert," ¶ 39.

82. Carelock, "Leaky House," 68. Ironically, Grand'Anse was not badly affected by the cholera outbreak: "45 Lynchings Over Cholera."

83. Human Rights Council, "Report of the Independent Expert," ¶ 39.

84. Ibid.

85. Human Rights Council, "National Report Submitted."

86. Human Rights Committee, "Consideration of Reports," ¶ 98.

87. Ibid., ¶ 115.

88. Human Rights Committee, "List of Issues," 4.

CHAPTER 2

1. Mike McPhate, "Gorilla Killed After Child Enters Enclosure at Cincinnati Zoo," *New York Times*, May 29, 2016, https://www.nytimes.com/2016/05/30/us/gorilla-killed-after-child-enters-enclosure-at-cincinnati-zoo.html.

2. These statistics come from KnowYourMeme.com, a wiki-like website where contributors can document the history and significance of various memes. See https://knowyourmeme.com/memes/harambe-the-gorilla.

3. Sheila Hurt, "Justice for Harambe," https://www.change.org/p/cincinnati-zoo-justice-for-harambe.

4. For example, Brittney Cooper, "The Conversation About Harambe Has Racist Undertones We Can't Ignore," *Cosmopolitan*, June 1, 2016, http://www.cosmopolitan.com/politics/news/a59261/harambe-gorilla-michelle-gregg/.

5. D. O'Brien, *Animal Sacrifice and Religious Freedom*, 33.

6. Ibid., 163.

7. Ibid., 164–68.

8. *Church of Lukumi Babalu Aye, Inc., v. City of Hialeah*, 723 F. Supp. 1467, 1486 (emphasis added).
9. Ibid., 1480.
10. *Church of Lukumi Babalu Aye, Inc., v. City of Hialeah*, 936 F.2d 586.
11. Ibid., 536–37.
12. Ibid., 534.
13. *Jose Merced v. Euless*, 577 F.3d 578, 582.
14. Ibid., 582–83.
15. Ibid., 583.
16. Affidavit of Jose Merced, *Jose Merced v. Kasson*, 2006 WL 4015958, 4.
17. Appellees' Brief, *Jose Merced v. Kasson*, 2008 WL 7241291, 4.
18. *Jose Merced v. Euless*, 577 F.3d 578, 584.
19. Ibid., 583–84.
20. "General Penalty," § 1–12, Euless Code of Ordinances, http://z2codes.franklinlegal.net/franklin/pdfs/euless_code.pdf.
21. *Jose Merced v. Euless*, 577 F.3d 578, 583.
22. Ibid., 586.
23. Appellees' Brief, *Jose Merced v. Kasson*, 2008 WL 7241291, 3 and 6.
24. *Jose Merced v. Euless*, 577 F.3d 578, 586.
25. Ibid., 581.
26. Ibid., 595.
27. Ibid.
28. Kimberly Thorpe, "If Nothing Else, We Learn That in a Fight Over a Goat Sacrifice, the Goat Always Loses," *Dallas Observer*, January 27, 2010.
29. Richard Fausset, "Religious Freedom Won't Be Sacrificed: A Santeria Priest Files a Lawsuit Stemming from a Police Raid During a Worship Ritual," *Los Angeles Times*, August 11, 2008, http://articles.latimes.com/2008/aug/11/nation/na-santeria11.
30. David Aelion, "News Release: Victory with Police in Pursuit of Religious Freedom," July 22, 2008, http://www.theaelionfirm.com/site/media/press-releases/59-victory-with-police-in-pursuit-of-religious-freedom.html.
31. Fausset, "Religious Freedom Won't be Sacrificed"; Tamara Lush, "Death in the City Beautiful," *Miami New Times*, July 11, 2007, http://www.miaminewtimes.com/2007-07-12/news/death-in-the-city-beautiful/6366936.
32. Aelion, "News Release."
33. J. D. Patterson, Miami-Dade Police Department, "Florida Law Enforcement Handbook: Miami-Dade County Edition" (2014), LG-30.
34. Ibid.
35. "Animal Sacrifices Found in Barbershop Basement," *New Zealand Herald*, August 19, 2011.
36. Associated Press, "Mass. Barber Closed After Animals Found at Site," *AP Regional State Report–Massachusetts*, August 17, 2011.
37. Ibid.
38. "Animal Sacrifices Found in Barbershop Basement," *New Zealand Herald*, August 19, 2011.
39. Associated Press, "New Bedford Barbershop Where Birds Found Reopens," *AP Regional State Report–Massachusetts*, August 24, 2011.
40. Tony Allen-Mills, "Chango the Voodoo God Faces Trial in Miami," *Sunday Times* (London), August 4, 1996; "Santeria Priest Apologizes for Sacrifices," *UPI Archive: Domestic News*, July 2, 1993.
41. *State of Florida v. Rigoberto Zamora*, 3 Fla. L. Weekly Supp. 696b.
42. *State of Florida v. Rigoberto Zamora*, No. M95028476; Allen-Mills, "Chango the Voodoo God"; "Plea Deal in Animal Sacrifice Trial," *UPI Archive: Domestic News*, July 31, 1996.
43. "Santeria Priest Apologizes for Sacrifices."
44. *Jorge Badillo v. Victor Amato*, 2014 U.S. Dist. LEXIS 10210, 4–5.
45. Ibid., 4.
46. Ibid., 4–5. The latter is something that is controversial among devotees. Many believe that photos and videos should not be taken of shrines, particularly following a sacrifice.
47. Ibid., 5, 18–19.
48. Ibid., 5.
49. Complaint, *Jorge Badillo v. Victor Amato*, No. 3:13-cv-01553-FLW-TJB, 4.
50. *Jorge Badillo v. Victor Amato*, 2014 U.S. Dist. LEXIS 10210, 6.
51. Complaint, *Jorge Badillo v. Victor Amato*, No. 3:13-cv-01553-FLW-TJB, 5.
52. Settlement Agreement, *Jorge Badillo v. Victor Amato*, No. 3:13-cv-01553-FLW-TJB, 2.

53. Garrett Brnger, "'We're Not Cruel People': Couple Arrested in Santeria Ceremony Says Religion Is Misunderstood," *KSAT*, March 23, 2018, https://www.ksat.com/news/were-not-cruel-people-couple-arrested-during-santeria-ceremony-elaborates-on-religion.
54. Texas, Penal Code: Cruelty to Livestock Animals, §42.09.
55. Texas, Penal Code: Punishments, §12.21.
56. *Ramon Patino v. Nicolas Hood*, No. 2018CI05535.
57. Oro, "Sacrifice of Animals," 1.
58. Conte, "Umbanda," 49.
59. Ibid., 49; Oro, "Sacrifice of Animals," 2.
60. Oro, "Sacrifice of Animals," 2; Conte, "Umbanda," 49.
61. Oro, "Sacrifice of Animals," 4.
62. Ibid.
63. *Exmo. Sr. Dr. Procurador-Geral de Justiça v. Assembléia Legislativa*, No. 70010129690.
64. Gualberto, "Mapa da Intolerância Religiosa, 107–9.
65. Oro, "Sacrifice of Animals," 5–6.
66. Assembleia Legislativa, "Detalhes da Proposição, PL 21 2015."
67. Ibid.
68. *Extraordinary Remedy RE 494601*, No. 2006/68373.
69. Jorge Rueda, "Santeria: Venezuelans Increasingly Turn to Hybrid Religion for Spiritual Needs," *Winnipeg Free Press*, February 10, 2008.
70. Victoria Carrascosa, "Santeros dicen que sacrifican animales para salvar vidas," *El Nacional de Venezuela*, March 30, 2009.
71. Ibid.
72. Venezuela, Ley Para la Protección de la Fauna Doméstica Libre y en Cautiverio.
73. "Sacrifico de animales con fines rituales? Fe verdadera o lucro sin control?" *VTactual*, December 16, 2016, https://www.vtactual.com/es/sacrifico-de-animales-con-fines-rituales-fe-verdadera-o-lucro-sin-control/.
74. *Ordenanza sobre Tenencia, Control, Registro, Comercialización y Protección de Fauna Doméstica del Municipio Libertador*.
75. "Sacrifico de animales con fines rituales."
76. Carlos Ruperto Fermín, "El crecimiento del maltrato animal en Venezuela," *Aporrea*, March 25, 2015, http://www.aporrea.org/actualidad/a205050.html.
77. Ariana Guevara, "Santería: Profanaciones y sangre derramada," *El Estímulo*, June 27, 2016, http://elestimulo.com/climax/santeria-profanaciones-y-sangre-derramada/.
78. Ibid.
79. Ibid.
80. Roger López, "Demanda de nulidad contra la reforma de la Ordenanza sobre Tenencia, Control, Registro, Comercialización y Protección de Fauna Doméstica dictada por el Municipio Bolivariano Libertador del Distrito Capital" (n.d.), http://actualidadpenal.net/demanda-de-nulidad-contra-la-reforma-de-la-ordenanza-sobre-tenencia-control-registro-comercializacion-y-proteccion-de-fauna-domestica-dictada-por-el-municipio-bolivariano-libertador-del-distrito-ca/#more-1377.
81. *Exp. N° 15-0993*.
82. Vanessa Padron, "Prohíban Sacrificios De Animales Permanentemente," *SOS VOX*, July 21, 2016, https://www.sosvox.org/es/petition/prohiban-sacrificios-de-animales-permanentemente.html.
83. "Vida de preto não tem valor nenhum. Mas a galinha da religião de preto tem que ser radicalmente protegida." Quoted in Luiz Orlando Carneiro and Matheus Teixeira, "STF tem dois votos para permitir sacrifício de animais em rituais religiosos," *JOTA*, August 8, 2018, https://www.jota.info/stf/do-supremo/stf-permitir-sacrificio-animais-religiosos-09082018.

CHAPTER 3

1. *United States v. Myrlene Severe*, No. 06–6053-SNOW.
2. Complaint, *United States v. Myrlene Severe*, No. 06–60097 CR-COHN, 3.
3. Ibid., 1.
4. Statements or entries generally, 18 US Code § 1001; Transporting hazardous material, 49 US Code § 46312; Smuggling goods into the United States, 18 U.S. Code § 545. The section on smuggling goods was amended in 2006. The new penalty is up to twenty years' imprisonment.
5. Brian Haas and Macollvie Jean-François, "No Bones About It: You Just Can't Bring a

Skull Through Customs," *Sun Sentinel* (Ft. Lauderdale, FL), February 11, 2006.

6. Complaint, *United States v. Myrlene Severe*, No. 06-60097 CR-COHN. Severe was charged with violating Florida Statute Section 497.386 governing the "storage, preservation, and transportation of human remains."

7. Haas and Jean-François, "No Bones About It."

8. Martin, "Removal and Reinterment of Remains," 14.

9. Long, *Spiritual Merchants*, 11.

10. Ibid., 12.

11. Martin, "Removal and Reinterment of Remains," 15–16.

12. Ibid., 17.

13. Ibid., 10.

14. Ibid., 12.

15. Ibid., 23.

16. For example, see Washington, Revised Code: Unlawful Disposal of Remains; Massachusetts, General Laws: Permanent Disposition of Dead Bodies or Remains; South Carolina, Code of Laws Unannotated: Destruction or Desecration of Human Remains or Repositories.

17. Halperin, "The Poor, the Black, and the Marginalized," 489; Frank, "Body Snatching," 400.

18. Willoughby, "Pedagogies of the Black Body," 202.

19. Ibid., 203.

20. Halperin, "The Poor, the Black, and the Marginalized," 490–91.

21. Washington, *Medical Apartheid*, 126.

22. P. Clark, "Prejudice and the Medical Profession," 121.

23. Ibid.; Washington, *Medical Apartheid*, 126.

24. Washington, *Medical Apartheid*, 131.

25. Halperin, "The Poor, the Black, and the Marginalized," 493.

26. Ibid.

27. Washington, *Medical Apartheid*, 120–21.

28. Ibid., 126.

29. Ibid., 127.

30. Ibid., 130.

31. Halperin, "The Poor, the Black, and the Marginalized," 490.

32. Washington, *Medical Apartheid*, 85.

33. Ibid., 86; Willoughby, "Pedagogies of the Black Body," 198.

34. Washington, *Medical Apartheid*, 86.

35. Willoughby, "Pedagogies of the Black Body," 198; Washington, *Medical Apartheid*, 88.

36. Willoughby, "Pedagogies of the Black Body," 194.

37. Washington, *Medical Apartheid*, 136; Young, "Black Body as Souvenir," 639–57.

38. Young, "Black Body as Souvenir," 649–50.

39. For example, see Brian M. Vazquez, "Kansas Dead Body Law," https://ksbma.ks.gov/resources/legislation/dead-body-law; North Dakota, Century Code: Care and Custody of the Dead.

40. Parrinder, *African Traditional Religion*, 99, 136.

41. Chireau, *Black Magic*, 48.

42. Long, *Spiritual Merchants*, 55, 89.

43. Chireau, *Black Magic*, 62.

44. Mbiti, *African Religions and Philosophy*, 160.

45. Ibid.; Parrinder, *African Traditional Religion*, 98–99.

46. Smith, "Gede Rising," 78–79, 85.

47. Olmos and Paravisini-Gebert, *Creole Religions*, 79–80.

48. M. A. Clark, "Palo Monte," 306.

49. V. Gomez, "Matamoros 'Drug Cult' Murders," 7.

50. Ibid., 6–7.

51. Ibid., 7, 12.

52. Schutze, *Cauldron of Blood*, 116.

53. Ibid., 117–22.

54. Bartkowski, "Claims-Making and Typifications of Voodoo," 559, 562–63, 571; V. Gomez, "Matamoros 'Drug Cult' Murders," 80.

55. Holmes and Holmes, *Profiling Violent Crimes*.

56. Ibid., 229.

57. Kail, *Narco-Cults*, 56.

58. For instance, in the biggest Palo Mayombe case in the state of New Jersey, one of the primary officers involved, Garabrandt, testified that he had attended a workshop on ritualistic crime scenes with such scholars about six weeks before this case. April 15, 2004 transcript, *State v. Miriam Miraballes*, No. A-0404-05T4, 185–87.

59. William Kleinknecht, "Body Snatching Is Mark of a Cult: Newark Man Received Probation But Other Cases Are Resolved," *Star-Ledger* (Newark, NJ), May 1, 2002.

60. "Tomb-Rob Horror—N.J. Cult Used Remains in Rituals," *New York Post*, May 3, 2004.

61. "Voodoo Furor in Body Snatch," *New York Post*, October 10, 2002.

62. "Cult Member Mum in Graveyard Body-Snatching Case," *Jersey Journal* (Jersey City, NJ), November 15, 1999.

63. Kleinknecht, "Body Snatching Is Mark of a Cult."

64. "Cult Member Mum."

65. Laura Italiano, "Ghouls Selling Babies' Corpses," *New York Post*, August 30, 2000.

66. Ibid.

67. "Cult Member Mum"; Italiano, "Ghouls Selling Babies' Corpses."

68. *State of New Jersey v. Miraballes*, 392 N.J.Super. 342, 345.

69. Ibid., 345–47.

70. April 15, 2004 transcript, *State of New Jersey v. Miraballes*, No. A-0404-05T4, 41–43.

71. Defendant-Appellant's Brief, *State of New Jersey v. Miraballes*, No. A-0404-05T4.

72. Ibid.

73. April 15, 2004 transcript, *State of New Jersey v. Miraballes*, No. A-0404-05T4, 95–96.

74. Ibid.

75. State-Appellee's Brief, *State of New Jersey v. Miraballes*, No. A-0404-05T4.

76. April 13, 2004 transcript, *State of New Jersey v. Miraballes*, No. A-0404-05T4, 84.

77. Indictment, *State of New Jersey v. Ramon L. Gonzalez, Miriam Miraballes, et al.* No. 2003-4-1426.

78. William Kleinknecht, "Grave Robber Recalls Theft of Human Head," *Star-Ledger* (Newark, NJ), January 15, 2004.

79. Ibid.

80. William Kleinknecht, "Human and Animal Remains Are Shown to Jury," *Star-Ledger* (Newark, NJ), January 14, 2004.

81. Kleinknecht, "Grave Robber Recalls Theft of Human Head."

82. William Kleinknecht, "Palo Priest Convicted of Possessing Crypt Bones," *Star-Ledger* (Newark, NJ), January 27, 2004.

83. *State of New Jersey v. Oscar Cruz*, No. 02008126.

84. April 15, 2004 transcript, *State of New Jersey v. Miraballes*, No. A-0404-05T4, 89; "Voodoo Furor in Body Snatch."

85. "Voodoo Furor in Body Snatch."

86. Ronald Smothers, "2 Accused of Storing Stolen Remains for Rituals," *New York Times*, October 9, 2002.

87. William Kleinknecht, "Looking for Answers: Cult Ties to '99 Crypt Theft Probed," *Star-Ledger* (Newark, NJ), October 9, 2002.

88. Maya Kremen, "Spirits of the Dead: Palo Mayombe, a Mixture of African and Catholic Beliefs, Stirs Controversy," *Herald News* (Passaic County, NJ), October 17, 2002.

89. Ibid.

90. Smothers, "2 Accused of Storing Stolen Remains for Rituals."

91. State-Appellee's Brief, *State of New Jersey v. Miraballes*, No. A-0404-05T4.

92. Ibid.

93. *State of New Jersey v. Miraballes*, 392 N.J.Super. 342, 349–50.

94. Transcript, *State of New Jersey v. Miraballes*, 392 N.J.Super. 342, 44–45

95. Ibid., 48–49.

96. Ibid., 49.

97. Ibid., 63.

98. Ibid.

99. *State of New Jersey v. Miraballes*, 392 N.J.Super. 342, 351.

100. "Tomb-Rob Horror."

101. Transcript, *State of New Jersey v. Miraballes*, 392 N.J.Super. 342, 37.

102. Ibid., 43.

103. *State of New Jersey v. Miraballes*, 392 N.J.Super. 342, 350. April 22, 2004 transcript, *State v. Miraballes*, Docket No. A-0404-05T4, 95.

104. *State of New Jersey v. Miraballes*, 392 N.J.Super. 342, 350.

105. April 2004 transcript, *State v. Miraballes*, No. A-0404-05T4, 122.

106. Ibid., 141–42.

107. Ibid., 143.

108. State-Appellee's Brief, *State of New Jersey v. Miraballes*, Docket No. A-0404-05T4.

109. William Kleinknecht, "Woman on Trial in Grave Robberies," *Star-Ledger* (Newark, NJ), April 15, 2005.

110. Statement of Reasons, *State v. Miraballes*, No. A-0404-05T4.

111. State-Appellee's Brief, *State v. Miraballes*, No. A-0404–05T4, 54,

112. Ibid.

113. Gary Murray, "Suppression of Evidence Sought By Man Who Allegedly Stole Remains from Worcester Mausoleums," *Worcester Telegram and Gazette*, November 24, 2017.

114. City of Worcester Press Release, "Missing Skeletal Remains from Hope Cemetery Located in Hartford Connecticut," December 5, 2015, http://www.worcesterma.gov/wpd-press-releases/missing-skeletal-remains-from-hope-cemetery-located-in-hartford-connecticut#idu9_XRltKVk4v21apcuCY3w.

115. "Police: Santeria Priest Raided Cemetery, Took Remains of 5," *UWIRE Text*, December 7, 2015.

116. Scott Croteau, "Who Was Entombed in the Worcester Mausoleum Where 5 Skeletal Remains Were Stolen?," *Mass Live*, December 7, 2015.

117. Nina Golgowski, "Human Remains Stolen from Cemetery Found in Man's Home, Police Say," *Huffington Post*, December 7, 2015; City of Worcester Press Release, "Missing Skeletal Remains."

118. Jim Smith, "Family 'Shocked' by Theft of Remains from Worcester Cemetery," *CBS Boston*, December 12, 2015.

119. Brief of Amador Medina, *Commonwealth v. Amador Medina*, No. SJC-12830, 12–16; Brief of the Commonwealth, *Commonwealth v. Amador Medina*, No. SJC-12830, 9–12.

120. *Commonwealth v. Amador Medina*, No. SJC-12830.

CHAPTER 4

1. Statement of Dr. Rosiane Rodrigues, on file with author.

2. D. O'Brien, *Animal Sacrifice and Religious Freedom*, 90.

3. *Church of Lukumi Babalu Aye, Inc., v. City of Hialeah*, 723 F. Supp. 1467, 1474.

4. Ibid., 1475.

5. Ibid., 1476.

6. Ibid.

7. Ibid., 1485–86.

8. The City of Hialeah chose not to focus on this in their brief because the Eleventh Circuit had not adopted this reasoning. However, they reminded the Supreme Court that the animal rights groups had addressed the purported psychological harm to children in their briefs and that the "court could, if necessary, rely on that aspect of the district court's decision." Respondent's Brief, *Church of the Lukumi Babalu Aye v. City of Hialeah*, 1992 U.S. S. Ct. Briefs LEXIS 534, 8, footnote 4.

9. Brief for the Human Society of the United States, et al., *Church of the Lukumi Babalu Aye v. City of Hialeah*, 1992 U.S. S. Ct. Briefs LEXIS 537, 45.

10. Ibid., 46.

11. *In the Matter of the Adoption of Vincent*, 602 N.Y.S.2d 303.

12. *In re M.A. v. Ronald A.*, 2010 WL 705521.

13. The surname of the father, the children, and the foster family are limited to the first initial in juvenile court records to preserve anonymity.

14. *In re M.A. v. Ronald A.*, 2010 WL 705521, 2.

15. Ibid.

16. Ibid., 5.

17. Ibid.

18. *New Jersey Division of Youth and Family Services v. Y.C.*, 2011 N.J. Super. Unpub. LEXIS 1366.

19. John Petrick, "Mother Guilty in Bloody Rituals," *Record* (Bergen County, NJ), May 24, 2011.

20. *New Jersey Division of Youth and Family Services v. Y.C.*, 2011 N.J. Super. Unpub. LEXIS 1366, 4.

21. Olmos and Paravisini-Gebert, *Creole Religions*, 85. Palo initiation "involves a series of rituals known as rayamientos (markings), a name derived from the cutting made during the rite with a knife or sharp object on the body of the neophyte."

22. *New Jersey Division of Youth and Family Services v. Y.C.*, 2011 N.J. Super. Unpub. LEXIS 1366, 4.

23. Ibid., 4–6.

24. Petrick, "Mother Guilty in Bloody Rituals."

25. *New Jersey Division of Youth and Family Services v. Y.C.*, 2011 N.J. Super. Unpub. LEXIS 1366, 5.

26. Ibid., 7.

27. Ibid., 9–10.
28. Ibid., 2.
29. Ibid., 6.
30. Ibid., 12, footnote 3.
31. *State of New Jersey v. Miriam Miraballes*, 392 N.J.Super. 342.
32. Ibid., 349–50.
33. *New Jersey Division of Youth and Family Services v. Y.C.*, 2011 N.J. Super. Unpub. LEXIS 1366, 12.
34. Ibid., 4–6.
35. John Petrick, "Judge Rejects Religious Freedom Defense in Palo Mayombe Trial," *Record* (Bergen County, NJ), January 22, 2011.
36. Ibid.
37. Petrick, "Mother Guilty in Bloody Rituals," L01.
38. Ibid.
39. "Sentence Disposition," *New Jersey v. Yenitza Colichon*, No. 09003395.
40. Nicola White, "Santeria Priest Goes Public with Animal Sacrifice; Slaughters Two Chickens in Passaic Ceremony," *Record* (Bergen County, NJ), October 21, 2003.
41. Ibid.
42. Ibid.; "ASPCA & HSUS Demand Cruelty Charges in Passaic, New Jersey Animal Sacrifice," *Charity Wire*, October 24, 2003.
43. White, "Santeria Priest Goes Public with Animal Sacrifice."
44. For example, see Emma Perez-Trevino, "Remembering Mark J. Kilroy: Years Ago, Grisly Murders That Claimed His and Others' Lives Terrified Everyone," *Brownsville Herald* (Texas), March 8, 2009.
45. "Situação de conflitos religiosos no Brasil equipara-se à França, ao Sudão e à Bósnia, alerta antropóloga," *JusBrasil.com*, November 16, 2015, http://dp-rj.jusbrasil.com.br/noticias/256209191/situacao-de-conflitos-religiosos-no-brasil-equipara-se-a-franca-aosudao-e-a-bosnia-alerta-antropologa; Comissão de Combate à Intolerância Religiosa, "Por causa de sua fé."
46. Ibid.
47. Hollanda, "Mãe é ameaçada de perder a guarda da filha."
48. Inter-American Commission on Human Rights, "Report on the Situation of Human Rights in Brazil," chapter V.
49. *AOM v. RDDL*, No. 70051844082.
50. *Petition Number PET 10595305*.
51. *André Amâncio Fogaça v. Luciana Soeiro Purissmo*, No. 1009615–85.2015.8.26.0126.

SECTION II

1. Desilver and Masci, "World's Muslim Population."
2. Diouf, *Servants of Allah*, 20; M. Gomez, *Reversing Sail*, 29.
3. M. Gomez, *Reversing Sail*, 32.
4. Lawrence, "Mandinga Voyages Across the Atlantic," 202.
5. Ibid., 227–28.
6. Diouf, *Servants of Allah*, 217–18.
7. Ibid., 219–20.
8. Ibid., 221.
9. Ibid., 222.
10. Mohamed Younis, "Perceptions of Muslims in the United States: A Review," December 11, 2015, https://news.gallup.com/opinion/gallup/187664/perceptions-muslims-united-states-review.aspx.
11. Pew Research Center, "U.S. Muslims Concerned About Their Place in Society, but Continue to Believe in the American Dream," July 26, 2017, https://www.pewforum.org/2017/07/26/findings-from-pew-research-centers-2017-survey-of-us-muslims/. The percentage of African-descended Muslims in the United States is likely much higher; however, US census categories frame North Africans as "whites," making this population more difficult to identify.
12. Akinyi Ochieng, "Black Muslims Face Double Jeopardy, Anxiety in the Heartland," NPR, February 25, 2017, https://www.npr.org/sections/codeswitch/2017/02/25/516468604/black-muslims-face-double-jeopardy-anxiety-in-the-heartland.
13. Scales-Trent, "African Women in France," 708.
14. Viorst, "Muslims of France," 78.
15. Research on Islam and Muslims in Africa (RIMA), "Numbers and Percentage of Muslims in African Countries," https://muslimsinafrica.wordpress.com/numbers-and-percentage-of-muslims-in-african-countries/; Insee, "Immigrant and Foreign Population," https://www.ined.fr/en/everything_about_population

/data/france/immigrants-foreigners/immigrants-foreigners/.

16. Pew Research Center, "The Future of the Global Muslim Population," January 27, 2011, http://www.pewforum.org/2011/01/27/the-future-of-the-global-muslim-population/.

17. Pew Research Center, "The Future of the Global Muslim Population: Interactives, Sub-Saharan Africa," http://www.pewforum.org/interactives/muslim-population-graphic/#/Sub-Saharan%20Africa.

18. This includes Somalia, Niger, Comoros, Djibouti, Senegal, Mauritania, Gambia, and Mali.

19. Amer, *What Is Veiling?*, 5–6.

20. Ibid., 6–7.

21. Ibid., 7–8.

22. Hashmi, "Too Much to Bare?," 411.

23. Ibid.

24. Abdo, "Legal Status of Hijab," 448.

25. Ibid.; Hashmi, "Too Much to Bare?," 412.

26. Abdo, "Legal Status of Hijab," 449; Hashmi, "Too Much to Bare?," 412.

27. Abdo, "Legal Status of Hijab," 448.

28. Ibid., 449.

29. Morris, "Covering Islam," 4.

30. Abdo, "Legal Status of Hijab," 449; Hashmi, "Too Much to Bare?," 414–15.

31. Abdo, "Legal Status of Hijab," 449.

32. Hashmi, "Too Much to Bare?," 415.

33. Ibid., 416.

34. Abdo, "Legal Status of Hijab," 447.

35. Olmos and Paravisini-Gebert, *Creole Religions*, 184.

36. Ibid., 185; Mhango, "Constitutional Protection," 221.

37. Barrett, *Rastafarians*, 1.

38. Ibid., 1–3.

39. Ibid., chapter 4; Mhango, "Constitutional Protection," 221; Pretorius, "Significance of the Use of Ganja," 1014.

40. Taylor, "Soul Rebels," 1607; Olmos and Paravisini-Gebert, *Creole Religions*, 186.

41. Taylor, "Soul Rebels," 1608; Olmos and Paravisini-Gebert, *Creole Religions*, 201; Mhango, "Constitutional Protection," 222.

42. Taylor, "Soul Rebels," 1608; Mhango, "Constitutional Protection," 222.

43. Kuumba and Ajanaku, "Dreadlocks," 230.

44. Ibid., 234–35; O'Brien and Carter, "Chant Down Babylon, 225.

45. Campbell, *Rasta and Resistance*, 72–73; Murrell, *Afro-Caribbean Religions*, 310.

46. Olmos and Paravisini-Gebert, *Creole Religions*, 193.

47. Taylor, "Soul Rebels," 1609; Mhango, "Constitutional Protection," 222.

48. Pretorius, "Significance of the Use of Ganja," 1012.

49. Ibid., 1023.

50. O'Brien and Carter, "Chant Down Babylon," 220.

51. Kuumba and Ajanaku, "Dreadlocks," 231; Olmos and Paravisini-Gebert, *Creole Religions*, 188.

52. Olmos and Paravisini-Gebert, *Creole Religions*, 188.

53. Ibid., 187.

54. Ibid., 188.

55. Barrett, *Rastafarians*, ix.

CHAPTER 5

1. California Legislature, Senate Bill No. 188.

2. Trica Keaton has explained that the veil is not really "a threat to French secularism" but is rather "associated with old wounds and current fears rooted in a bitter and bloody French history with the Muslim world dating from the invasions of southern France by the Saracens until their defeat in the eighth century, colonization and decolonization, the Algerian war, and attacks on French soil identified with Islamic fundamentalism during the 1980s and 1990s." Keaton, "Arrogant Assimilationism," 418.

3. Moruzzi, "Problem with Headscarves," 653–54, 658.

4. Jones, "Religious Freedom in Secular Society," 218.

5. Ibid., 220–21.

6. Ibid., 221–22.

7. Viorst, "Muslims of France," 86.

8. Hashmi, "Too Much to Bare?," 421n109.

9. Jones, "Religious Freedom in Secular Society," 223–24.

10. Ibid., 219.

11. Ibid. 236.

12. Osman, "Legislative Prohibitions on Wearing a Headscarf," 1321.

13. Hashmi, "Too Much to Bare?," 422; Ezekiel, "French Dressing," 256.
14. Hashmi, "Too Much to Bare?," 423.
15. Jones, "Religious Freedom in Secular Society," 231.
16. Ibid., 232.
17. Ibid.
18. Ibid.
19. P. O'Brien, "Veil," 105.
20. Scales-Trent, "African Women in France," 726.
21. P. O'Brien, "Veil," 125.
22. Scales-Trent, "African Women in France," 726.
23. Ibid., 708.
24. Ibid., 710–11.
25. Ibid., 708–10.
26. Viorst, "Muslims of France," 78.
27. Ibid.
28. Ibid., 80.
29. Scales-Trent, "African Women in France," 725.
30. Davis, "Reacting to France's Ban," 222; Ezekiel, "French Dressing," 260.
31. Keaton, "Arrogant Assimilationism," 417.
32. Ezekiel, "French Dressing," 268.
33. Ibid., 267.
34. Weil, "Symposium: Constitutionalism and Secularism," 2699–714.
35. Viorst, "Muslims of France," 85–86.
36. Moruzzi, "Problem with Headscarves," 659.
37. Insee, "Immigrant and Foreign Population."
38. RIMA, "Numbers and Percentage of Muslims in African Countries."
39. Insee, "Immigrant and Foreign Population." There were 1,761,254 immigrants from Algeria, Morocco, and Tunisia, constituting 67.89 percent of African immigrants. Another 238,671 immigrants were from countries that are at least 85 percent Muslim (Senegal: 91,949; Mali: 68,826; Comores: 30,893; Guinee: 31,179; Mauritania: 15,824). Therefore, 1,999,925 immigrants came from North Africa and other predominantly Muslim countries.
40. *Dzvova v. Minister of Education*, No. 291/06.
41. Ibid., ¶ 8.
42. Ibid.
43. Ibid., ¶ 41–42.
44. Ibid., ¶ 58.
45. *G v. the Head Teacher*, 2011 EWHC 1452.
46. Ibid., ¶ 48–49.
47. Ibid., ¶ 53–59.
48. "School Involved in High Court Battle Banned Second Boy Because of His Hairstyle," *North West London Times*, May 26, 2011.
49. Harvey Day, "School Threatens to Suspend Son if He Doesn't Cut Dreads," *Daily Mail Online*, September 14, 2017.
50. Ibid.
51. "Religious Discrimination in Fulham Boys School: Rasta Child Ordered to Cut Hair," AVAAZ, https://secure.avaaz.org/en/petition/Fulham_boys_school_in_London_W14_9LY_Change_hair_policy_in_Fulham_Boys_School.
52. James Rodger, "Rastafarian Pupil Told to Cut His Dreadlocks Off by His School," *Birmingham Mail*, November 2, 2017.
53. "Rastafarians Call for Equality in Malawi Schools," *Face of Malawi*, September 28, 2012, http://www.faceofmalawi.com/2012/09/rastafarians-call-for-equality-in-malawi-schools/; Centre for Human Rights, "Shadow Report," 17–18.
54. Centre for Human Rights, "Shadow Report," 17–18.
55. Watipaso Mzungu, "Renounce Faith in Pursuit of Education?," *The Nation*, July 28, 2013, http://mwnation.com/renounce-faith-in-pursuit-of-education/.
56. United States Department of State, "2016 International Religious Freedom Report—Malawi," 2.
57. Lameck Masina, "Malawi Rastafarians Push for Dreadlocks in Schools," *VOA News*, September 18, 2013, https://www.voanews.com/a/malawi-rastafarians-push-for-dreadlocks-in-schools-as-a-right/1751999.html.
58. United States Department of State, "2016 International Religious Freedom Report—Malawi," 1, 3.
59. Elijah Phimbi, "Malawi Govt Maintains Ban of Dreadlocks and Hijabs in Public Schools," *Nyasa Times*, March 27, 2017, https://

www.nyasatimes.com/malawi-govt-maintains-ban-dreadlocks-hijabs-public-schools/.

60. Ibid.

61. *Grant & Anor v. The Principal*, 3 CHRLD 138.

62. Ibid.

63. "British Virgin Islands Repeals Order Banning Rastafarians, Hippies," CNN, October 3, 1999.

64. *Grant & Anor v. The Principal*, 3 CHRLD 138.

65. *D.A. v. Governing Body*, No. 3791/00.

66. Ibid., 2.

67. Ibid., 5–6.

68. Ibid. 6.

69. *Lerato Radebe v. Principal of Leseding Technical School*, No. 1821/2013.

70. Ibid., 7.

71. Ibid., 3.

72. Thando Sipuye, "Why No Outrage at Treatment of Dreadlocked Pupils?," *Cape Argus* (South Africa), September 14, 2016, https://www.iol.co.za/capeargus/why-no-outrage-at-treatment-of-dreadlocked-pupils-2068130.

73. "Rasta Boy Misses School Over Hair; Mother Says Her Grade 8 Son Has Dreadlocks for Religious Reasons," *Cape Argus* (South Africa), January 19, 2016.

74. Prega Govender, "Several States and Private Schools Have Bans on Dreadlock, Afros, and Braid," *IOL* (Cape Town, South Africa), September 2, 2016, https://www.iol.co.za/news/south-africa/western-cape/rasta-boy-misses-school-over-dreads-1972722.

75. Sipuye, "Why No Outrage."

76. Izsák, "Report of the Special Rapporteur," ¶ 28; Working Group of Experts on People of African Descent, "Report of the Working Group," ¶ 16.

77. Working Group of Experts on People of African Descent, "Report of the Working Group," ¶ 37.

78. Gualberto, "Mapa da Intolerãncia Religiosa," 136–38.

79. "Livro sobre lendas da Umbanda gera polêmica em escola no Rio," *Terra*, October 27, 2009, https://www.terra.com.br/noticias/educacao/livro-sobre-lendas-da-umbanda-gera-polemica-em-escola-no-rio,891937dab d9ea310VgnCLD200000bbcceb0aRCRD.html.

80. Ibid.

81. Ibid.

82. Marques, "Lendas de Exu sob os holofotes da educação."

83. United States Department of State, "2010 International Religious Freedom Report—Brazil."

84. R. Garcia, "Aula sobre mitos africanos gera polêmica."

85. United States Department of State, "2013 International Religious Freedom Report—Brazil." 3.

86. Ibid. 2.

87. Andrade and Teixeira, "School, Religion, and Intolerance," 594.

88. Ibid., 593–94.

89. Ibid., 590.

90. Ibid., 591–92; Conte, "Umbanda," 57.

91. Conte, "Umbanda," 57.

92. Ibid.

CHAPTER 6

1. Sarah Strickland, "Attitude of Judge in Race Case Queried," *The Independent* (London), December 17, 1991.

2. David Pannick, "Beware When a Judge's Power Goes to His Head," *The Times* (London), June 11, 2002.

3. Ross McCarthy, "I'll Eat My Hat! Stunned Rastafarian Is Locked Up for Refusing to Take Off Headgear in Court," *Birmingham Evening Mail*, May 29, 2002.

4. Ibid.

5. *Muhammad v. Paruk*, 553 F.Supp.2d 893.

6. Ibid., 896.

7. Ibid.

8. David Ibata, "Muslim Woman, Douglasville Settle Lawsuit Over Her Hijab," *Atlanta Journal-Constitution*, August 10, 2012, https://www.ajc.com/news/local/muslim-woman-douglasville-settle-lawsuit-over-her-hijab/5EYnj9fIkTD9KyOGQi11XN/.

9. "Complaint," *Lisa Valentine v. City of Douglasville*, No. 1:10-mi-99999-UNA, 6.

10. Ibid., 8.

11. Ibid., 9.

12. Ibid., 11–12.

13. John Barker, "City Pays Settlement Over Headgear," *Patch*, October 6, 2011, https://patch

.com/georgia/douglasville/city-pays-settlement-over-headcovering.

14. *Lisa Valentine v. City of Douglasville*, No. 1:10-mi-99999-UNA.

15. Barker, "City Pays Settlement Over Headgear."

16. Paul Woolverton, "Fayetteville Man Believes Judge Violated His Right to Practice Voodoo," *Fayetteville Observer*, July 8, 2015.

17. Ibid.

18. Paul Woolverton, "Courthouse Blog: Transcript of Man Being Detained for Wearing Voodoo Beads in Court," *Fayetteville Observer*, July 8, 2015.

19. The *Fayetteville Observer* explains that the prisoner's box "is a secure, windowed area of the courtroom where jail inmates sit while they wait for their turn to appear before the judge." Woolverton, "Fayetteville Man Believes Judge."

20. Ibid.

21. Ibid.; David Milward, "Man Locked Up for Wearing Voodoo Beads in US Court," *The Telegraph Online* (United Kingdom), July 20, 2015.

22. Paul Woolverton, "Fayetteville Man with Voodoo Beads Again Clashes with Judge," *Fayetteville Observer*, July 16, 2015.

23. Ibid.

24. Ibid.

25. Milward, "Man Locked Up for Wearing"; Woolverton, "Fayetteville Man with Voodoo Beads."

26. Diogo Costa and Giulia Marquezini, "Estudante é expulso de fórum por se recusar a tirar adereço do candomblé," *Correio*, April 1, 2015, http://www.correio24horas.com.br/noticia/nid/estudante-e-expulso-de-forum-por-se-recusar-a-tirar-adereco-do-candomble/; "Estudante diz que foi expulso de Fórum por não tirar adereço do candomblé," *O Dia*, April 2, 2015, http://odia.ig.com.br/noticia/brasil/2015-04-02/estudante-diz-que-foi-expulso-de-forum-por-nao-tirar-adereco-do-candomble.html.

27. *In re Chikweche*, No. CA 626/93.

28. Ibid., 7.

29. Ibid., 8.

30. *Garreth Anver Prince v. President of the Law Society*, No. CCT 36/00 (2000).

31. Ibid., 8.

32. *Garreth Anver Prince v. President of the Law Society*, No. CCT 36/00 (2002).

33. Ibid., 32. Despite these strong observations about the stigmatization of Rastafarians in South Africa, even the dissenting judges would not have simply found in Prince's favor. They believed that it was for the legislature to determine how cannabis should be regulated. They would not have forced the Law Society to admit Prince until cannabis was no longer a crime.

34. Ibid., 98.

35. Ibid., 100.

36. *Garreth Anver Prince / South Africa*, No. 255/02.

37. Ibid., 6–7.

38. Ibid., 7.

39. *Garreth Anver Prince / South Africa*, No. 1474/2006.

40. Ibid., 14.

41. Court documents do not specify that Webb is African American. However, Seval Yildirim, a scholar who worked on Webb's case, explained that she used terminology for her head covering that was common in "Philadelphia's African American Muslim community." Yildrim includes a photo of Webb that show her as a darker-skinned woman, and she emphasizes that Webb's case challenges the idea of Muslim women as foreigners or immigrants. Yildirim, "Freeman v. Dep't of Highway Safety," 301, 303, 307.

42. *Webb v. City of Philadelphia*, 562 F.3d 256, 258.

43. Yildrim, "Freeman v. Dep't of Highway Safety," 302.

44. *Webb v. City of Philadelphia*, 562 F.3d 256, 258.

45. Yildrim, "Freeman v. Dep't of Highway Safety," 302; *Webb v. City of Philadelphia*, 2007 U.S. Dist. Lexis 46872, 4–5.

46. *Webb v. City of Philadelphia*, 2007 U.S. Dist. Lexis 46872, 6.

47. Ibid., 6.

48. *Webb v. City of Philadelphia*, 562 F.3d 256, 261.

49. Ibid., 262.

50. *Niles Dodd v. SEPTA*, No. 2:06-cv-04213-GEKP.

51. "Complaint," *Niles Dodd v. SEPTA*, No. 2:06-cv-04213-GEKP, 3.

52. Ibid.

53. Ibid.
54. "Order to Dismiss," *Niles Dodd v. SEPTA*, No. 2:06-cv-04213-GEKP.
55. *Lord Osunfarian Xodus v. Wackenhut Corporation*, 626 F. Supp. 2d 861; *Lord Osunfarian Xodus v. Wackenhut Corporation*, 619 F.3d 683.
56. EEOC, "Grand Central Partnership Settles EEOC Religious and National Origin Discrimination Suit," August 7, 2009, https://www.eeoc.gov/eeoc/newsroom/release/archive/8-7-09.html; EEOC, "Grand Central Partnership to Pay $135k to Settle EEOC Lawsuit for Retaliation," March 5, 2013, https://www.eeoc.gov/eeoc/newsroom/release/3-5-13.cfm.
57. *Police and Prisons Rights Union ("POPCRU") and Others v. The Department*, No. C544/2007; *Department of Correctional Services v POPCRU*, [2013] ZASCA 40.
58. *Department of Correctional Services v POPCRU*, [2013] ZASCA 40, 3.
59. Ibid., 7.
60. Ibid.
61. *POPCRU v. The Department of Correctional Services*, No. C544/2007, 39.
62. Ibid., 47. However, the union representative countered that there had not been a case of a Rastafarian smuggling drugs in the last twenty years.
63. Ibid., 87.
64. *Department of Corrections v. POPCRU*, [2013] ZASCA 40), 11.
65. *Jevon Hicks v. Hudson County Correctional Center*, 2007 N.J. Super. Unpub. Lexis 1035.
66. For example, see *Jonathan Booth v. Maryland*, 2006 U.S. Dist. Lexis 49313; *Nigel LeBlanc et al. v. Community Education Centers et al.*, No. 10–3704.
67. Council on American Islamic Relations, letter to Governor Brian P. Kemp, April 29, 2019 (on file with author).
68. Memorandum, Linton Deloach to Jalanda Calhoun, Rogers State Prison, February 22, 2019 (on file with author).
69. Jalanda Calhoun, Employment Discrimination Complaint, Georgia Commission on Equal Opportunity, April 22, 2019 (on file with author).

70. *Daniels and Others v Minister of Police*, [2015] ZAGPPHC 317.
71. Veronica Rocha, "Muslim Woman Awarded $85,000 After Her Hijab Was Forcibly Removed by Long Beach Police Officer," *Los Angeles Times*, August 10, 2017, http://www.latimes.com/local/lanow/la-me-ln-muslim-woman-hijab-removed-settlement-20170810-story.html; AFP, "Payout for US Muslim Woman Whose Hijab Was Removed by Police," *Times of Israel*, August 11, 2017, https://www.timesofisrael.com/payout-for-us-muslim-woman-whose-hijab-was-removed-by-police/.

SECTION III

1. Olmos and Paravisini-Gebert, *Creole Religions*, 131.
2. Ibid., 131, 133.
3. Ibid., 136–37; Murrell, *Afro-Caribbean Religions*, 239.
4. Olmos and Paravisini-Gebert, *Creole Religions*, 141; Murrell, *Afro-Caribbean Religions*, 239.
5. Olmos and Paravisini-Gebert, *Creole Religions*, 131.
6. Handler and Bilby, "On the Early Use," 90–91.
7. Ibid., 92.
8. Ibid., 87.
9. Jamaica, "An Act to Remedy," 2:55.
10. Ibid.
11. Paton, "Obeah Acts," 5–7.
12. Ibid., 1–2; Paton, *Cultural Politics of Obeah*, 1–2; Murrell, *Afro-Caribbean Religions*, 225–26.
13. Murrell, *Afro-Caribbean Religions*, 57.
14. Ibid., 59; Gaston agrees that it means "spirit" or "deity" in Fon. Gaston, "Case of Voodoo," 111.
15. Boaz, "Voodoo Cult of Detroit," 19.
16. Ibid.
17. St. John, *Hayti or the Black Republic*, 187–257.
18. Fandrich, "Yorùbá Influences," 786.
19. Ibid.
20. Ibid., 785. Gaston, "Case of Voodoo," 115, 127, 134.
21. Fandrich, "Yorùbá Influences," 786.

22. Gaston, "Case of Voodoo," 134–35; Fandrich, "Yorùbá Influences," 787.
23. Long, *Spiritual Merchants*, 50.
24. Ibid.
25. Gaston, "Case of Voodoo," 129–33.
26. Ibid., 131.
27. Ibid. 137.
28. Roberts, *Voodoo and Power*, 17–18.
29. Gaston, "Case of Voodoo," 137.
30. Ibid.
31. Ibid., 142.

CHAPTER 7

1. These countries are Belize, the Bahamas, Guyana, Jamaica, Dominica, Antigua and Barbuda, Grenada, St. Christopher and Nevis, the British Virgin Islands, Montserrat, St. Vincent and the Grenadines, and Turks and Caicos, as well as the Cayman Islands. See Handler and Bilby, *Enacting Power*, 45–101. The US Virgin Islands also maintains anti-Obeah legislation. Virgin Islands, Code Annotated: Miscellaneous Acts of Vagrancy.
2. Several scholars have discussed the complex relationship between Obeah legislation and English laws regarding witchcraft and vagrancy. See Paton, "Obeah Acts," 4–7; Handler and Bilby, *Enacting Power*, 18–19.
3. Beier, "'New Serfdom,'" 45–51.
4. England, "An Act for Punishment of Rogues, " 45.
5. These laws have been reprinted in Gibson, *Witchcraft and Society*, 1–8.
6. Sharpe, *Instruments of Darkness*, 125.
7. Ibid., 64–66.
8. Ibid., 85.
9. For example, see "An Act against Conjuration, Enchantments and Witchcrafts," in Gibson, *Witchcraft and Society*, 3–5; Sharpe, *Instruments of Darkness*, 66–68; Macfarlane, *Witchcraft in Tudor and Stuart England*, 126.
10. Sharpe, *Instruments of Darkness*, 223–27.
11. Ibid., 237–41.
12. This law actually went into effect in 1736 but, according to the law's own short title, was called "The Witchcraft Act of 1735."
13. England, "The Witchcraft Act of 1735," 15:549.
14. Ibid.

15. Davies, *Witchcraft, Magic and Culture*, 50.
16. Paton, *Cultural Politics of Obeah*, 17–42; Rucker, *River Flows On*, 44–45; Brown, *Reaper's Garden*, 147–50.
17. Jamaica, "An Act to Remedy," 2:52.
18. Ibid.
19. Ibid.
20. Dominica, "An Act for the Encouragement," 24; Barbados, "An Act for the Better Prevention," 25:269.
21. Jamaica, "An Act to Remedy," 2:52.
22. For example, see Paton, "Obeah Acts," 5; Paton, *Cultural Politics of Obeah*, 120–22; Bilby and Handler, *Enacting Power*, 18–19.
23. England, An Act for the Punishment of Idle and Disorderly Persons.
24. England, "Sixth Report from the Select Committee," 13:135–69.
25. Diana Paton, Jerome Handler, and Kenneth Bilby have discussed this in detail. Paton, "Obeah Acts," 5–7; Paton, *Cultural Politics of Obeah*, 120–22; Bilby and Handler, *Enacting Power*, 18–19.
26. Guyana, "Obeah Ordinance 1855," 476.
27. Jamaica, "An Act to Explain," 44.
28. Bahamas, Penal Code 1927; Grenada, Criminal Code 1958; Guyana, Summary Jurisdiction (Offenses) Law.
29. For example, see Bahamas, Penal Code 1927; Grenada, Criminal Code 1958; Belize, Summary Jurisdiction (Offences) Act 2000.
30. Antigua and Barbuda, Obeah Act 1904; Bahamas, Penal Code 1927; Guyana, Summary Jurisdiction (Offenses) Law.
31. Bechuanaland, "The Witchcraft Proclamation 1927."
32. Lesotho, "The Native Medicine Men and Herbalists Proclamation 1948."
33. Zambia, The Witchcraft Act 1914; Tanzania, The Witchcraft Act 1928; Botswana, An Act to Suppress the Imputation or Practice of Pretended Witchcraft 1927; Uganda, The Penal Code 1950; Seychelles, The Penal Code 1955.
34. Boaz, "Fraud, Vagrancy," 54–84.
35. This is based on my own research spanning hundreds of witchcraft and Obeah cases. In Africa, persons were charged with using

witchcraft to harm others, but there were separate provisions in witchcraft statutes that governed such offenses.

36. The language about reasonable beliefs "in these days of advanced knowledge" comes from *Penny v. Hanson*, 18 QBD 478. Justice Lawrence expressed similar sentiments in *Stonehouse v. Masson*, explaining that he could not imagine that any person who professed to communicate with spirits did not commit intentional fraud. *Stonehouse v. Masson*, 2 KB 818.

37. *Rex v. Duncan and Others*, KB 713.

38. For instance, see Collins, "Spiritualism and the Law," 158–62.

39. England, "Fraudulent Mediums Bill 1950," §1454.

40. Ibid., §1474, §1522.

41. Ibid., §1471.

42. Ibid., §1518. However, "rare" enforcement is a relative term. Mr. Ede reported that in 1949 there were "only" thirty-nine people prosecuted for this type of violation of the Vagrancy Act. Ibid., §1486.

43. England, Fraudulent Mediums Act 1951.

44. *Regina v. Molly Brodie*, 6 J.L.R. 129, 22.

45. Ibid.

46. Ibid., 23.

47. Ibid., 24.

48. Diana Paton, "Welcome Plan to Go Easy on Obeah," *Jamaica Observer*, February 25, 2013, http://www.jamaicaobserver.com/None/Welcome-plan-to-go-easy-on-Obeah_13699379.

49. The Jamaican Watchman, "Supporting Obeah Is Disturbing," *Jamaica Observer*, February 26, 2013, http://www.jamaicaobserver.com/columns/Supporting-Obeah-is-disturbing_13722107.

50. Ibid.

51. Ibid.

52. Concerned Citizen, "Why the Increase in 'Alternative Practices'?," *Jamaica Observer*, June 2, 2016, http://www.jamaicaobserver.com/letters/Why-the-increase-in--alternative-practices--_62846.

53. Ibid.

54. Ibid.

55. Linton Gordon, "The Rise of These Newcomer 'Healers' and 'Problem-Solvers,'" *Jamaica Observer*, September 19, 2017, http://www.jamaicaobserver.com/opinion/the-rise-of-these-newcomer-8216-healers-8217-and-8216-problem-solvers-8217-_111311.

56. Ibid.

57. Ibid.

58. Jediael Carter, "Obeah or Astrology?," *Jamaica Observer*, December 17, 2017, http://www.jamaicaobserver.com/front-page/Obeah-or-astrology-concern-raised-over-rise-in-number-of-indian-astrologers-advertising-their-talent-in-jamaican-media_119494.

59. "Settle This Obeah Issue Once and For All," *Jamaica Observer*, December 18, 2017, http://www.jamaicaobserver.com/editorial/settle-this-Obeah-issue-once-and-for-all_120204?profile=1100.

60. Ibid.

61. Ibid.

62. "Obeah Law could be repealed soon," *Loop Jamaica*, June 5, 2019, https://www.loopjamaica.com/content/obeah-law-could-be-repealed-soon.

63. United States Department of State, "2019 International Religious Freedom Report—Jamaica," 5.

64. Trinidad and Tobago, "An Ordinance for rendering certain offences punishable on Summary Conviction 1902," 130–31. I have been unable to locate an earlier version of this law from 1868 to confirm that the language is identical. However, this law is described in another work in sufficient detail to suggest that the language was at least very similar, if not the same. Handler and Bilby, *Enacting Power*, 59.

65. Trinidad and Tobago, The Miscellaneous Laws Act of Trinidad and Tobago 2000.

66. Ibid.

67. For example, see Trinidad and Tobago (House of Representatives), "Orisa Marriage Bill," 568.

68. Trinidad and Tobago (Senate), "Orisa Marriage Bill," 377–78.

69. Trinidad and Tobago (House of Representatives), "Miscellaneous Laws Bill 2000," 22.

70. Trinidad and Tobago (Senate), "Miscellaneous Laws Bill 2000," 98–100.
71. Trinidad and Tobago (House of Representatives), "Miscellaneous Laws Bill 2000," 35.
72. Ibid., 59–61.
73. Ibid., 60.
74. Ibid., 62.
75. Ibid., 70.
76. Ibid.
77. South Africa, "Regulations for the Government of the Transkei 1879," 6.
78. South Africa, "Native Territories' Penal Code 1886," 2:2388.
79. "Witchcraft," Ordinance No. 26, 1904, 151.
80. South Africa, Witchcraft Suppression Act 1957.
81. South African Pagan Rights Alliance, "Review of Witchcraft Suppression Act Update," http://www.paganrightsalliance.org/review-of-witchcraft-suppression-act-update/; South African Law Reform Commission, "Review of the Witchcraft Suppression Act 3 of 1957," 1.
82. Ibid., 1–2.
83. Ibid., 6–7.
84. South African Law Reform Commission, "Review of the Witchcraft Suppression Act 3 of 1957," [2014].
85. South African Law Reform Commission, "Review of the Witchcraft Suppression Act 3 of 1957," [2016].
86. Ibid., 42.
87. Ibid., 25.
88. Ibid., 84.
89. Ibid., 70–71.
90. Ibid., 71.
91. Canada, Criminal Code.
92. Bakht and Palmer, "Modern Law, Modern Hammers," 129.
93. Canada (House of Commons), "Bill C-51 Debate," [148, No. 194], 16:09–16:16.
94. Ibid.
95. Canada (House of Commons), "Bill C-51 Debate," [148, No. 249], 12:28–12:45.
96. Ibid., 13:24–13:31.
97. Canada (House of Commons), "Bill C-51 Debate," [148, No. 195], 20:30–20:40.
98. Ibid., 20:30–20:40.
99. Ibid., 18:25–18:45.
100. Ibid., 19:19–19:29.

CHAPTER 8

1. *Taekwon Taylor v. Anthony Bruno*, 2008 WL 5481128.
2. Ibid., 1.
3. Ibid., 4.
4. Ibid., 5.
5. Motion to Suppress, *United States of America v. Alberto Duncan*, No. 08-2394-CR-Seitz/O'Sullivan.
6. "Brief for the United States," *United States of America v. Alberto Duncan*, No. 08-16825-AA, 4.
7. Ibid.; "District Court's Order on Defendant's Motion to Suppress," *United States of America v. Alberto Duncan*, No. 08-20394-CR-Seitz/O'Sullivan, 1–2.
8. "Indictment & Penalty Sheet," *United States of America v. Alberto Duncan*, No. 08-20394-CR-Seitz/O'Sullivan.
9. Olmos and Paravisini-Gebert, *Creole Religions*, 61.
10. Ibid., 49–50, 61–62; Murrell, *Afro-Caribbean Religions*, 109–10.
11. "Proposed Jury Instruction on Religious Freedom of Restoration Act," *United States of America v. Alberto Duncan*, No. 08-2394-CR-Seitz/O'Sullivan.
12. "Transcript," *United States of America v. Alberto Duncan*, No. 08-2394-CR-Seitz/O'Sullivan (July 29, 2008), 50.
13. Ibid., 32–33.
14. Ibid., 112–14.
15. Ibid., 115.
16. Ibid., 128.
17. "Transcript," *United States of America v. Alberto Duncan*, No. 08-2394-CR-Seitz/O'Sullivan (July 30, 2008), 71.
18. Ibid., 48.
19. Ibid., 51.
20. Ibid., 54.
21. Ibid., 79–83.
22. "Brief for the United States," *United States of America v. Alberto Duncan*, No. 08-16825-AA, 13.
23. "Defendant's Reply Brief," *United States of America v. Alberto Duncan*, No. 08-16825-AA, 6.

24. Ibid., 8.
25. *United States of America v. Alberto Duncan*, No. 08-16825, 253–54.
26. *Queen v. Marlon Rowe*, 2006 CanLII 14235.
27. Ibid., 4.
28. Ibid., 3.
29. Ibid., 4.
30. Lawes was finally apprehended approximately two years after the robbery, but it does not appear that "Brownman" was ever conclusively identified or charged with the robbery.
31. *Queen v. Marlon Rowe*, 2006 CanLII 14235; Bob Mitchell, "'Con Man' Psychic In Line to Receive $200,000 Reward; Got Crucial Information from Defendant in Nancy Kidd Murder Trial," *Toronto Star*, December 27, 2000.
32. *Queen v. Marlon Rowe*, 2006 CanLII 14235, 13.
33. Ibid., 10.
34. *Queen v. Welsh*, 2013 ONCA 190.
35. Ibid., 10.
36. Ibid., 14–16.
37. *Queen v. Marlon Rowe*, 2006 CanLII 14235, 4.
38. *Queen v. Welsh*, 2013 ONCA 190, 31.
39. *Queen v. Ruben Pinnock*, 2007 CanLII 13943, 9.
40. *Queen v. Welsh*, 2013 ONCA 190, 14 (emphasis added).
41. Ibid., 20.
42. Ibid., 20–21. This test about whether the religious practice furthers the interest of the community is significant. Aisha Khan has previously argued that part of the reason that Obeah has never earned the classification of "religion" in Western interpretations is because it was "viewed as lacking the coherence (social glue) that could produce 'community' because of an alleged raison d'être based on an individual-oriented operation." Khan, "Dark Arts and Diaspora," 53. Khan emphasizes that principles of freedom of religion have shielded faiths that are constructive and practiced as a community (ibid., 56–57).
43. *Queen v. Welsh*, 2013 ONCA 190, 21.
44. *Rothman v. The Queen*, 1 SCR 640, 642.
45. Ibid., 697.
46. *Queen v. Marlon Rowe*, 2006 CanLII 14235, 14.

47. J. Brent Crosson explains the significance of the use of the word "sin" in these cases. He argues that the discussion of "a specifically Euro-Christian concept of sin and salvation structured the exercise of legal power and state protection" demonstrates "that certain Euro-Christian religious ideas deeply underpinned the exercise of law." Crosson, "What Obeah Does Do," 163–64.
48. *Queen v. Welsh*, 2013 ONCA 190, 39.
49. Ibid., 30.
50. Murrell, *Afro-Caribbean Religions*, 229–30.
51. Olmos and Paravisini-Gebert, *Creole Religions*, 140.
52. Ricardo de Mattos, "About Umbanda and Candomblé," *Digestivo Cultural*, June 23, 2014; "MPF pede que Google tire do ar vídeos que discriminam religiões africanas," *Migalhas*, February 27, 2014, http://www.migalhas.com.br/Quentes/17,MI196313,51045-MPF+pede+que+Google+tire+do+ar+videos+que+discriminam+religioes.
53. *Ministério Público Federal v. Google Brasil*, No. 0004747-33.2014.4.02.5101; *Ministério Público Federal v. Google Brasil*, No. 0101043-94.2014.4.02.0000, 4.
54. *Ministério Público Federal v. Google Brasil*, No. 0101043-94.2014.4.02.0000, 4–5.
55. Ibid.
56. *Ministério Público Federal v. Google Brasil*, No. 0004747-33.2014.4.02.5101.
57. Ibid.
58. Ibid.
59. *Ministério Público Federal v. Google Brasil*, No. 0004747-33.2014.4.02.5101.
60. Comitê Nacional de Respeito à Diversidade Religiosa (CNRDR), "Nota de Comitê defende diversidade religiosa."
61. *Ministério Público Federal v. Google Brasil Internet Ltda*, No. 0101043-94.2014.4.02.0000, 2, 19.
62. Ibid., 14.
63. Ibid., 2.
64. Ibid., 2, 22.
65. CNRDR, "Relatório sobre Intolerância e Violência Religiosa," 84.
66. United States Department of State, "2013 International Religious Freedom Report—Brazil," 3.

67. United Nations General Assembly, "Report of the Chair of the Working Group," ¶ 17.
68. United States Department of State, "2014 International Religious Freedom Report—Brazil," 4.
69. "Umbandistas atacados vão cobrar indenização na Justiça," *Globo1*, June 6, 2008, http://g1.globo.com/Noticias/Rio/0,,MUL588075-5606,00-UMBANDISTAS+ATACADOS+VAO+COBRAR+INDENIZACAO+NA+JUSTICA.html.
70. Patricia Iglecio, "Delegado é atacado por religiosos após audiência por intolerância no Rio," *Dossiê Intolerância Religiosa*, September 6, 2014, http://intoleranciareligiosadossie.blogspot.com/2014/09/delegado-e-atacado-por-religiosos-apos.html.
71. United States Department of State, "2014 International Religious Freedom Report—Brazil," 3.
72. "Feliciano pode ser preso por crime de preconceito contra religião," *Geledes*, March 27, 2014, https://www.geledes.org.br/feliciano-pode-ser-preso-por-crime-de-preconceito-contra-religiao/.

CHAPTER 9

1. Carli Teproff, "Man Arrested in Ollie the Pit Bull's Killing Linked to Voodoo, Animal Sacrifices," *Miami Herald*, November 22, 2007.
2. Ibid.
3. Ibid.; Susannah Bryan, "Man, 31, Arrested in Death of Pit Bull," *Sun Sentinel* (Ft. Lauderdale, FL), November 23, 2017.
4. See *Autopsy*, "Autopsy 6: Secrets of the Dead," aired in 1999 on HBO. (Sutton's name also appears as "Suttle" in reports.)
5. *Paula Albritton v. State of Florida*, No. 2D99-2008; Manatee County Human Services, "Burial Assistance: Human Services Benefit Programs."
6. *Paula Albritton v. State of Florida*, No. 2D99-2008.
7. *Autopsy*, "Autopsy 6: Secrets of the Dead."
8. *Paula Albritton v. State of Florida*, No. 2D99-2008.
9. Ibid.; Kristi Ceccarossi, Jeremy Wallace, and L. W. Kong, "Revisiting a Bizarre Case,"

Sarasota Herald Tribune, June 2, 2004, http://www.heraldtribune.com/news/20040602/revisiting-a-bizarre-case.
10. *Paula Albritton v. State of Florida*, No. 2D99-2008.
11. *Autopsy*, "Autopsy 6: Secrets of the Dead."
12. *Paula Albritton v. State of Florida*, No. 2D99-2008.
13. Ibid.
14. *State of Florida v. Jimmie Lee Clark*, No. 1998-SA-011423.
15. *Paula Albritton v. State of Florida*, No. 2D99-2008.
16. Ibid.
17. "Docket," *State of Florida v. Paula Albritton*, No. 1998-SA-008094.
18. Ibid.
19. Kellie McMaster, "Funeral Home Investigation: Expert's Report Confirms Ritual Was Voodoo Practice," *Sarasota Herald Tribune*, August 5, 1998.
20. Ibid.
21. Ibid.
22. "Mortician Guilty of Abusing Body," *Los Angeles Times*, March 7, 1999, http://articles.latimes.com/1999/mar/07/news/mn-14697.
23. *Autopsy*, "Autopsy 6: Secrets of the Dead."
24. Ceccarossi, Wallace, and Kong, "Revisiting a Bizarre Case."
25. "Long Term Jail for Haitian Mother Who Set Daughter Ablaze in Voodoo Ritual" *CANAnews* (Barbados), June 7, 2011.
26. Christina Carrega-Woodby, "Voodoo Mom Sentenced to 17 Years in Prison for Burning Daughter," *New York Post*, June 6, 2011, https://nypost.com/2011/06/06/voodoo-mom-sentenced-to-17-years-in-prison-for-burning-daughter/.
27. "Long Term Jail for Haitian Mother"; Carrega-Woodby, "Voodoo Mom Sentenced."
28. Carrega-Woodby, "Voodoo Mom Sentenced."
29. Ibid.
30. Ibid.
31. "Haitian Mother in New York Burns Child in Voodoo Ritual; Faces Deportation," *Dominica News Online*, May 19, 2011, http://dominicanewsonline.com/news/homepage/news/international-news/haitian-mother-in-new-york-burns-child-in-voodoo-ritual-faces-deportation/ ; "Mother Admits to Burning

Child in Voodoo Ritual," *Sydney Morning Herald*, May 20, 2011, https://www.smh.com.au/world/mother-admits-to-burning-child-in-voodoo-ritual-20110520-1evep.html; "'Voodoo Mum' Sentenced to 17 Years Behind Bars for Setting Fire to Six-Year-Old Daughter in Exorcism Ritual," *Daily Mail Online*, June 7, 2011, https://www.dailymail.co.uk/news/article-2000009/Voodoo-mum-sentenced-17-years-bars-burning-year-old-daughter.html.

32. "Voodoo Child-Burning Grandma Going to Prison," *Queens Chronicle*, April 14, 2011, http://www.qchron.com/editions/eastern/voodoo-child-burning-grandma-going-to-prison/article_103d33db-4f6a-5ebe-86e3-6d06d4fc92f9.html?mode=story.

33. Dan Bilefsky, "Voodoo, an Anchor, Rises Again," *New York Times*, April 8, 2011, http://sites.middlebury.edu/themoderncaribbean/files/2011/02/Voodoo-Spiritual-Anchor-Rises-Again-in-New-York-NYTimes.com_.pdf.

34. Ibid.

35. Alanna Durkin Richer and Philip Marcelo, "Believers Fear Backlash from 'Voodoo' Claims—Practitioners Say Religion Does Not Sanction Violence," *Berkshire Eagle* (Pittsfield, MA), February 13, 2018; "Women Accused of Burning 5-Year-Old Girl in Voodoo Ritual," *New York Post*, February 4, 2018, https://nypost.com/2018/02/04/women-accused-of-burning-5-year-old-girl-in-voodoo-ritual/.

36. Caroline Mortimer, "Five-Year-Old Girl Tied Down and Burned to Rid Her of 'Demon' in 'Voodoo' Ritual, Police Say," *Independent on Sunday* (London), February 3, 2018; Sara Cline, "East Bridgewater Women Disfigure Child in Voodoo Ritual, Say Police," *Enterprise News* (Brockton, MA), February 1, 2018, http://www.enterprisenews.com/news/20180201/east-bridgewater-women-disfigure-child-in-voodoo-ritual-say-police.

37. Mortimer, "Five-Year-Old Girl Tied Down."

38. "Women Accused of Burning 5-Year-Old Girl."

39. Ibid.; Lisa Marie Segarra, "5-Year-Old Permanently Disfigured in Voodoo Ritual, Police Say," *Time*, February 3, 2018, http://time.com/5132317/child-burned-voodoo-ritual/.

40. Segarra, "5-Year-Old Permanently Disfigured."

41. Cline, "East Bridgewater Women Disfigure Child."

42. Cleve R. Wootson Jr., "A Child Was Taken to a Voodoo Practitioner for Discipline. Police Say She Will Be Permanently Disfigured," *Washington Post*, February 4, 2018, https://www.washingtonpost.com/news/true-crime/wp/2018/02/04/a-misbehaving-child-was-taken-to-a-voodoo-practitioner-police-say-she-will-be-permanently-disfigured/.

43. "Police: Child Burned in Voodoo Ritual in Massachusetts, 2 Women Charged," *VOA News*, February 3, 2018, https://www.voanews.com/a/police-say-child-burned-voodoo-ritual-massachusetts/4238162.html.

44. Associated Press, "Police: 5-Year-Old Girl Burned in Voodoo Ritual; 2 charged," *UK Business Insider*, February 3, 2018, http://uk.businessinsider.com/ap-police-5-year-old-girl-burned-in-voodoo-ritual-2-charged-2018-2; Chris Kitching, "Sisters 'Burn Five-Year-Old Girl's Face During VOODOO Ritual to Get Rid of Evil Spirit Inside Her Body,'" *The Mirror*, February 3, 2018, https://www.mirror.co.uk/news/us-news/sisters-burn-five-year-old-11964753.

45. Wootson, "Child Was Taken."

46. Ibid.

47. "Police: Child Burned in Voodoo Ritual."

48. Cody Shepard, "Was It Voodoo? Massachusetts Mother Charged in Macabre Murders of Sons," *Topsail Advertiser*, February 7, 2018, https://www.topsailadvertiser.com/zz/news/20180207/was-it-voodoo-massachusetts-mother-charged-in-macabre-murders-of-sons.

49. Ibid.

50. Richer and Marcelo, "Believers Fear Backlash."

51. Ibid.

52. Van Dijk, "'Voodoo' on the Doorstep," 563.

53. Cole, "Reducing the Damage," 217–19.

54. For instance, see Rucker, *River Flows On*, 83–84; Agyekum, "*Ntam* 'Reminsciential Oath' Taboo," 318; Luongo, *Witchcraft and Colonial Rule*, 167–68.

55. Scholars often use this language of "voodoo" in their article titles. For instance, see Van Dijk, "'Voodoo' on the Doorstep," and Baarda, "Human Trafficking." News articles

often use this language in titles as well. See "Spanish Police Arrest 23 People for 'Using Voodoo Curses,'" *The Telegraph*, May 22, 2009, https://www.telegraph.co.uk/news/worldnews/europe/spain/5364373/Spanish-police-arrest-23-people-for-using-voodoo-curses.html.

56. Garcia, "Voodoo, Witchcraft and Human Trafficking in Europe," 1.

57. Ibid., 7.

58. Ezeilo, "Report of the Special Rapporteur," 4.

59. Van Dijk, "'Voodoo' on the Doorstep," 564.

60. Ibid., 572.

61. Baarda, "Human Trafficking," 263–65.

62. Ojo, "Incorporation of Ayelala," 995.

63. Ibid., 996.

64. Ibid., 998.

65. Ibid., 999; Similarly, in Dr. Akhilomen Don's blog post about the Ayelala in Benin, there is no mention of the words "voodoo" or "vodun." Akhilomen Don, "The Resurgence of Ayelala in Benin Kingdom: An Indictment of the Conventional Dispensation of Justice in Nigeria," September 25, 2009, https://ihuanedo.ning.com/profiles/blogs/the-resurgence-of-ayelala-in.

66. Van der Watt and Kruger, "Exploring 'Juju' and Human Trafficking," 77.

67. Ibid., 78.

68. Ibid., 73.

69. Ibid., 76.

7. Ibid., ¶ 33–39.

8. Marcelo Silva De Sousa, "Rio City Council Votes Against Opening Impeachment of Mayor," *AP News*, July 12, 2018.

9. Elaine Brum, "How a Homophobic, Misogynist, Racist 'Thing' Could Be Brazil's Next President," *The Guardian*, October 6, 2018, https://www.theguardian.com/commentisfree/2018/oct/06/homophobic-mismogynist-racist-brazil-jair-bolsonaro.

10. Jen Kirby, "4 Things to Know About Jair Bolsonaro, Brazil's New Far-Right President," *Vox*, October 29, 2018, https://www.vox.com/2018/10/29/18037728/bolsonaro-brazil-election-guide.

11. Ernesto Londoño, "Right-Wing Presidential Contender in Brazil Is Charged with Inciting Hatred," *New York Times*, April 14, 2018.

12. Ibid.

13. Van Der Schyff, "Ritual Slaughter and Religious Freedom"; Gliszczyńska-Grabias and Sadurski, "Freedom of Religion"; Delahunty, "Does Animal Welfare"; Reuters Staff, "Belgian Region's Plan to Ban Ritual Slaughter Upsets Religious Minorities," *Reuters*, March 30, 2017.

CONCLUSION

1. Kehinde Andrews, "Brexit and the Racial Fault Line Awakened in Britain," *Montray Kréyol*, http://www.montraykreyol.org/article/brexit-and-the-racial-fault-line-awakened-in-britain.

2. Ibid.

3. Ibid.

4. Achiume, "End of Mission Statement," ¶ 62.

5. Ibid., ¶ 58.

6. Ibid.

Bibliography

STATUTES AND OTHER LEGISLATIVE MATERIALS

Antigua and Barbuda. Obeah Act 1904, c. 298, § 2-11. http://laws.gov.ag/acts/chapters/cap-298.pdf.
Assembleia Legislativa, Estado do Rio Grande do Sul. "Detalhes da Proposição, PL 21 2015." http://www.al.rs.gov.br/legislativo/ExibeProposicao.aspx?SiglaTipo=PL&NroProposicao=21&AnoProposicao=2015&Origem=Dx.
Bahamas. Penal Code 1927, c. 84, § 232. http://laws.bahamas.gov.bs/cms/en/.
Barbados. "An Act for the Better Prevention of the Practice of Obeah 1818." In *State Papers, Session: 21 November 1826–2 July 1827*, 25:269. London: H. G. Clarke, 1827.
Bechuanaland. "The Witchcraft Proclamation 1927." In *The Laws of the Bechuanaland Protectorate*, ed. A. C. Thompson, 1:489-90. Cape Province, South Africa: Cape Times Ltd., 1959.
Belize. Summary Jurisdiction (Offences) Act 2000, c. 98, pt. II, § 3(1)(viii). http://www.belizelaw.org/web/lawadmin/.
Botswana. An Act to Suppress the Imputation or Practice of Pretended Witchcraft 1927, c. 09:02. http://www.elaws.gov.bw/law.php?id=512.
California. Senate Bill No. 188 2019, c. 58. https://leginfo.legislature.ca.gov/faces/billTextClient.xhtml?bill_id=201920200SB188.
Canada. Criminal Code, pt. IX, § 365 (repealed 2018). https://laws-lois.justice.gc.ca/eng/acts/C-46/page-81.html.
Canada (House of Commons). "Bill C-51 Debate." In *Hansard Proceedings and Debates* 148, no. 194 (June 14, 2017). https://www.ourcommons.ca/DocumentViewer/en/42-1/house/sitting-194/hansard.
———. "Bill C-51 Debate." In *Hansard Proceedings and Debates* 148, no. 195 (June 15, 2017). https://www.ourcommons.ca/DocumentViewer/en/42-1/house/sitting-195/hansard.
———. "Bill C-51 Debate." In *Hansard Proceedings and Debates* 148, no. 249 (Dec. 11, 2017). https://www.ourcommons.ca/DocumentViewer/en/42-1/house/sitting-249/hansard.
Dominica. "An Act for the Encouragement, Protection, and Better Government of Slaves 1788." In *Copies of Several Acts for the Regulation of Slaves, Passed in the West India Islands*, 24. N.p., 1789.
England. "An Act for Punishment of Rogues, Vagabonds, and Sturdy Beggers." In *Certaine Statutes Especially Selected, and Commanded by His Majestie*. 45. London: Robert Barker & John Bill, 1630.
———. An Act for the Punishment of Idle and Disorderly Persons, and Rogues and Vagabonds 1824, 5 Geo. 4. c. 83. http://www.legislation.gov.uk/ukpga/1824/83/pdfs/ukpga_18240083_en.pdf.
———. Fraudulent Mediums Act 1951, c. 33 (repealed 2008). http://www.legislation.gov.uk/ukpga/Geo6/14-15/33/enacted.
———. "Fraudulent Mediums Bill 1950." In *Hansard Proceedings and Debates* 481. https://api.parliament.uk/historic-hansard/commons/1950/dec/01/fraudulent-mediums-bill.

———. "Sixth Report from the Select Committee on Sugar and Coffee Planting." In *Reports from Committees: Sugar and Coffee Planting*, 13:135–69. N.p., 1848.

———. "The Witchcraft Act of 1735." In *Statutes of Practical Utility Passed from 1902 to 1907*, ed. J. M. Lely and W. H. Aggs, 15:549. London: Sweet and Maxwell, 1908.

Grenada. Criminal Code 1958, c. 72A, §§ 98(b), 143. http://laws.gov.gd/.

Guyana. "Obeah Ordinance 1855." In *The Magisterial Law of British Guiana*, ed. Alfred Pound, 476. Demerara: The Royal Gazette Establishment, 1877.

———. Summary Jurisdiction (Offenses) Law, c. 8:02, §§ 145(1)-(2). http://www.legalaffairs.gov.gy/information/laws-of-guyana/.

Jamaica. "An Act to Explain the Fourth Victoria, Chapter Forty-Two, and the Nineteenth Victoria, Chapter Thirty, and for the More Effectual Punishment of Obeah and Myalism." In *The Statutes and Laws of the Island of Jamaica*, ed. Hon. C. Ribton Curran, 4:44. Jamaica: Government Printing Establishment, 1890.

———. "An Act to Remedy the Evils Arising from Irregular Assemblies of Slaves 1760." In *Acts of Assembly Passed in the Island of Jamaica, From the Year 1681 to the Year 1769*, 2:52. Saint Jago de la Vega, Jamaica: Lowry and Sherlock, 1791.

Lesotho. "The Native Medicine Men and Herbalists Proclamation 1948." In *Revised Edition of the Laws of Basutoland in Force on the 1st Day of January, 1949*, ed. J. G. Kneen and H. C. Juta, 1:611–13. London: Waterlow & Sons Ltd., 1950.

Massachusetts. General Laws: Permanent Disposition of Dead Bodies or Remains, pt. I, tit. XVI, c. 114, § 43M. https://malegislature.gov/Laws/GeneralLaws/PartI/TitleXVI/Chapter114/Section43M.

North Dakota. Century Code: Care and Custody of the Dead, c. 23-06, §§ 14–15. https://www.legis.nd.gov/cencode/t23c06.pdf.

Seychelles. The Penal Code 1955, c. 158, § 303. https://greybook.seylii.org/w/se/CAP158.

South Africa. "The Native Territories' Penal Code 1886." In *Statutes of the Cape of Good Hope, 1652–1905*, ed. E. M. Jackson, 2:2388. Cape Town: Cape Town Limited, 1906.

———. "Ordinance No. 26 1904." In *The Laws and Regulations Specially Relating to the Native Population of the Transvaal*, 151. Pretoria: Government Printing and Stationery Office, 1907.

———. "Regulations for the Government of the Transkei 1879." In *Proclamations of Laws for Native Territories Annexed to the Colony of the Cape of Good Hope*, 6. Cape Town: Saul Solomon & Co., 1880.

———. The Witchcraft Suppression Act 3 1957. https://www.justice.gov.za/legislation/acts/1957-003.pdf.

South African Law Reform Commission. "The Review of the Witchcraft Suppression Act 3 of 1957." Discussion Paper 139, Project No. 135 (2016).

———. "The Review of the Witchcraft Suppression Act 3 of 1957." Issue Paper 29, Project No. 135 (2014).

South Carolina. Code of Laws Unannotated: Destruction or Desecration of Human Remains or Repositories, tit. 16, c. 17, § 600. https://www.scstatehouse.gov/code/t16c017.php.

Tanzania. The Witchcraft Act 1928, c. 18. http://www.icla.up.ac.za/images/un/use-of-force/africa/Tanzania/The%20Witchcraft%20Act.pdf.

Texas. Penal Code: Cruelty to Livestock Animals, §42.09. https://statutes.capitol.texas.gov/Docs/PE/htm/PE.42.htm.

———. Penal Code: Punishments, §12.21. https://statutes.capitol.texas.gov/Docs/PE/htm/PE.12.htm.

Trinidad and Tobago. The Miscellaneous Laws Act of Trinidad and Tobago 2000. http://www.ttparliament.org/legislations/a2000-85.pdf.

———. "An Ordinance for rendering certain offences punishable on Summary Conviction 1902." In *Laws of Trinidad and Tobago*, 1:123, 130–31. Port-of-Spain, Trinidad: Government Printing Office, 1902.

——— (House of Representatives). Miscellaneous Laws Bill 2000. In *Hansard Proceedings and Debates*. http://www.ttparliament.org/hansards/hh20001011.pdf.

——— (House of Representatives). Orisa Marriage Bill 1999. In *Hansard Proceedings and Debates*. http://www.ttparliament.org/hansards/hh19990730.pdf.

——— (Senate). Miscellaneous Laws Bill 2000. In *Hansard Proceedings and Debates*. http://www.ttparliament.org/hansards/hs20001019.pdf.

——— (Senate). Orisa Marriage Bill 1999. In *Hansard Proceedings and Debates*. http://www.ttparliament.org/hansards/hs19990810.pdf.

Uganda. The Penal Code 1950, c. 120, § 311. https://ulii.org/ug/legislation/consolidated-act/120/.

Venezuela. Ley Para la Protección de la Fauna Doméstica Libre y en Cautiverio 2010. In *La Gaceta Oficial* 39338. http://www.saber.ula.ve/bitstream/123456789/30813/1/articulo5.pdf.

Virgin Islands. Code Annotated: Miscellaneous Acts of Vagrancy, tit. 14, c. 111, § 2221.

Washington. Revised Code: Unlawful Disposal of Remains, c. 68.50, §130. https://app.leg.wa.gov/RCW/default.aspx?cite=68.50.130.

Zambia. The Witchcraft Act 1914, c. 90. https://www.zambialii.org/node/7864.

COURT CASES

André Amâncio Fogaça v. Luciana Soeiro Purissmo. No. 1009615-85.2015.8.26.0126. Court of Justice of the State of São Paulo (Jan. 12, 2017).

AOM v. RDDL. No. 70051844082. Court of Justice of Rio Grande do Sul TJ-RS (Dec. 13, 2012).

Church of the Lukumi Babalu Aye, Inc., v. City of Hialeah. 723 F. Supp. 1467. United States District Court for the Southern District of Florida (Oct. 5, 1989).

Church of the Lukumi Babalu Aye, Inc., v. City of Hialeah. 936 F.2d 586. United States Court of Appeals for the Eleventh Circuit (June 11, 1991).

Church of the Lukumi Babalu Aye, Inc. v. City of Hialeah. 1992 U.S. S. Ct. Briefs LEXIS 537. United States Supreme Court (July 31, 1992).

Commonwealth v. Amador Medina. No. 2018-P-0544. Commonwealth of Massachusetts Appeals Court (June 17, 2019).

Commonwealth v. Amador Medina. No. SJC-12830. Supreme Judicial Court for the Commonwealth of Massachusetts (filed Oct. 21, 2019).

D.A. v. Governing Body, et al. No. 3791/00. High Court of South Africa, Cape of Good Hope Provincial Division (Feb. 8, 2002).

Damian Belfonte v. Attorney General of Trinidad and Tobago. 2004 TTHC 22. High Court of Justice for Trinidad and Tobago (June 11, 2004).

Daniels and Others v Minister of Police. [2015] ZAGPPHC 317. High Court of South Africa, Gauteng Division, Pretoria (Feb. 26, 2015).

Department of Correctional Services v POPCRU. [2013] ZASCA 40. Supreme Court of South Africa (Mar. 28, 2013).

Dzvova v. Minister of Education, Sports and Culture et al. No. 291/06. Supreme Court of Zimbabwe (Jan. 10, 2007).

Exmo. Sr. Dr. Procurador-Geral de Justiça v. Assembléia Legislativa do Estado do Rio Grande do Sul and Exmo. Sr. Governador do Estado do Rio Grande do Sul. No. 70010129690. Court of Justice in the State of Rio Grande do Sul (Apr. 18, 2005).

Exp. N° 15-0993. Supreme Tribunal of Justice of the Republic of Venezuela (May 18, 2016).

Extraordinary Remedy RE 494601. No. 2006/68373. Supreme Federal Tribunal of Brazil (May 26, 2006).

G v. the Head Teacher and Governors of St. Gregory's Catholic Science College. 2011 EWHC 1452. High Court of Justice, Queen's Bench Division, England (June 17, 2011).

Garreth Anver Prince v. President of the Law Society of the Cape of Good Hope and Others. No. CCT 36/00. Constitutional Court of South Africa (Dec. 12, 2000; Jan. 25, 2002).

Garreth Anver Prince / South Africa. No. 255/02. African Commission on Human and Peoples' Rights (Nov. 23–Dec. 7, 2004).

Garreth Anver Prince / South Africa. No. 1474/2006. Human Rights Committee. U.N. Doc. CCPR/C/91/D/1474/2006 (Nov. 14, 2007).

Grant & Anor v. The Principal, John A. Cumber Primary School and Others. 3 CHRLD 138; [2001] CILR 78. Court of Appeal, Cayman Islands (2001).

In re Chikweche. No. CA 626/93. Zimbabwe Supreme Court (Mar. 27, 1995).

In re M.A. v. Ronald A. 2010 WL 705521. Court of Appeal, Second District, California (Mar. 2, 2010).

In the Matter of Jevon Hicks. 2013 N.J. Agen. LEXIS 36. State of New Jersey Office of Administrative Law (Feb. 11, 2013).

In the Matter of the Adoption of Vincent. 602 N.Y.S.2d 303. Family Court, New York County, New York (Aug. 3, 1993).

Jevon Hicks v. Hudson County Correctional Center. 2007 N.J. Super. Unpub. LEXIS 1035. Superior Court of New Jersey Appellate Division (Aug. 29, 2007).

Jonathan Booth v. Maryland Department of Public Safety and Correctional Services. 2006 U.S. Dist. LEXIS 49313. United States District Court for the District of Maryland (July 7, 2006).

Jorge Badillo v. Victor Amato, et al. No. 3:13-cv-01553-FLW-TJB. United States District Court for the District of New Jersey (filed Mar. 13, 2013).

Jorge Badillo v. Victor Amato, et al. 2014 U.S. Dist. LEXIS 10210. United States District Court for the District of New Jersey (Jan. 28, 2014).

Jose Merced v. Kurt Kasson, et al. 577 F.3d 578. United States Court of Appeals, Fifth Circuit (July 31, 2009).

Lerato Radebe et al. v. Principal of Leseding Technical School et al. No. 1821/2013. Free State High Court, Republic of South Africa (May 30, 2013).

Lisa Valentine v. City of Douglasville, et al. No. 1:10-mi-99999-UNA. United States District Court for the Northern District of Georgia (filed Dec. 14, 2010).

Lord Osunfarian Xodus v. The Wackenhut Corporation. 619 F.3d 683. United States Court of Appeals for the Seventh Circuit (Apr. 15, 2010).

Lord Osunfarian Xodus v. The Wackenhut Corporation. 626 F. Supp. 2d 861. United States District Court for the Northern District of Illinois, Eastern Division (Apr. 24, 2009).

Maheshwar Singh v. The State of Himachal Pradesh. No. 32595/2014. The Supreme Court of India (Aug. 10, 2014).

Ministério Público Federal v. Google Brasil Internet Ltda. No. 0004747-33.2014.4.02.5101. 17th Federal Court of Rio de Janeiro (Apr. 28, 2014; May 20, 2014).

Ministério Público Federal v. Google Brasil Internet Ltda. No. 0101043-94.2014.4.02.0000. Federal Regional Tribunal of the 2nd Region (Sep. 4, 2014).

Muhammad v. Paruk. 553 F.Supp.2d 893. United States District Court, Eastern District of Michigan (May 12, 2008).

New Jersey v. Yenitza Colichon. No. 09003395. Superior Court of New Jersey (June 24, 2011).

New Jersey Division of Youth and Family Services v. Y.C. 2011 N.J. Super. Unpub. LEXIS 1366. Superior Court of New Jersey, Appellate Division (May 27, 2011).

Nigel LeBlanc et al. v. Delaware County Board of Prison Inspectors et al. No. 10-3704, 2011 U.S. Dist. LEXIS 75919. United States District Court for the Eastern District of Pennsylvania (July 14, 2011).

Niles Dodd v. SEPTA et al. No. 2:06-cv-04213-GEKP, 2008 U.S. Dist. LEXIS 56301.

U.S. District Court for the Eastern District of Pennsylvania (July 24, 2008).

Patson Makhiwa v. Minister of Education, Sport and Culture, et al. No. HC 51/13. High Court of Zimbabwe (Jan. 24, 2013).

Paula Albritton v. State of Florida. No. 2D99-2008. District Court of Appeal of Florida, Second District (Sept. 20, 2000).

Penny v. Hanson. 18 QBD 478. Queen's Bench Division of the High Court of Justice, England (Feb. 25, 1887).

Petition Number PET 10595305. Court of Justice of Paraná TJ-PR, Brazil (Nov. 13, 2013).

Police and Prisons Rights Union ("POPCRU") and others v. The Department of Correctional Services and another. No. C544/2007. Labour Court of South Africa at Cape Town (May 11, 2010).

Queen v. Marlon Rowe. 2006 CanLII 14235. Court of Appeal for Ontario (Dec. 14, 2005).

Queen v. Ruben Pinnock. 2007 CanLII 13943. Superior Court of Justice for Ontario (Jan. 29, 2007).

Queen v. Welsh. 2013 ONCA 190. Court of Appeal for Ontario (Dec. 18–20, 2012).

Ramon Patino et al. v. Nicolas Hood et al. No. 2018CI05535. Bexar County Court, Texas (Mar. 26, 2018).

Regina v. Molly Brodie. 6 J.L.R. 129. Supreme Court of Judicature of Jamaica (July 30, 1952).

Rex v. Duncan and Others. KB 713. Court of Criminal Appeal (June 10, 1944).

Rothman v. The Queen. 1 SCR 640. Supreme Court of Canada (Mar. 2, 1981).

State v. Rigoberto Zamora. No. M95028476. County Court for Miami Dade County, Florida (1995).

State of Florida v. Brendan Evans. No. 17013069CF10A. County Court for Broward County, Florida (Nov. 16, 2017).

State of Florida v. Jimmie Lee Clark. No. 1998-SA-011423. County Court for Manatee County, Florida (July 1, 1998).

State of Florida v. Paula Albritton. No. 1998-SA-008094. County Court for Manatee County, Florida (June 30, 1998).

State of Florida v. Rigoberto Zamora. No. M95028476. 3 Fla. L. Weekly Supp. 696b. County Court for Miami Dade County, Florida (Feb. 14, 1996).

State of New Jersey v. Miriam Miraballes. 392 N.J.Super. 342. Superior Court of New Jersey, Appellate Division (Apr. 25, 2007).

State of New Jersey v. Oscar Cruz. No. 02008126. Essex County Court, New Jersey (May 4, 2004).

Stonehouse v. Masson. 2 KB 818. King's Bench Division of the High Court of Justice, England (Apr. 19, 1921).

Taekwon Taylor v. Anthony Bruno et al. and Omar J. Miller v. Anthony Bruno et al. 2008 WL 5481128. Superior Court of Connecticut, Hartford (Nov. 25, 2008).

United States of America v. Alberto Duncan. No. 08-16825-AA. United States Court of Appeals, Eleventh Circuit (Dec. 8, 2009).

United States of America v. Alberto Duncan. No. 08-2394-CR-Seitz/O'Sullivan. United States District Court, Southern District of Florida (May 2, 2008).

United States of America v. Myrlene Severe. No. 06-6053-SNOW. United States District Court, Southern District of Florida (Feb. 10, 2006).

United States of America v. Myrlene Severe. No. 06-60097 CR-COHN. United States District Court, Southern District of Florida (Mar. 31, 2006).

Webb v. City of Philadelphia. 562 F.3d 256. United States Court of Appeals for the Third Circuit (Apr. 7, 2009).

Webb v. City of Philadelphia. 2007 U.S. Dist. LEXIS 46872. United States District Court for the Eastern District of Pennsylvania (June 27, 2007).

HUMAN RIGHTS REPORTS

Achiume, E. Tendayi. "End of Mission Statement of the Special Rapporteur on Contemporary Forms of Racism, Racial Discrimination, Xenophobia and Related Intolerance at the Conclusion of Her Mission to the United Kingdom of Great Britain and Northern Ireland" (2018). https://www.ohchr.org/EN/NewsEvents/Pages/DisplayNews.aspx?NewsID=23073&LangID.

Brazil. "Combating Intolerance, Negative Stereotyping, Stigmatization, Discrimination, Incitement to Violence and Violence Against Persons, Based on Religion or Belief." U.N. Doc. A/HRC/34/35 (Mar. 15, 2016).

Centre for Human Rights and Rehabilitation and Centre for the Development of People. "A Shadow Report to the Malawi Government's First Periodic Report on the Implementation of the International Covenant on Civil and Political Rights" (2013). https://tbinternet.ohchr.org/Treaties/CCPR/Shared%20Documents/MWI/INT_CCPR_NGO_MWI_14672_E.pdf.

Comitê Nacional de Respeito à Diversidade Religiosa. "Nota de Comitê defende diversidade religiosa" (May 27, 2014). http://www.mdh.gov.br/noticias/2014/maio/nota-de-comite-defende-diversidade-religiosa.

———. "Nota Pública N. 04 2016" (April 4, 2016). http://www.sdh.gov.br/sobre/participacao-social/cnrdr/notas-publicas/NOTAPUBLICA04CNRDR.pdf.

———. "Recentes casos de agressão de lideranças e depredação de espaços de culto de religiões de matriz africana" (April 4, 2016). https://www.mdh.gov.br/sdh/noticias/2016/abril/comite-nacional-de-respeito-a-diversidade-religiosa-divulga-nota-publica-contra-preconceito-discriminacao-e-violencia.

———. "Relatório sobre Intolerância e Violência Religiosa no Brasil (2011–2015)" (2016). http://www.mdh.gov.br/informacao-ao-cidadao/participacao-social/cnrdr/pdfs/relatorio-de-intolerancia-e-violencia-religiosa-rivir-2015/view.

Committee on the Rights of the Child. "Concluding Observation on the Report Submitted by the United Kingdom." U.N. Doc. CRC/C/OPSC/GBR/CO/1 (July 8, 2014).

Ezeilo, Joy. "Report of the Special Rapporteur on Trafficking in Persons, Especially Women and Children, on Her Mission to Italy." U.N. Doc. A/HRC/26/37/Add.4 (Apr. 1, 2014).

Garcia, Ana Dols. "Voodoo, Witchcraft and Human Trafficking in Europe." New Issues in Refugee Research: Research Paper No. 263. UNHCR. (2013).

Governo do Rio de Janeiro. "Secretário de Direitos Humanos cria Comissão para apurar casos de intolerância religiosa em Nova Iguaçu" (Sept. 28, 2017). http://www.rj.gov.br/web/sedhmi/exibeconteudo?article-id=4258439.

Gualberto, Marcio Alexandre M. "Mapa da Intolerância Religiosa: Violação ao Direito de Culto no Brasil" (2011). http://www.acaoeducativa.org.br/fdh/wp-content/uploads/2012/11/Mapa-da-intoler%C3%A2ncia-religiosa.pdf.

Hollanda, Adriana. "Mãe é ameaçada de perder a guarda da filha por ser candomblecista." Comissão de Combate à Intolerância Religiosa (May 27, 2010).

Human Rights Committee. "Consideration of Reports Submitted by States Parties Under Article 40 of the Covenant, Initial Reports of States Parties: Haiti." U.N. Doc. CCPR/C/HTI/1 (Jan. 23, 2013).

———. "List of Issues in Relation to the Initial Report of Haiti." U.N. Doc CCPR/C/HTI/Q/1 (Apr. 23, 2014).

Human Rights Council. "National Report Submitted in Accordance with Paragraph 15 (a) of the Annex to the Human Rights Council Resolution 5/1: Haiti." U.N. Doc. A/HRC/WG.6/12/HTI/1 (July 19, 2011).

———. "Report of the Independent Expert on the Situation of Human Rights in Haiti, Michel Forst." U.N. Doc. A/HRC/17/42 (Apr. 4, 2011).

Inter-American Commission on Human Rights. "Report on the Situation of Human Rights in Brazil." Doc. OEA/Ser.L/V/II.97 (Sept. 29, 1997). http://www.cidh.org/countryrep/brazil-eng/index%20-%20brazil.htm.

International Commission to Combat Religious Racism. "Twenty Years of Religious Racism in Brazil" (Nov. 8, 2019). https://www.religiousracism.org/brazil.

Izsák, Rita. "Report of the Special Rapporteur on Minority Issues on Her Mission to Brazil." U.N. Doc. A/HRC/31/56/Add.1 (Feb. 9, 2016).

Ministry of Human Rights. "Balanço–Disque 100." https://www.mdh.gov.br/informacao-ao-cidadao/ouvidoria/balanco-disque-100.

United Nations General Assembly. "Report of the Chair of the Working Group of Experts on People of African Descent." U.N. Doc. A/69/318 (Aug. 15, 2014).

United States Department of State. "2010 International Religious Freedom Report—Brazil." https://www.state.gov/j/drl/rls/irf/2010/148738.htm.

———. "2013 International Religious Freedom Report—Brazil." https://2009-2017.state.gov/documents/organization/222573.pdf.

———. "2014 International Religious Freedom Report—Brazil." https://2009-2017.state.gov/documents/organization/238738.pdf.

———. "2015 International Religious Freedom Report—Brazil." https://2009-2017.state.gov/documents/organization/256549.pdf.

———. "2017 International Religious Freedom Report—Brazil." https://www.state.gov/wp-content/uploads/2019/01/Brazil-2.pdf.

———. "2019 International Religious Freedom Report—Jamaica." https://www.state.gov/wp-content/uploads/2020/06/JAMAICA-2019-INTERNATIONAL-RELIGIOUS-FREEDOM-REPORT.pdf.

———. "2012 International Religious Freedom Report—Malawi." https://www.state.gov/documents/organization/208380.pdf.

———. "2016 International Religious Freedom Report—Malawi." https://www.state.gov/documents/organization/268912.pdf.

Working Group of Experts on People of African Descent. "Report of the Working Group of Experts on People of African Descent on its Fourteenth Session: Mission to Brazil." U.N. Doc. A/HRC/27/68/Add.1 (Sept. 4, 2014).

SECONDARY SOURCES

Abdo, Aliah. "The Legal Status of Hijab in the United States: A Look at the Sociopolitical Influences on the Legal Right to Wear the Muslim Headscarf." *Hastings Race and Poverty Law Journal* 5 (2008): 441–507.

Agyekum, Kofi. "*Ntam* 'Reminiscential Oath' Taboo in Akan." *Language in Society* 33, no. 3 (2004): 317–42.

Amer, Sahar. *What Is Veiling?* Chapel Hill: University of North Carolina Press, 2014.

Amoah, Jewel, and Tom Bennett. "The Freedoms of Religion and Culture Under the South African Constitution: Do Traditional African Religions Enjoy Equal Treatment?" *Journal of Law and Religion* 24, no. 1 (2008): 1–20.

Andrade, Marcelo, and Pedro Teixeira. "School, Religion, and Intolerance: On Laic School and Religious Conflicts in Brazil." In *Second International Handbook of Urban Education*, edited by William T. Pink and George W. Noblit, 1:585–611. Cham, Switzerland: Springer International Handbooks of Education, 2017.

Baarda, C. S. "Human Trafficking for Sexual Exploitation from Nigeria into Western Europe: The Role of Voodoo Rituals in the Functioning of a

Criminal Network." *European Journal of Criminology* 13, no. 2 (2016): 257–73.

Bakht, Natasha, and Jordan Palmer. "Modern Law, Modern Hammers: Canada's Witchcraft Provision as an Image of Persecution." *Windsor Review of Legal and Social Issues* 36 (2015): 139.

Barrett, Leonard. *The Rastafarians*. Boston: Beacon Press, 1977.

Bartkowski, John P. "Claims-Making and Typifications of Voodoo as a Deviant Religion: Hex, Lies, and Videotape." *Journal for the Scientific Study of Religion* 37, no. 4 (1998): 559–79.

Behrens, Kevin G. "Tony Yengeni's Ritual Slaughter: Animal Anti-Cruelty vs. Culture." MA thesis, University of the Witwatersrand, Johannesburg, 2008.

Beier, A. L. "'A New Serfdom': Labor Laws, Vagrancy Statutes, and Labor Discipline in England, 1350–1800." In *Cast Out: Vagrancy and Homelessness in Global and Historical Perspective*, edited by A. L. Beier and Paul Ocobock, 35–63. Athens: Ohio University Press, 2008.

Bellegarde-Smith, Patrick. "A Man-Made Disaster: The Earthquake of January 12, 2010—A Haitian Perspective." *Journal of Black Studies* 42, no. 2 (2011): 264–75.

Beynon, Erdmann Doane. "The Voodoo Cult Among Negro Migrants in Detroit." *American Journal of Sociology* 43, no. 6 (1938): 894–907.

Boaz, Danielle. "Fraud, Vagrancy and the 'Pretended' Exercise of Supernatural Powers in England, South Africa and Jamaica." *Law and History* 5, no. 1 (2018): 54–84.

———. "The Voodoo Cult of Detroit: Race, Human Sacrifice, and the Nation of Islam from the 1930s to the 1970s." *Journal of Interreligious Studies* 23 (2018): 17–30.

Brown, Vincent. *The Reaper's Garden: Death and Power in the World of Atlantic Slavery*. Cambridge: Harvard University Press, 2008.

Campbell, Horace. *Rasta and Resistance: From Marcus Garvey to Walter Rodney*. Trenton, NJ: Africa World Press, 1987.

Carelock, Nicole Payne. "A Leaky House: Haiti in the Religious Aftershock of the 2010 Earthquake." PhD diss., Rice University, 2012.

Chester, Colby M. "Haiti: A Degenerating Island." *National Geographic Magazine* 19 (1908): 201–11.

Chireau, Yvonne. *Black Magic: Religion and the African American Conjuring Tradition*. Berkeley: University of California Press, 2003.

Clark, Mary Ann. "Palo Monte." In *African American Religious Cultures*, edited by Anthony Pinn, 303–7. Santa Barbara, CA: ABC-CLIO, 2009.

Clark, Peter A. "Prejudice and the Medical Profession: A Five-Year Update." *Journal of Law, Medicine, and Ethics* 37, no. 1 (2009): 118–33.

Cole, Jeffrey. "Reducing the Damage: Dilemmas of Anti-Trafficking Efforts Among Nigerian Prostitutes in Palermo." *Anthropologica* 48, no. 2 (2006): 217–28.

Collins, B. Abdy. "Spiritualism and the Law." *Modern Law Review* 8, no. 3 (1945): 158–62.

Comissão de Combate à Intolerância Religiosa. "Por causa de sua fé, candomblecista perde a guarda do filho e é chamada de 'parideira.'" Nov. 2, 2009. http://ccir.org.br/por-causa-de-sua-fe-candomblecista-perde-a-guarda-do-filho-e-e-chamada-de-parideira/ (accessed May 4, 2018).

Conte, Andreza. "Umbanda: Apontamentos sobre a interferência da religião no estado e o estudo da lei." Bachelor of law thesis, University of Santa Cruz do Sul, 2016.

Crosson, J. Brent. "What Obeah Does Do: Healing, Harm, and the Limits of Religion." *Journal of Africana Religions* 3, no. 2 (2015): 151–76.

Davies, Owen. *Witchcraft, Magic and Culture, 1736–1951*. Manchester: Manchester University Press, 1999.

Davis, Derek H. "Reacting to France's Ban: Headscarves and Other Religious Attire in American Public Schools." *Journal of Church and State* 46 (2004): 221–35.

Delahunty, R. J. "Does Animal Welfare Trump Religious Liberty? The Danish Ban on Kosher and Halal Butchering." *San Diego International Law Journal* 16 (2015): 341–79.

Desilver, Drew, and David Masci. "World's Muslim Population More Widespread Than You Might Think." Pew Research Center. Jan. 31, 2017. http://www.pewresearch.org/fact-tank/2017/01/31/worlds-muslim-population-more-widespread-than-you-might-think/.

Dijk, Rijk van. "'Voodoo' on the Doorstep: Young Nigerian Prostitutes and Magic Policing in the Netherlands." *Africa: Journal of the International African Institute* 71, no. 4 (2001): 558–86.

Diouf, Sylvaine Anna. *Servants of Allah: African Muslims Enslaved in the Americas*. New York: New York University Press, 2013.

Dodson, Jualynne. *Sacred Spaces and Religious Traditions in Oriente Cuba*. Albuquerque: University of New Mexico Press, 2008.

Edmonds, Ennis B., and Michelle A. Gonzalez. *Caribbean Religious History: An Introduction*. New York: New York University Press, 2010.

Ezekiel, Judith. "French Dressing: Race, Gender, and the Hijab Story." *Feminist Studies* 32, no. 2 (2006): 256–78.

Fandrich, Ina J. "Yorùbá Influences on Haitian Vodou and New Orleans Voodoo." *Journal of Black Studies* 37, no. 5 (2007): 775–91.

Frank, Julia Bess. "Body Snatching: A Grave Medical Problem." *Yale Journal of Biology and Medicine* 49 (1976): 399–410.

Frerichs, Ralph. *Deadly River: Cholera and Cover-Up in Post-Earthquake Haiti*. Ithaca: Cornell University Press, 2016.

Garcia, Rosane. "Aula sobre mitos africanos gera polêmica." Secretaria Da Educação, Governo do Estado do Paraná. Nov. 19, 2009. http://www.ensinoreligioso.seed.pr.gov.br/modules/noticias/article.php?storyid=221.

Gaston, Jessie Ruth. "The Case of Voodoo in New Orleans." In *Africanisms in American Culture*, edited by Joseph Holloway, 111–49. Bloomington: Indiana University Press, 2005.

Germain, Felix. "The Earthquake, the Missionaries, and the Future of Vodou." *Journal of Black Studies* 42 (2011): 247–63.

Gibson, Marion, ed. *Witchcraft and Society in England and America, 1550–1750*. Ithaca: Cornell University Press, 2003.

Gliszczyńska-Grabias, Aleksandra, and Wojciech Sadurski. "Freedom of Religion Versus Humane Treatment of Animals: Polish Constitutional Tribunal's Judgment on Permissibility of Religious Slaughter." *European Constitutional Law Review* 11, no. 3 (2015): 596–608.

Gomez, Michael A. *Reversing Sail: A History of the African Diaspora*. Cambridge: Cambridge University Press, 2004.

Gomez, Victor. "The Matamoros 'Drug Cult' Murders: Borderland Perceptions and the Shaping of Belief." MA thesis, University of Texas–Pan American, 2005.

Grimaud, Jérôme, and Fedia Legagneur. "Community Beliefs and Fears During a Cholera Outbreak in Haiti." *Intervention* 9, no. 1 (2011): 26–34.

Hale, Lindsay. *Hearing the Mermaid's Song: The Umbanda Religion in Rio de Janeiro*. Albuquerque: University of New Mexico Press, 2009.

Halperin, Edward. "The Poor, the Black, and the Marginalized as the Source of Cadavers in United States Anatomical Education." *Clinical Anatomy* 20 (2007): 489–95.

Handler, Jerome S., and Kenneth Bilby. *Enacting Power: The Criminalization of Obeah in the Anglophone Caribbean, 1760–2011*. Kingston: University of the West Indies Press, 2012.

———. "On the Early Use and Origin of the Term 'Obeah' in Barbados and the

Anglophone Caribbean." *Slavery and Abolition* 22, no. 2 (2001): 87–100.

Hashmi, Hera. "Too Much to Bare? A Comparative Analysis of the Headscarf in France, Turkey, and the United States." *University of Maryland Law Journal: Race, Religion, Gender, and Class* 10 (2010): 409–45.

Hebblethwaite, Benjamin. "The Scapegoating of Haitian Vodou Religion: David Brooks's (2010) Claim That 'Voodoo' Is a 'Progress-Resistant' Cultural Influence." *Journal of Black Studies* 46, no. 1 (2015): 3–22.

Holmes, Ronald, and Stephen Holmes, *Profiling Violent Crimes: An Investigative Tool*. Thousand Oaks, CA: Sage Publications, 2009.

Houk, James. *Spirits, Blood, and Drums: The Orisha Religion in Trinidad*. Philadelphia: Temple University Press, 1995.

Johnson, Paul Christopher. "Law, Religion and 'Public Health' in the Republic of Brazil." *Law and Social Inquiry* 26 (2001): 9–33.

———. *Secrets, Gossip, and Gods: The Transformation of Brazilian Candomblé*. Oxford: Oxford University Press, 2005.

Jones, Nicky. "Religious Freedom in Secular Society: The Case of the Islamic Headscarf in France." In *Freedom of Religion Under Bills of Rights*, edited by Paul Babie and Neville Rochow, 239–52. Adelaide: University of Adelaide Press, 2012.

Kail, Tony. *Narco-Cults: Understand the Use of Afro-Caribbean and Mexican Religious Cultures in the Drug Wars*. Boca Raton, FL: CRC Press, 2015.

Keaton, Trica. "Arrogant Assimilationism: National Identity Politics and African-Origin Muslim Girls in the Other France." *Anthropology and Education Quarterly* 36, no. 4 (2005): 405–23.

Khan, Aisha. "Dark Arts and Diaspora." *Diaspora: A Journal of Transnational Studies* 17, no. 1 (2013): 40–63.

Kuumba, M. Bahati, and Femi Ajanaku. "Dreadlocks: The Hair Aesthetics of Cultural Resistance and Collective Identity Formation." *Mobilization: An International Journal* 3, no. 2 (1998): 227–43.

Lammoglia, Jose. "Legal Aspects of Animal Sacrifice Within the Context of Afro-Caribbean Religions." *St. Thomas Law Review* 20 (2008): 710–20.

Lawrence, Harold G. "Mandinga Voyages Across the Atlantic." In *African Presence in Early America*, edited by Ivan Van Sertima, 169–214. Transaction Publishers, 1992.

Long, Carolyn. *Spiritual Merchants: Religion, Magic, and Commerce*. Knoxville: University of Tennessee Press, 2001.

Luongo, Katherine. *Witchcraft and Colonial Rule in Kenya, 1900–1955*. New York: Cambridge University Press, 2011.

Macfarlane, Alan. *Witchcraft in Tudor and Stuart England: A Regional and Comparative Study*. New York: Harper and Row, 1970.

Manatee County Human Services. "Burial Assistance: Human Services Benefit Programs." https://www.mymanatee.org/home/government/departments/community-services/human-services-benefit-programs.html.

Marques, Maria Cristina. "Lendas de Exu sob os holofotes da educação." Thesis, Centro Federal de Educação Tecnológica Celso Suckow da Fonseca, 2014.

Martin, R. F. "Removal and Reinterment of Remains." *American Law Reports*, 2nd ed., 21 (1952): 472–535. [Subsequently updated weekly.]

Mbiti, John. *African Religions and Philosophy*. New York: Frederick Praeger, 1969.

McCarthy-Brown, Karen. "Afro-Caribbean Spirituality: A Haitian Case Study." In *Vodou in Haitian Life and Culture: Invisible Powers*, edited by Claudine Michel and Patrick Bellegarde-Smith, 1–26. New York: Palgrave Macmillan, 2006.

Mhango, Mtendeweka Owen. "The Constitutional Protection of Minority Religious Rights in Malawi: The

Case of Rastafari Students." *Journal of African Law* 52, no. 2 (2008): 218–44.
Morris, Paul. "Covering Islam—Burqa and Hijab: Limits to the Human Right to Religion." *Human Rights Research* (2004): 1–22.
Moruzzi, Norma Claire. "A Problem with Headscarves: Contemporary Complexities of Political and Social Identity." *Political Theory* 22, no. 4 (November 1994): 653–72.
Murphy, Joseph. *Santería: African Spirits in America*. Boston: Beacon Press, 1993.
———. *Working the Spirit: Ceremonies of the African Diaspora*. Boston: Beacon Press, 1994.
Murray, Virginia H. "A 'Right' of the Dead and a Charge on the Quick: Criminal Laws Relating to Cemeteries, Burial Grounds and Human Remains." *Journal of the Missouri Bar* 56 (2000): 115–20.
Murrell, Nathaniel Samuel. *Afro-Caribbean Religions: An Introduction to Their Historical, Cultural, and Sacred Traditions*. Philadelphia: Temple University Press, 2010.
O'Brien, David M. *Animal Sacrifice and Religious Freedom: Church of the Lukumi Babalu Aye v. City of Hialeah*. Lawrence: University of Kansas Press, 2004.
O'Brien, Derek, and Vaughan Carter. "Chant Down Babylon: Freedom of Religion and the Rastafarian Challenge to Majoritarianism." *Journal of Law and Religion* 18, no. 1 (2002–3): 219–48.
O'Brien, Peter. "Veil." In *The Muslim Question in Europe: Political Controversies and Public Philosophies*, 104–43. Philadelphia: Temple University Press, 2016.
Ojo, Matthias Olufemi Dada. "Incorporation of Ayelala Traditional Religion into Nigerian Criminal Justice System: An Opinion Survey of Igbesa Community People in Ogun State, Nigeria." *Issues in Ethnology and Anthropology* 9, no. 4 (2014): 995–1014.
Olmos, Margarite Fernández, and Lizabeth Paravisini-Gebert. *Creole Religions of the Caribbean: An Introduction from Vodou and Santería to Obeah and Espiritismo*. 2nd ed. New York: New York University Press, 2011.
Oro, Ari Pedro. "The Sacrifice of Animals in Afro-Brazilian Religions: Analysis of a Recent Controversy in the Brazilian State of Rio Grande Do Sul." *Religião e Sociedade* 1, 2nd ed. (2006): 1–14.
Ortiz, Renato. "Ogum and Umbandista Religion." In *Africa's Ogun: Old World and New*, edited by Sandra Barnes, 90–102. Bloomington: Indiana University Press, 1989.
Osman, Fatima. "Legislative Prohibitions on Wearing a Headscarf: Are They Justified?" *Potchefstroom Electronic Law Journal* 17, no. 4 (2014): 1317–49.
Palmié, Stephan. *Wizards and Scientists: Exploration in Afro-Cuban Modernity and Tradition*. Durham: Duke University Press, 2002.
Parrinder, Geoffrey. *African Traditional Religion*. Westport, CT: Greenwood Press, 1976.
Paton, Diana. *The Cultural Politics of Obeah: Religion, Colonialism and Modernity in the Caribbean World*. Cambridge: Cambridge University Press, 2015.
———. "Obeah Acts: Producing and Policing the Boundaries of Religion in the Caribbean." *Small Axe* 28 (2009): 1–18.
———. "Witchcraft, Poison, Law, and Atlantic Slavery." *William and Mary Quarterly* 69, no. 2 (2012): 235–64.
Paton, Diana, and Maarit Forde. *Obeah and Other Powers: The Politics of Caribbean Religion and Healing*. Durham: Duke University Press, 2012.
Perlmutter, Dawn. "The Forensics of Sacrifice: A Symbolic Analysis of Ritualistic Crime." *Anthropocentric: The Journal of Generative Anthropology* 9, no. 2 (2003/2004). http://anthropoetics.ucla.edu/apo902/sacrifice-2.
Pretorius, S. P. "The Significance of the Use of Ganja as a Religious Ritual in the Rastafari Movement." *Verbum et Ecclesia* 27, no. 3 (2006): 1012–30.
Prichard, Hesketh. *Where Black Rules White: A Journey Across and About Hayti*. New York: Charles Scribner's Sons, 1900.

Ramsey, Kate. *The Spirits and the Law: Vodou and Power in Haiti*. Chicago: The University of Chicago Press, 2011.

Roberts, Kodi. *Voodoo and Power: The Politics of Religion in New Orleans, 1881–1940*. Baton Rouge: Louisiana State University Press, 2015.

Roman, Reinaldo. *Governing Spirits: Religion, Miracles and Spectacles in Cuba and Puerto Rico, 1898–1956*. Chapel Hill: University of North Carolina Press, 2007.

Rucker, Walter C. *The River Flows On: Black Resistance, Culture, and Identity Formation in Early America*. Baton Rouge: Louisiana State University Press, 2006.

Sandoval, Mercedes Cros. *Worldview, the Orichas, and Santería: Africa to Cuba and Beyond*. Gainesville: University Press of Florida, 2006.

Scales-Trent, Judy. "African Women in France: Immigration, Family, and Work." *Brooklyn Journal of International Law* 24 (1999): 705–37.

Schutze, Jim. *Cauldron of Blood: The Matamoros Cult Killings*. New York: Avon Books, 1989.

Schyff, Gerhard van der. "Ritual Slaughter and Religious Freedom in a Multilevel Europe: The Wider Importance of the Dutch Case." *Oxford Journal of Law and Religion*, 3, no. 1 (2014): 76–102.

Sharpe, James. *Instruments of Darkness: Witchcraft in Early Modern England*. Philadelphia: University of Pennsylvania Press, 1997.

Smith, Katherine Marie. "Gede Rising: Haiti in the Age of *Vagabondaj*." PhD diss., University of California, Los Angeles, 2010.

Stansky, Victoria. "Persecution and Permanence: Re-Negotiating Brazil's Identity, Religious Intolerance, and Consuming Candomblé." MA thesis, University of California, Santa Barbara, 2012.

St. John, Spenser. *Hayti or the Black Republic*. London: Smith, Elder, 1889.

Taylor, Timothy B. "Soul Rebels: The Rastafarians and the Free Exercise Clause." *Georgetown Law Journal* 72 (1984): 1605–35.

Viorst, Milton. "The Muslims of France." *Foreign Affairs* 75, no. 5 (1996): 78–96.

Voeks, Robert. "African Medicine and Magic in the Americas." *Geographical Review* 83, no. 1 (1993): 66–78.

Washington, Harriet. *Medical Apartheid: The Dark History of Medical Experimentation on Black Americans from Colonial Times to the Present*. New York: Doubleday, 2006.

Watt, Marcel van der, and Beatri Kruger. "Exploring 'Juju' and Human Trafficking: Towards a Demystified Perspective and Response." *South African Review of Sociology* 48, no. 2 (2017): 70–86.

Weil, Patrick. "Symposium: Constitutionalism and Secularism in an Age of Religious Revival: The Challenge of Global and Local Fundamentalisms Religious Symbols in the Public Space." *Cardozo Law Review* 30 (2009): 2699–714.

Willoughby, Christopher. "Pedagogies of the Black Body: Race and Medical Education in the Antebellum United States." PhD diss., Tulane University, 2016.

Yildirim, Seval. "Freeman v. Dep't of Highway Safety and Motor Vehicles and Webb v. City of Philadelphia: Accommodation Tangles in the Laws Over Hair." In *Law and Religion: Cases in Context*, edited by Leslie Griffin, 293–310. New York: Aspen, 2010.

Young, Harvey. "The Black Body as Souvenir in American Lynching." *Theatre Journal* 57, no. 4 (2005): 639–57.

Zoethout, Carla M. "Ritual Slaughter and the Freedom of Religion: Some Reflections on a Stunning Matter." *Human Rights Quarterly* 35, no. 3 (2013): 651–72.

Index

Afro-Brazilian religions. *See* Brazil; Candomblé; Umbanda
animal sacrifice, 12, 71, 136, 164, 180, 190
    attempts to restrict, 8, 35–52, 58–59, 193
    relationship to child custody, 73–83, 86

Barrett, Leonard, 93
Bellegarde-Smith, Patrick, 31
Bilby, Kenneth, 136, 145–46
Brazil, 5, 13–14, 87, 89, 192–93
    animal sacrifice controversies in, 46–49, 52
    boundaries of "religion" in, 160, 174–79
    child custody controversies in, 72–73, 83–86
    controversies over religious attire in, 110, 112–13, 120–21
    definition of "religious racism" in, 2, 3
    religion and education in, 110–13
    religious intolerance in, 7–8, 19–30, 34
Bwa Kayiman, 30, 31, 89

Candomblé, 1, 13, 15, 20, 175–77
    animal sacrifice and, 47
    child custody and, 72–73, 84–85
    right to education for devotees of, 110–13
    right to wear religious attire and devotees of, 110, 112–13, 120–21
    violence against devotees of, 8, 23–28, 34
    See also Brazil
Canada, 1, 141, 157–59, 160, 166–74, 178, 193
Carelock, Nicole Payne, 31, 32, 33
Catholics (Catholic Church, Catholicism), 14, 86, 100, 103, 138, 171, 178
    and the persecution of Africana religions, 3–5
    and Afro-Brazilian religions in schools, 111, 112
Cayman Islands, 101, 106–7
Church of the Lukumi Babalu Aye, Inc., 8, 166
    animal sacrifice litigation and, 36–38, 40, 41, 42, 43, 46, 47

child custody and animal sacrifice litigation regarding, 73–77, 81, 83
"Civilization," narratives about, 3, 4, 6, 46, 100, 191
Cuba, 5–6, 7, 14–17, 49, 59
    Cuban immigrants in the United States, 17, 59, 61, 63–64
    See also Palo Mayombe; Santeria
"cults," 6, 82, 150, 165, 175, 176, 189
    "narco-cults," 58–60, 179
    stereotypes of Palo Mayombe as, 58–60, 65, 66, 67, 82

Dahomey, 12, 137, 138
devil worship (Satan), derogatory references to, 96, 159, 156
    Afro-Brazilian religions and, 27, 28, 111, 112, 113, 177
    Obeah and, 136, 143, 150, 151, 153–54, 157
    Palo Mayombe and, 59, 65, 68
    Vodou and, 31, 32, 185
    Voodoo and, 137, 138, 185, 189
Dodson, Jualynne, 16
dreadlocks, 92, 191, 192
    right to education and, 9, 95, 101–9, 191
    justice system controversies and, 115, 116, 121–22, 125–33

England. *See* United Kingdom
Evangelical Christianity (Protestants), 7, 19, 47, 174–77, 192–93
    intolerance in Brazilian schools and, 110, 111, 112, 113
    Evangelized drug gangs in Rio de Janeiro, 24–25, 179
    Haiti and, 31, 32, 34
    physical attacks on Afro-Brazilian religious communities and, 23, 24–25, 27, 28–29, 30

Fandrich, Ina, 138
Florida, 163–66
    animal sacrifice cases in, 36–38, 41, 42–43, 74–76
    child custody cases in, 74–76
    human remains cases in, 62, 65
    myths of Africana religions in, 180–84
France, 12, 30, 31, 89, 96–01, 137

ganja. *See* marijuana
Germain, Felix, 32

Haiti, 3–5, 7, 11–12, 58, 89, 137, 138,
    violence against Africana religions in, 8, 19, 30–33, 34
Haitian-Americans, 53, 184–88
Handler, Jerome, 136, 145–46
Harambe (the gorilla), 35, 51
Hashmi, Hera, 91
Hoodoo, 139
human sacrifice, rumors of, 51
    African American Muslims and, 6
    Brazil and, 48, 84
    Cuba and, 5
    Haiti and, 4, 137
    Palo Mayombe and, 59, 66, 67

International Commission to Combat Religious Racism (ICCRR), 23, 24, 25, 110
Islam, 2, 21, 87–91, 193
    African American Muslims, 6, 89
    animal sacrifice/slaughter and, 37, 47
    justice system controversies and, 117–19, 125–26, 127, 130–31, 132–33
    right to education and, 96–101, 105–6, 113
Izsák, Rita (United Nations special rapporteur on minority issues), 23, 29

Jamaica, 87, 93, 143–44, 147–51, 154, 161
    Jamaican Immigrants in Canada, 1, 166–74
Johnson, Paul C., 5, 14

Kongo, 13, 14, 15–16, 58, 138

Laveau, Marie, 138–39
Lucumi. *See* Santeria
lwa (loa), 12, 31, 184–85

Malawi, 101, 105–6, 145
marijuana (ganja, dagga), 62, 92–93
    right to education and, 106–7, 108, 109

justice system controversies and, 122–24, 128, 129–30, 132
Massachusetts, 41–42, 69–70, 185–87
Matamoros, Mexico, murders in, 58–60, 66, 82–83
Miraballes, Miriam, 62–63, 65–69, 79, 82
Murrell, Nathaniel, 15, 136–37
Muslims. *See* Islam

Nation of Islam, 6, 89
New Orleans, 12, 137–39, 185, 188
New Jersey, 43–45, 60–69, 77–83
New York, 57, 66, 76–77, 81, 184–85
nganga, 16, 58, 59, 61, 63, 67

Obeah, 9, 135–36, 138
    proscription of, 141–54, 157, 159, 190
    court cases involving, 160–62, 166–74, 178
Olmos, Margarite Fernandez, 11
Ortiz, Renato, 14

Palo Mayombe, 2, 15–6
    animal sacrifice controversies and, 42, 77– 83
    child custody controversies and, 74, 77– 83
    possession of human remains and, 8, 9, 53, 58–71
Pew Research Center, 20–21, 90, 101
Paravisini-Gebert, Lizabeth, 11
Paton, Diana, 145, 149
public health ("public morality"), 7, 113, 122, 127, 173, 190
    animal sacrifice and, 36–40, 46, 48, 50, 51
    historical suppressions of Africana religions and narratives of, 5, 11
    proscription of Obeah and, 114, 145

Rastafarians, 2, 87, 92–93, 153, 191
    right to education and, 101–2, 104–9, 110, 113
    justice system controversies and, 116–17, 121–33
religious attire, 96, 113, 131, 133, 190, 191
    eketé, 120–21
    headscarves (hijab), generally, 90–91; in schools, 9, 95–101, 105–6; in the justice system, 115, 118–19, 125–26, 127, 131, 132–33
    ilekes (Candomblé necklaces), 24, 27, 112–13
    Rastafarians/tams, 107, 116–17
    veils (niqab), 90–91, 96–01, 117–18
    "Voodoo" necklaces, 119–20

Religious Land Use and Institutionalized Persons Act (RLUIPA), 39, 132
religious racism, 7, 9, 23–28, 34, 83, 112, 114
    definition of, 2–3
    future of, 191–94
    ICCRR report on, 23–24, 110
Roman, Reinaldo, 6

Santeria (Lucumi), 1, 14–15, 17
    animal sacrifice and, 36–41, 42–45, 49–51
    boundaries of religion and, 160, 161, 163–66, 173, 178
    child custody and, 74–77, 78, 79, 81, 82–83
    controversies about the possession of human remains and, 58, 59, 65, 66, 67, 68
"sorcery," 4–5, 27, 33, 171, 177
    proscription of witchcraft and, 143–46, 153, 155, 157–58
South Africa, 189
    right to education in, 101, 107–10
    justice system controversies in, 121, 122–24, 127–30, 131–32, 133
    witchcraft laws in, 141, 154–57
"superstition," 3–6, 137, 143–45, 151–52, 158, 162

Trinidad and Tobago, 151–54

Umbanda, 1, 13–14, 175, 177
    child custody and, 85–86
    right to education and devotees of, 110–11
    violence against devotees of, 8, 19, 23–25, 27
United Kingdom (England, Britain), 191–92
    justice system controversies in, 116–17
    possession of human remains in, 54, 55
    right to education in, 101, 103–05, 106
    vagrancy and witchcraft laws in, 141–44, 146–49, 151–55, 157
United States. *See* Florida; Massachusetts; New Jersey; New Orleans; New York

vagrancy, 141–43, 146–48, 151
veils. *See* religious attire
Venezuela, 8, 14, 46, 49–51, 193
Vodou, 2, 4–5, 11–12, 138
    possession of human remains and, 53–70
    rumors and stereotypes about, 180, 185–87, 188
    violence against devotees of, 8, 30–34
Voodoo, 2, 59, 135, 136–39, 150
    boundaries of religion and, 166, 171, 173
    myths and rumors of, 4, 6, 180–89
    religious attire controversies and, 117, 119–20
    used as alternate spelling to Vodou, 12, 31, 32, 33, 53

Wicca, 141, 154, 156–57, 159
witches/witchcraft (brujos), 15
    proscription of, 9, 136, 141–59
    stereotypes of Africana religions as, 5, 59, 67, 76, 171, 173, 189
    violence against Africana religions and accusations of, 24, 32–33
Working Group of Experts on People of African Descent, 23, 110, 176–77

Yoruba, 1, 14, 49–51, 65, 138, 189
Young, Harvey, 57

Zimbabwe, 101, 102–03, 121–22, 124

www.ingramcontent.com/pod-product-compliance
Lightning Source LLC
Chambersburg PA
CBHW022051290426
44109CB00014B/1053